THE ROSENBERGS

THE ROSENBERGS

Collected Visions of Artists and Writers

Edited by Rob A. Okun

Universe Books
New York, N.Y.

CREDITS

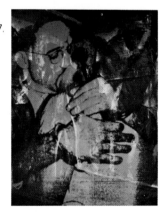

Published in the United States of America
by Universe Books
381 Park Avenue South, New York, NY 10016

© 1988 by Rob A. Okun

88 89 90 91 92 / 10 9 8 7 6 5 4 3 2 1

Printed in Hong Kong

Library of Congress Cataloging in Publication Data

The Rosenbergs : collected visions of artists and
   writers.

   Bibliography: p.
   1. Arts, American. 2. Arts, Modern—20th cen-
tury—United States. 3. Rosenberg, Julius, 1918-
1953—Influence. 4. Rosenberg, Ethel, 1915-1953—
Influence.
I. Okun, Rob A.
NX504.R67   1988   700'.9'04   88-14433
ISBN 0-87663-543-5 (pbk.)

In memory of my father and to my children

Art can . . . take our unexpressed
thoughts and desires and fling
them with clarity and coherence
on the wall, a screen, a sheet
of paper, or against the long
silence of history . . .

—Adrienne Rich

UNKNOWN SECRETS
Art and the Rosenberg Era

Rob A. Okun
Director

Nina Felshin
Curator

Heather Miller, Office Manager   Marion Kahan, Registrar

A central component of the Rosenberg Era Art Project (REAP) is a national exhibition of artwork done between the early Fifties and the late Eighties which examines the Rosenberg-Sobell case, the Cold War and McCarthyism. It can be viewed at the following institutions:

Hillwood Art Gallery
Long Island University
Greenvale, New York
September 9–October 23, 1988

Massachusetts College of Art North Gallery
Boston, Massachusetts
November 16–December 23, 1988

Olin Gallery
Kenyon College
Gambier, Ohio
January 8–February 5, 1989

Palmer Museum of Art
Pennsylvania State University
University Park, Pennsylvania
March 19–May 14, 1989

University of Colorado Art Gallery
Boulder, Colorado
June 8–August 12, 1989

Installation Gallery
San Diego, California
September 8–October 22, 1989

San Francisco Jewish Community Museum
San Francisco, California
January 7–March 30, 1990

Spertus Museum of Judaica
Chicago, Illinois
April 15–July 15, 1990

Aspen Art Museum
Aspen, Colorado
September 20–November 4, 1990

Contents

ACKNOWLEDGMENTS

It is staggering to look back over a five-year project such as this one and realize how many people have given it support. For *The Rosenbergs* is more than a book. Hundreds contributed to a direct-mail appeal in 1986 and 1987. Dozens more wrote or phoned in with leads and suggestions. Still others sent word of artists or activists to contact, helping to turn the project into both a detective story and a jigsaw puzzle. And, of course, many unexpected individual acts of kindness along the way helped remind me that what I had embarked upon was an adventure, not a chore.

So special thanks to: David and Emily Alman, Linda Backiel, Sally Baker, John Bauldie, Berkshire Forum Radical Writers Retreat, Ida Bernstein, Lynne Bobenhausen, Steven Borns, Bread and Roses Cultural Project, Nancy Buchanan, Paul Buhle, Wendy Cadden, Ceres Gallery, David Christiano, Janie Cohen, Mary Cohen, Bruce Cronin, Ross Curtis, Emile De Antonio, Rita Dibert, Morris Dickstein, Per Mauritz Eriksson, Karen Evans, James Farrell, Ronald Feldman, Seon and Dorothy Felshin, Fred Fierst, Moe Foner, Miriam Fredenthal, Meg Gage, Joanne Garland, Cheri Gaulke and Sue Maberry, Rabbi Robert Goldburg, Shifra Goldman, Harry Gottlieb, Marge Grevatt, Anna Gyorgy, Rhyena Halpern, Helen A. Harrison, Woody and Hanna Hastings, Jennifer Hastings, David and Michelle Holzapfel, Marjo Iken and Maarten van de Kamp, Willem Iken, Ken Isaacs, Randy Johnson, Doug Kahn, Judy Kaplan, Aaron Katz, Charles Keller, Arlette Klaric, Henry Klein, Sharon Kleinbaum, Irena Klepfisz, Lisa Kokin, Richard Kruger, Pat and Tex LaMountain, Julius Lazarus, Jack Levine, Herman and Betty Liveright, Pam McAllister, Media Network, Kate Meil, Julie Melrose, Peter Miller, Martha Millet, Ward Mintz, Viviana Muñoz, National Committee to Re-open the Rosenberg Case, Nancy Neel, Stuart Okun, Robert Pac,

Arthur Pettee, Ilene Philipson, John Polak, Ruth and Al Prago, Earl Price, Sylvia Price, Primary Color Lab, Andreas Randhahn, Julia Reichert and Jim Klein, Shoshana Rihn, Philip Reisman, Judy Rubenstein, Glenn Ruga, Jack Rutberg, Joel Saxe, Morris U. Schappes, Ken Schoen, Judith Shahn, Linn Shapiro, Robert Simpson, Sam Skillings, Berthe Small, Social and Public Art Resource Center (SPARC), Cecile Sportis, Peggy Strauss, Dan Scharlin and Harriet Schaeffer, Gary Tartakov, Terry Teagarden, Patricia Thompson, Sylvia Thompson, Ray Waterman, Ruth Weisberg, Ethel and Julius Weiser, Marc Weiss, Richard Weiss, Dorothy White, Rob Wilson, William Wolf, Marilyn Zeitlin, Bill Zimmerman, Rebecca Zurier.

A number of private foundations and individuals contributed generously to help bring the exhibition to fruition. Appreciation and thanks go to: Andreas C. Albrecht, Edward Asner, Robert and Frances Boehm Foundation, Courtney Cazden, Anna Cherney, the Lucius and Eva Eastman Fund, the Fairtree Foundation, Jeanne E. Giordano, Dr. Henry S. Kahn, Ben and Beatrice Goldstein, the Woody Guthrie Foundation, Alfred and Selma Knobler, Harold and Johnnie Kozupsky, Helen and Jack Kruger, Ben Kublin, Matthew Leighton, Harold and Beatrice Loren, Helen and Edgar J. Moore, Carl and Estelle Reiner, William Rothberg, the Reed Foundation, Aaron and Martha Schecter, Laurie Schecter and Gary Isaacson, Lionel Stander, the Tides Foundation, and Mickey and Mitzi Webber.

Other individual generous contributors include: Daniel and Carolyn Berger, Barbara R. Bick, Clara Binswanger, Harold Bloom, Harry Cagin, Samuel S. Chavkin, Annie Cheatham, Ken Coplon, L.J. Du Bartell, Jean M. Entine, Lillian Fortress, Allan Barry Freeman, Ruth V. Friedman, Ellen Grobman, Nina Greenspan, Abraham and Anna Hoffman, Harold

Levanthal, Al and Leah Lutzky, William Obrinsky and Elaine Allen, Reed and Marjorie MacBain, Elena and Harvey Meltzer, Judith Merbaum, Abraham and Mildred Miller, I. Sidney and Beatrice Milwe, Jean and Joseph Okun, Ruth Ost, Joseph and Gail Merrifield Papp, Fred Pasamanick, Albert Ruben, Laura Ross, Moss K. Schenck, Lenore Schreiber, Jean Shulman, June Steingart, Michael Krasnow and Sumru Tekin, John Thorne, Anne Wilson.

Early on in the project, I assembled an advisory board that included a number of artists, writers, actors, musicians, activists, and art and social historians. Their early support was vital. They include: James Aronson, Edward Asner, Peg Averill, Cedric and Mary Belfrage, Leonard Baskin, Steve Cagan, Ramsey Clark, Robert Coover, Ossie Davis, Ruby Dee, David Dellinger, Elinor Gadon, Ronnie Gilbert, Jack Gilford and Madeline Lee Gilford, Ben Goldstein, Alvin H. Goldstein, Steve Heller, Bruce Kaiper, Jerry Kearns, Deborah Kruger, David Kunzle, Lucy Lippard, Ellen and Robert Meeropol, Michael Meeropol, Holly Near, Grace Paley, Tony Randall, John Randolph, Adrienne Rich, Larry Rivers, Paul Robeson, Jr., Pete and Toshi Seeger, Dr. Helen L. Sobell, May Stevens, Studs Terkel, Paul Von Blum, and Howard Zinn.

The ongoing assistance and support of Ed Asner and his administrative assistant Kathy Royce proved crucial at many points along the way. Filmmaker Alvin Goldstein had ready answers to arcane questions, and art collector Ben Goldstein graciously shared his wealth of information about political art.

Almost from the outset, poet Adrienne Rich steadfastly supported the project, beginning when we were neighbors in western Massachusetts. Her contributions go far beyond her extraordinary poem, "For Ethel Rosenberg," and her friendship and wisdom continue to be a source of strength.

THE ROSENBERGS

Collected Visions of Artists and Writers

Edited by Rob A. Okun

With an introduction by Margaret Randall and an essay by Nina Felshin, curator of the Rosenberg exhibition "Unknown Secrets."

It has been 35 years since the trial and execution of Julius and Ethel Rosenberg. The moral and social questions raised by their martyrdom inflamed the imagination of artists and writers of the time and continue to spark the creative imagination of contemporary artists.

The Rosenbergs: Collected Visions of Artists and Writers brings together works by artists such as Picasso, Leger, and Alice Neel who were compelled to respond to the events as they were unfolding, as well as artists of today such as Robert Arneson, Rudolf Baranik, and Sue Coe. Moving excerpts from the memoirs of Arthur Miller, and from the fiction, poetry, and plays of E. L. Doctorow, Adrienne Rich, Robert Coover, Donald Freed, and Allen Ginsberg, underscore the hold the case has had on the literary imagination.

The art, prose, poetry, and plays in *The Rosenbergs* form a powerful synthesis of history, politics, and emotion that goes beyond simply capturing the cultural ethos of the time.

"Every so often the State supposes its citizens to be weary of fair play. As a sort of comic relief, it commits a spectacular injustice which it knows will be popular. Such an entertainment, such a departure from solemnity, in my opinion, was the electrocution of the Rosenbergs." — **Kurt Vonnegut**

"This book could not be merely commemorative, because the collective experience of the Rosenberg trial is still unfinished. Artists and writers are still dreaming that dream, and the consciousness of a new generation still moves in its shadow." — **Adrienne Rich**

"It was a time of scoundrels who disguised themselves, but that doesn't undo the awful injustice. This book helps us to remember." — **Tony Randall**

Published by Universe Books, New York. Distributed by St. Martin's Press. 160 pgs., 95 illustrations (25 color) $27.50

A powerful synthesis of art, history, politics, and emotion

Book Order Form

Yes!

I want to order *The Rosenbergs: Collected Visions of Artists and Writers*, by Rob A. Okun, at $27.50 each

20% OFF

Allow 4 Weeks For Delivery

Number of Books _____	$22.00	
	x ~~$27.50~~: $ _____	
	x $2.50: $ _____	
	Total Due: $ _____	

Please make check or money order payable to:

ROSENBERG ERA ART PROJECT

37 Ferry Road, Turners Falls

Massachu____

Name: _____

Street: _____

City: _____

State: _____ Zip: _____

...chusetts 01376
413-863-9402

Novelist Robert Coover searched his memory and his files for a rich, behind-the-scenes history of the troubled half-life of his fearsome epic, *The Public Burning.*

Los Angeles writer and teacher Prof. Paul Von Blum was another early supporter whose offer of lodging and advice was the start of a friendship between his family and mine.

Peter Selz, art historian at the University of California at Berkeley, was much too generous with his time—writing, advising, and lobbying on behalf of the exhibition. Boston University art history professor Patricia Hills also provided crucial, early support.

Space does not permit me to express the extent of my appreciation for Dr. Helen Sobell whose suggestions and help from the first proved essential in uncovering the historical works in the exhibition. Her struggle to free and to vindicate Morton Sobell and the Rosenbergs is both an inspiration and a testament to commitment.

Several key players in the Rosenberg-Sobell case, including attorney Marshall Perlin, historian Harold Fruchtbaum, and writers Bill Reuben, and Walter and Miriam Schneir all provided essential information and advice. Morton Sobell cooperated fully, offering valuable suggestions.

It is important for me also to acknowledge the support of several advisory board members who died during the five years it took to complete the project. Actors Sara Cunningham and Howard Da Siva, both victims of the Hollywood blacklist, writer John Wexley, author of the first major book to investigate the case, artist Raphael Soyer, and the writer-librarian couple Yuri and Isabel Suhl did more than just endorse this effort. In particular, although I visited them only a handful of times, Yuri and Isabel opened their home and hearts to me in a way only family could.

Good friends Bob Winston and Janet Walerstein Winston *were* like family to me throughout the five years it took to organize the exhibition and complete this book. Indeed, Janet's Rosenberg sketches, done years before I conceived of the exhibition, confirmed my

initial, unsubstantiated hunch that artists worldwide had created Rosenberg art. (Her subsequent twelve-painting series, "Rosenbergs Remembered," has been exhibited extensively.)

I am also grateful to artist Sue Coe and writer-photographer Margaret Randall for helping me to remember the goals of the exhibition at moments when my own vision faltered. Margery Rosenthal provided comfort to the weary traveller on many occasions.

Political art organizer and curator Reinhard Schultz served as a European ambassador for the exhibition, uncovering art, visiting artists, and providing transatlantic support.

Richard Corey's long-distance influence on the project has been profound. From video tapes and poetry books, photographs, and newspaper clips, he is a major archivist of the Rosenberg era and his contributions have touched virtually every aspect of the project.

During the exhibition's critical final two years, I was fortunate to have Heather Miller working with me. Her office management, bookkeeping, and therapeutic skills were essential to keeping the project on an even keel.

I am also grateful to exhibition registrar Marian Kahan for juggling an enormous array of technical details with good humor and aplomb.

No words could possibly convey the contributions of curator Nina Felshin. Her vision and ideas, more than any other, shaped the exhibition. Her knowledge of contemporary art and artists, particularly those engaged in addressing social issues, was crucial to bringing into focus the exhibition's Fifties/Eighties connection. Working with her has been an education from which I continue to benefit.

Frances Goldin, my literary agent, provided the right mix of encouragement and business sense, essential to completing the work. At Universe Books, my editor Adele Ursone and her associate, Margaux King, spent much time and energy in working with a challenging manuscript. Designer Harry Chester, produced a visually exciting final document.

Virtually all of my efforts in organizing the exhibition, and the writing and editing of this book, were completed at the Bloom Institute of Media Studies in Montague, Massachusetts. Home of Green Mountain Post Films, with whom I produced a documentary film on Rosenberg art and artists, I was fortunate to have the comaraderie of GMP's Chuck Light and Daniel Keller, and, in the final months, Lucky, Tulita Allen, and Steve Diamond.

When I initially conceived of organizing the exhibition, among the first people I discussed it with were the Rosenbergs's sons, Michael and Robby Meeropol, and Robby's wife, Elli. Their encouragement and support, and belief in me, was heartening. Robby, in particular, has been a tireless advocate. His advice on a myriad of details was unique and invaluable. Neither he nor his brother ever made any effforts to influence what was or wasn't included in the exhibition; I take full responsibility for any errors or omissions. My friendship of nearly a decade with Robby and his family remains an important part of my life.

My mother and father, Jean and Joseph Okun, taught me the value of family, an essential lesson underlying this effort and one I hope I can adequately pass on to my own children.

Indeed, the creation of my family coincided with the evolution of the exhibition. Since beginning work on this project in 1983, I also became the father of two children, Aviva and Jonah, whom I am privileged to share with my wife, Deborah Kruger. More than any other single individual, Deborah gave me the encouragement and love with which to carry out this arduous and joyful adventure. What else could anyone ask for?

—R. O.
Montague, Massachusetts
Spring 1988

Support for the exhibition *Unknown Secrets: Art and the Rosenberg Era* was provided in part by the New York State Council on the Arts and by the New England Foundation for the Arts, a nonprofit organization which develops and promotes the arts of the region.

The Rosenberg Era Art Project (REAP) was a sponsored program of the Alternative Media Information Center in New York City, which provided valuable technical support. REAP also gratefully acknowledges the assistance of the Center for the Arts, Northampton, Massachusetts.

Ongoing efforts related to the Rosenberg Era Art Project are being coordinated by Cultural Forecast of Montague, Massachusetts, which organizes speakers, programs, and exhibitions on art and society. Write to them at 37 Ferry Road, Turners Falls, Massachusetts 01376, (413) 863-9402.

Inquiries about the documentary film, *Unknown Secrets: Art and the Rosenberg Era*, should be directed to Green Mountain Post Films, P.O. Box 229, Turners Falls, Massachusetts 01376, (413) 863-4754.

Our Backbone Culture

MARGARET RANDALL

Two cultures. One, the culture of authority. A blanket of sameness, sterility, our potential for thought/feeling/creativity exploited in the blood (no, not only of the lamb, but) of our own unknowing sacrifice.

As the prizes are dangled before our eyes—the safety and security of no-think, the anesthesia of an easy win, the absolution of a future devoid of the need to take risks—it is not only our present tense, our here-and-now opportunity to do and make that is ripped from us. Our memory is blotted out as well. Our history is raped, distorted, sanitized, and then marketed so that it may be returned to us in a perfectly harmonious, manageable, odor-free package.

Depending on how we have been repressed or allowed to grow, we may hardly discern an opposing culture. Yet in a very vital living sense this opposing culture is our backbone, that which has kept us alive: mother to daughter, father to son, generation upon generation, life linked to life. Not only within our national family, but across borders as well. It is ultimately what places each of us within the human family. This other, *people's* culture is the very essence of our self-regeneration, the core of what is unique yet bonding, new yet ageless, known yet daring and experimental in our lives.

Editor's note:
As a contemporary victim of McCarthyism (described in this introduction), writer-photographer Margaret Randall provides a chilling link between domestic political persecution in the 1950s and in the 1980s. However, as she wishes to underscore, there is a marked distinction between the government's as yet unsuccessful efforts to deport her for her beliefs and its execution of Julius and Ethel Rosenberg for theirs.

Economic culture. Political culture. Spiritual culture. Artistic culture. Opportunism has been the name of their game, survival the name of ours, since history first assumed a human face.

In his story of how this exhibition came to be, Rob Okun tells us that the search for Rosenberg art has also been "a search, at first unwittingly, for a hidden culture." He reminds us the "work has had to assert itself from behind an iron curtain of censorship, both subtle and overt."

It is important that we ponder, if only for the moment contained within these notes, upon the ways in which not only our art but our *lives* must continually assert and reassert themselves from behind an ever more murky and intrusive curtain, a shroud so oppressive it can alter the human condition we share and would pass on.

On June 19, 1953, in the aftermath of a war whose history was even then being radically altered by establishment "historians," at the height of the cold-war hysteria we have labeled McCarthyism (as if it were a stain long since removed), a man and a woman were murdered in this country. There was no declared war, yet their alleged crime was called treason. Evidence was fabricated and ludicrous. A mockery was made of our justice system. Bigotry and guilt by allusion or association were allowed to overrule the checks and balances of even the most traditional court. The few years since the Soviet Union had been our heroic World War II ally were sufficient for anti-Communism to replace reason in its capacity for sealing people's minds and justifying the unjustifiable. A man and a woman were accused. And they added to their supposed crime another, more serious one: they maintained their innocence to the end.

Julius and Ethel Rosenberg would not say they were sorry for something they had not done. To preserve their honor—which by then was all they had left to leave to their two small children, their fellow citizens, their country—they went to a hideous death. A shock wave of disbelief, of despair, of horror and indignation ran through the consciences of people around the world.

I was sixteen years old when the Rosenbergs died, destined—as was most of my generation—to a recreation of self amid the shallow glitter and deceptive promises of the "good-time fifties." We jitterbugged and then rock 'n' rolled our way into young adulthood, learning all the lessons of conformity, "if you want to make it bad enough you will," just look around and do it like the Good Ole Boys.

Those of us who were the wrong class, the wrong color, or the wrong gender to be Good Ole Boys; those of us who were groomed as cannon fodder but somehow survived Korea and Vietnam; those of us who went away in order to survive or stayed in order to survive, quickly or not so quickly found holes in the Great American Dream.

We began to ask questions. We found answers to some of them. And our images of the Rosenbergs—Julius in the police van, his shackled arms around his wife, Ethel's clear sweet voice through the walls of a Sing Sing cell, her body forcing them to kill it twice, the absolute sureness in her poem to her sons—those images ripped through the media sensationalism of establishment injustice. Our real people's culture anchored us to our

lives in ways that were increasingly recognizable as time asserted its corrective arm.

The culture of life continues to fight the death culture in arenas ranging from the international to the intensely personal. Holocausts humankind would "never forget" are written out of history by men who dare to name themselves "experts," and so we must fight again and again simply to "prove" that fascism exists and that it kills. Jewish descendants of six million victims open fire on the Palestinian inhabitants of Gaza, and we are reminded that we must continue to take a stand. We twice elect an actor turned FBI informant president of the United States, and are surprised when we are asked to swallow his deadly double-talk vis-à-vis Nicaragua, South Africa, the Iran-Contra affair, or any of dozens of other issues affecting our lives. Invasion becomes our national password to "posterity," and we listlessly record the fact that 80 percent of all women in the United States will confront some form of sexual abuse in our lives.

The Rosenbergs were murdered. Some of us were deeply changed by the event, others barely remember it as news; still others are too young to be aware of it except through the memory recreated by a few dogged historians or artists of responsibility.

Who are our artists of responsibility? Many of them, in their work, people the pages of this book and the successive exhibition halls displaying this important show. This collection is a monument to our culture that refuses to disappear; to our culture that inevitably surfaces to remind us of our strengths, in spite of the untold damage of censorship, persecution, erasure.

Some of the pieces were produced while the Rosenbergs were still alive; they were made in the spirit of protest, to condemn the perpetrators of the crime, to rouse us, force us to remember, urge us to action. Others were created in the years immediately following the event; they became memories refusing to lie down in spite of galleries that would not show them or publishers who would not help them

into print. Many more were born more recently, as artists of later generations came to resent the covert or overt chill placed by officialdom not only upon our creativity but upon our very knowledge of *who we are.*

The Rosenbergs had been framed and "legally" put to death. Hundreds, if not thousands, of artists, filmmakers, teachers, writers, and others had been called up before a committee invested with the power to try to force them to condemn themselves and implicate their friends and colleagues in an invented conspiracy to "do America in." Many were imprisoned, denied passports, or lost jobs during the Fifties. But that was another time. An earlier, less responsible time. After all, a nation grows up, learns its lessons. Doesn't it?

I have said I was sixteen when the Rosenbergs were murdered. I had my own road to travel, my own search to discern what is real from what is sanitized and plastic-coated to keep us from ourselves. I left this country in 1961 and went to Mexico, where a raw national identity choking on dependent capitalism began teaching me how issues of international domination and control play themselves out in ordinary lives.

I continued to write poetry, became a feminist, was deeply involved in gathering oral histories of women in Cuba, Nicaragua, and other parts of Latin America. I began to make photographic images and wanted them to transmit the common voice in all its multiple dimensions. I began to see myself as a bridge: between the poets of two continents, the lives of two social systems, the voices of women traditionally silenced or ignored and a reading public ready to listen to what they have to say.

When I returned to the United States in 1984, because I had assumed Mexican citizenship back in the Sixties, I had to petition for residency in the land where I was born. I was still naive enough to believe that (at least for the white, middle-class "majority"), the United States remains a nation that can pride itself on being a model free marketplace for even dissenting ideas.

I believed that we honor our constitution and possess a system of justice through which obvious wrongs can be righted.

I encountered my first tangible evidence that the McCarthy era is still very much alive in this country when I came to an interview requested by the U.S. Immigration and Naturalization Service (INS) at its Albuquerque office and saw copies of some of my published books with sentences and whole paragraphs brightly set off with yellow magic-marker ink. The investigator asked what I meant by what I had written: criticism of U.S. policy in Southeast Asia, criticism of U.S. policy in Central America, the articulation of my concern over the racism and misogyny evident in aspects of this country's domestic life.

I responded that I meant exactly what I had said. And that I believed I had a right to my ideas. Three years later INS is still trying to deport me *solely on the basis of my written opinions.* And I, in my ongoing battle to remain in this country of my birth, continue to defend both my opinions and my right to express them.

Mine is a clear case of freedom of expression, involving the most obvious abuse of the First Amendment. The government's case against me is based on the McCarran-Walter Immigration and Nationality Act, passed by a McCarthyite Congress over President Truman's veto in 1952. Recently there has been some momentum in Congress around revising the more unconstitutional and antiquated clauses of McCarran-Walter. Interim legislation looks like it may have a favorable effect on my case as well as on others; more importantly, public as well as congressional sentiment leans toward more in-depth modifications that may, finally, cleanse our books of this legislation which has made the United States the butt of cynicism in the capitalist as well as the socialist worlds.

But the damage that cannot be erased is the chill, the censorship, the *self-censorship,* that tempered our thought and creativity back when the Rosenbergs were executed—when speaking out, in whatever way, might somehow imply guilt by association. That tempered our thought and creativity for many years afterward. And that continues to do so today in an *atmosphere that has itself been nurtured by an ongoing conspiracy of silencing forces.*

These paintings and prints, these poems and novels, the theatre, posters, and other art in this collection represent the best of that which has resisted this conspiracy of silence. From my personal experience I know how difficult it is to daily resolve to live inside my own voice, against the forces that urge me, subtly and brutally, to give up, give in, repent. It is an effort that must be renewed every day.

"… that daughter of a family/like so many/needing its female monster/she, actually wishing to be an *artist*/wanting out of poverty/possibly also really wanting revolution…." These lines from Adrienne Rich's extraordinary poem "For Ethel Rosenberg" take on particular meaning, become a special amulet, an immediate source of strength, in a struggle such as the one in which I am engaged.

This work is important beyond its worth as an excellent collection of committed art. The voices and images that are its separate parts are born out of an event that continues to both shame and inspire us. But in its entirety this show is also part and parcel of our most energizing culture. It restores our memory. It places us once more within our lives.

Hartford, Connecticut
Winter 1988

HAUNTED MEMORIES
The Rosenberg Era Art Project

ROB A. OKUN

I remember the evening in 1953 when Julius and Ethel Rosenberg were executed. There was a big meeting and I still remember the scene and the big, red sun was going down in the city streets. I wanted to paint it, but I never got to it. It was too much for me—too emotional. Rouault would have painted a scene like that.

—Raphael Soyer, in an interview with art historian Patricia Hills

One night in the spring of 1983, I had a dream. The artist Pablo Picasso was talking to Robby Meeropol, the younger son of Julius and Ethel Rosenberg.

Picasso was gesturing; Robby was nodding his head. I was too far away to hear what they were saying. They were inside the large foyer of what looked like an old French villa, and Picasso was pointing out the artwork on the walls. It was his work, and I remember feeling frustrated that I couldn't hear his descriptions.

They lingered before one piece, a double portrait of Robby's parents (fig. 2). It was a lithograph capturing, I thought, the dignity and conviction with which the couple lived through their three-year nightmare. Picasso pointed to the dedication: *Pour Michael et Robby Rosenberg.* After a moment, they moved on, opening a set of doors onto a patio and an expanse of closely cropped lawn. They walked for a moment and then descended out of view. As eerily as it began, my dream ended.

More than two years passed before I remembered that dream and by then I was deeply involved in organizing the exhibition *Unknown Secrets: Art*

and the Rosenberg Era. Whether it was some subconscious interpretation of what Picasso and Robby were discussing or a more rational explanation that sparked this project, I can't say. I do know that once the idea took hold, there was no letting go.

The hunt for Rosenberg art began with a half-dozen names on a list Robby Meeropol drew up for me. It included the activists Ethel and Julius Weiser in Washington, D.C., and the writer-editors Yuri Suhl and James Aronson, the latter a cofounder and editor of the *National Guardian,* the first newspaper to fully investigate the case (thanks to the efforts of reporter Bill Reuben). Along with their wives, Isabel Suhl and Grambs Miller, Yuri and Jim drew upon memories and personal relationships to help me uncover what all believed would be an important cache of art capturing the horror of the times. Accompanied by my wife, artist Deborah Kruger, we spent a long, sunny August afternoon on the deck of Yuri and Isabel's cottage on Martha's Vineyard talking about the Rosenberg case, and about art and politics. For Yuri and Jim—who were among the trustees of the Rosenberg Children's Fund—the idea of the exhibition evoked special, unspoken memories. In the course of four years' work organizing the exhibition, I would meet many artists and activists who repeatedly impressed me with the level of warmth and humanity that seemed especially triggered by the tragic story of Julius and Ethel Rosenberg.

The artwork of the Rosenberg era serves as a visual diary of one of the most horrific political events of the 1950s. My search for its far-flung

pages—and the later, important decision to invite artists to create new work—has taught me a great deal about an underground social history missing from the official chapters on those years. For people who didn't live through that era, it is almost impossible to fully grasp the enormity of the paranoia and repression that held the nation in its ugly grip, a time when people were afraid to speak their minds or express their deeper beliefs, an era unique in American history.

In the thirty-eight years since Ethel and Julius Rosenberg and Morton Sobell were arrested for conspiring to pass the so-called secrets of the atomic bomb to the Soviets, a staggering number of books and articles have been written about the case. The legal aspects have been hashed and rehashed, with a multitude of sides and perspectives presented in print. Less well known have been the poems and plays, films and novels, songs and stories produced in response to the chilling events of what I choose to call the Rosenberg era. But virtually unheard of has been the *artwork* produced as a result of their trial and execution.

In the Rosenberg case, a number of major issues were unfurled, not all of them addressed or understood at the time; all of them are still with us today: *the arms race, the right to dissent, capital punishment, anti-semitism, the treatment of political prisoners, espionage, anti-communism.*

What artists see and record—and what we learn from their work—is at the heart of this book and exhibition. Despite all the books, the story of the Rosenbergs and Morton Sobell (encapsulated here by Walter and Miriam

Fig. 2. A limited number of Picasso's portraits were sold to raise money for the Rosenbergs's defense. Pablo Picasso, *Untitled*, 1952, lithograph, 14 x 20".

Schneir from their book *Invitation to an Inquest*), is still a misunderstood chapter in modern history. It is a story of a rigid, paranoid nation afraid of its new-found atomic power nearly as much as it was of those who might acquire that power. Ultimately, it is a story of a fear of communism, a fear of the "other" so all pervasive and uncontrollable that perhaps the only way it could have been assuaged was by ritualistic murder, or as novelist Robert Coover would so aptly frame it, "the public burning."

Regardless of one's attitude about the trio's guilt or innocence, it is indisputable that Julius and Ethel Rosenberg and Morton Sobell were among the first American casualties of the nuclear arms race. Their punishment was the highwater mark in a flood of scapegoating, blacklisting, and witch-hunting spanning nearly a decade and a half, uprooting tens of thousands of lives and in many cases destroying them completely, and, finally, altering the political and sociocultural landscape in its wake.

Five years ago, in 1983, when a debate on the topic "Were the Rosenbergs Framed?" was staged at New York's Town Hall by two very different magazines, *The Nation* and *The New Republic*, more than 3,000 people tried to squeeze into a hall that held only 1,500. The evening was as much theatre as debate, and when the audience, a mix of old, new, and used leftists, finally left five hours later, it seemed to many that the case was thirty *days* old, rather than thirty years.

In each decade since the arrests, artists have created work inspired by what happened to this couple from the Lower East Side of Manhattan. From a lithograph by Picasso, a savage painting by Karel Appel, or the plays, *Le Peur* (The Fear) by French playwright Georges Soria, and the Polish writer Leon Kruczjowski's *Ethel and Julius* (all created by the end of 1953), to E. L. Doctorow's searing novel, the poetry of Adrienne Rich, and songs by Bob Dylan and other songwriters—various artists in a mix of media made art out of what occurred, or didn't occur, or might have. Each artist may have had a different motivation, but I believe that underlying each creation is an insistence on the artist's responsibility and right to creatively address our political, social, and spiritual predicament. The artwork in the exhibition

Fig. 3. This drawing by internationally acclaimed social realist Renato Gutusso was reproduced on posters and leaflets all over Italy. Renato Guttuso, *Julius and Ethel Rosenberg*, 1953, pencil on paper.

and represented throughout this book is indicative of much, but not all, of the worldwide artistic expression about the Rosenberg case.

When I began working on this project I was searching for that which already existed. And there was quite a lot. In addition to work on the East and West coasts of the United States, I discovered that artists in Mexico, Sweden, Holland, Germany, Italy, and France made Rosenberg art in the 1950s. Nagging at the back of my mind, though, was the idea of putting out a call for new work. I resisted, unsure how to proceed, especially when I had no venues in which to exhibit the old work, let alone the new. It was only after I began working closely with curator Nina Felshin in 1986 that the exhibition evolved into its present form.

And, as the art itself makes chillingly clear when we view it, there are many connections to be drawn between the Fifties and the Eighties.

The search for Rosenberg art has also been a search, at first unwittingly, for a hidden culture. The breadth of contributions by leftists to all of the arts has, by and large, been downplayed or dismissed by mainstream chroniclers. Such work has had to assert itself from behind an iron curtain of censorship, both subtle and overt—it can be explained in part by the number of artists and writers driven out of the country, blacklisted from their professions because of their political beliefs and affiliations.

I discovered pockets of this hidden culture in a variety of places: at a

"red-diaper" baby conference for children of communists in the New Hampshire mountains; in the exhibitions of art created for Artists Call, an action network; in the work of organizations such as the Alliance for Cultural Democracy, PADD (Political Art Documentation/Distribution), Bread and Roses Cultural Project, Heresies, Redwood Records, and the Shadow Project, among others, groups bridging the gap between the hidden and the mainstream. I also found many traces of it during long afternoons and evenings spent with artists and activists who survived the Rosenberg era.

Sitting at his kitchen table, not long after he had moved to New York in 1985, painter Arnold Mesches told me in vivid detail how his Los Angeles studio was broken into in the mid-Fifties

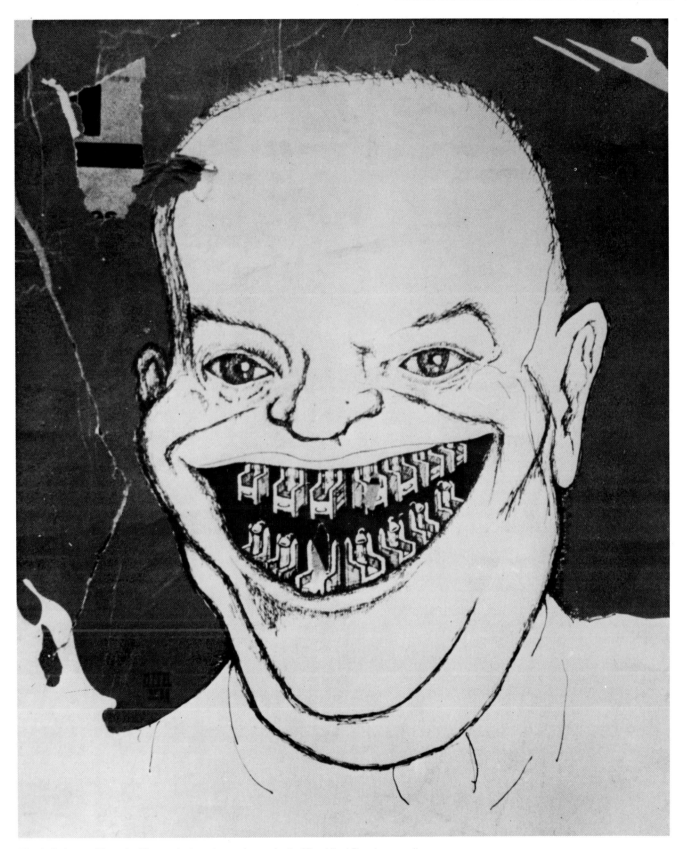

Fig. 4. Outraged French citizens plastered a poster portrait of President Eisenhower all over Paris. Louis Mittelberg, *His Famous Smile*, 1952, pencil on paper. (Photo courtesy State Historical Society of Wisconsin.)

and several of his Rosenberg paintings were stolen. "I don't doubt the FBI was involved," Mesches recalled.

Another painter, Anthony Toney, also had stories to tell during a visit I paid him at his home in Katonah, New York. A veteran of the Abraham Lincoln Brigade in the Spanish Civil War, Toney has been painting and exhibiting nationally for half a century. After lunch with Toney and his wife Edna—author of the Rosenberg-inspired play, *Danny Boy*, the artist recounted with ironic pleasure that his Rosenberg painting, *Procession*, resided in the permanent collection of the Whitney Museum of American Art.

It was a blustery March day in 1985 when artists Rudolf Baranik and May Stevens shared their feelings of outrage with me about what had happened to the Rosenbergs. Sitting in Baranik's SoHo loft, Stevens remembered painting a portrait of the two young Rosenberg children, but told me the painting had been lost years before. Later, Baranik pulled out his 1953 Rosenberg-inspired canvas, *Banners*, recounting how important it had been to him to make the painting.

From these conversations and others, as well as by becoming more familiar with a diverse and growing number of contemporary cultural workers making social and political connections in a variety of art forms, I came to believe that a rich heritage of social-issue art is flourishing in America. Happily, it is making its way into Hollywood and the New York art scene with more and more frequency—an encouraging development, I believe. But it is more often found out of the glare of the commercial spotlight. Perhaps this exhibition and book, in a small way, can help to direct some light on art made outside of the mainstream.

Support for social art and artists reached its zenith during the Depression, fostered by the federal government through the Works Project Administration (WPA). But such support had dried up by the end of World War II. The political climate of the Thirties, exposing as it did the emptiness of capitalism, fueled a compelling mix

of social art and literature attacking poverty and fascism, most notably the war drums beating in Spain. A host of artists—Ben Shahn, Jack Levine, William Gropper, Isabel Bishop, the Soyer brothers, Phillip Evergood—continued, after the war to till the fields of social realism, along with powerful photographers like Dorothea Lange and Margaret Bourke-White—but most are best known for their work before the war.

"Social realism as a force in American art did not outlive the Thirties though some of the artists remained loyal to its precepts," wrote art historian Milton Brown in a 1981 catalogue essay commemorating the ACA Galleries' fiftieth anniversary exhibition. "[They] continued to work in that vein beyond World War II in spite of the political atmosphere of the Cold War and

> Support for social art and artists reached its zenith during the Depression.

McCarthyism and a hostile aesthetic ambience."

But that hostile ambience didn't deter the first wave of artists who would reflect the Rosenberg case—Karel Appel, Rudolf Baranik, Angel Bracho and Celia Calderon, Fred Ellis, Adelyne Cross-Eriksson, Hugo Gellert, Renato Guttuso, Rockwell Kent, Fernand Léger, Louis Mittelberg, Francisco Mora, and Picasso. Their work, all completed by the year of the Rosenbergs' execution, 1953, represented, in many cases, a merger of art and activism. Limited editions of Picasso's and Léger's portraits were sold to raise money for the couple's defense. Mora, Bracho, and Calderon were all members of Mexico City's *Taller de Grafica Popular*, a left-wing graphics cooperative that produced posters with explanatory text about the case and plastered them by the thousands all over the city. (This take-the-message-to-the-streets tradition has been carried on often in contemporary time, most recently by Los Angeles artist Robby Conal, who

created a series of ghoulish poster portraits of the principals in the Iran-Contra scandal and had them hung by the thousands in major cities across the country.)

Ellis and Gellert drew for *The Daily Worker*, the Communist paper, among others, and published political cartoons protesting what was happening to the Rosenbergs. Guttuso, a well-known Italian social realist who exhibited internationally, did a riveting portrait of the handcuffed couple before a bloody map of North America (fig. 3). It was later reproduced with text on street leaflets in Rome.

Among the most powerful images created at the high point of the hysteria was Louis Mittelberg's portrait of President Eisenhower, his famous wide smile revealing a mouthful of electric chairs in place of teeth (fig. 4). Drawn originally for the French Communist newspaper *L'Humanité*, it was plastered all over Paris. Today, Mittelberg refuses to discuss the drawing, his politics having taken a sharp turn to the right. He continues to draw and is an illustrator for the French weekly *L'Express.* He told a colleague in Paris assisting me with the exhibition that he wanted no part in the show.

It is curious to note that throughout the intensive research that went into uncovering the historical pieces, I was unable to locate any anti-Rosenberg art or editorial cartoons. I was intrigued by the prospect of uncovering such work, as it, too, would say much about the era. Indeed, I did learn about some scathing editorial page illustrations, but was unable to put my hands on any, despite contact with major cartoon syndicates and newspapers around the country. Of course there was no dearth of virulent anti-Rosenberg sentiment— counter-demonstrators in front of the White House carried picket signs suggesting not "frying" the couple because they would stink too much.

Like Robet Minor, best known for biting political illustrations done earlier in this century, Hugo Gellert believed that the newspaper was "the poor man's art gallery." In those years, too,

Gellert's political drawings were a mainstay in newspapers and magazines in New York City. His illustrations of Tom Mooney, the Scottsboro Boys, Sacco and Vanzetti, among others, were well known. Gellert had turned sixty when he did the first of several Rosenberg and Sobell drawings, not all of which have survived. I spoke to him in 1984, a year before he died at age ninety-three.

"I remember this mass meeting on Union Square—15th Street, really. It was the night of the execution. We were tied up by a cordon of police between Fifth Avenue and Union Square. There were a good many cops. And from where we stood, we could see the clock on the tower of the Metropolitan Life Insurance Company building. We were watching it because we knew the execution was slated for eight o'clock. When it got close, the crowd was worked up, really worked up. We scared the cops to death. I can't remember it even now without being moved, even at this late date."

During a long winter's afternoon conversation at his home in Freehold, New Jersey, interrupted with apple pie and coffee, Gellert looked younger and more sprightly than his years as he recalled a lifetime of artmaking wedded to political activism. Gellert organized auctions of artwork as fundraisers for the Rosenberg-Sobell defense committee, once receiving a drawing of Michael and Robby "by a young girl who turned out to be (the New York artist) May Stevens," he told me with an amused smile.

Although he drew for *The New York Times*, the *New York Post*, and, for twenty years, *The New Yorker*, Gellert is best known for his work in left-wing publications such as *The Daily Worker*, *The Masses, and Masses & Mainstream*.

By June 1953, Gellert had already done a number of Rosenberg drawings. But after the shocked and brokenhearted vigil had received official word that the executions had in fact occurred, he walked through the crowd to his studio just off Union

Square and did one more. "I went right up and did the drawing of them embraced by a figure I call posterity. So that's what I called the drawing, *Embraced by Posterity*."

Gellert says work done after the Rosenbergs were executed is different from art created while they were still alive. As a political activist and an artist involved in the major issues of the day, he led the artists' strike picketing John D. Rockefeller after the industrialist removed Diego Rivera's mural at Rockefeller Center for including an image of Lenin. (E. B. White wrote a poem about the incident in which Rivera complains, "It's my mural," to which Rockefeller replies, "But it's my wall.")

To Gellert, artists who created Rosenberg art for the leftist press or the

> What is intriguing about the Rosenberg paintings is how the political climate affected them.

committee working to free the couple, were an important part of the struggle. Those who did their work afterward were recording history. "It's not that it isn't valuable," he told me, "It's just not the same. Too many artists were afraid to be counted."

Whatever one believes about this analysis, the fact that young artists, some only children or teenagers at the time of the trial, chose, years later, to make art about the case, contributes much more than a record of a historical event. By keeping the issue alive it offers a reference point for beginning to understand our present situation.

One of the artists in the exhibition, Leon Marcus, was visited on a number of occasions in the Fifties by the FBI. Not about his art but about his politics. The harassment became so frequent that Marcus set up his easel in his living room and began painting the scene of the agents standing in the doorway questioning his wife with the couple's small children nearby. He would leave the painting-in-progress in the doorway so the agents would be forced to

confront it when they came calling. One day, Marcus became so exasperated with the harassment that he lost his temper and chased them away with a baseball bat. Surprisingly, they never returned.

Marcus's son, the young boy hanging close to his mother in the painting, grew up to become a political artist himself, Paul Marcus. He is one of the contemporary artists who created new work for the exhibition.

In my conversations with several of the artists, they revealed a sophisticated understanding of how society operated in the McCarthy years. None created Rosenberg art because a dealer or patron had suggested it. On the contrary, making such images bucked prevailing political and art-world norms.

"What I knew about the whole process going on against Julius and Ethel Rosenberg, right from the beginning, I considered it completely unjust," recalled Francisco Mora, the Mexican artist and member of the *Taller de Grafica Popular* graphics cooperative. I interviewed him and his American-born wife, sculptor Elizabeth Catlett, when they were visiting the U.S. from their home in Mexico. Catlett served as interpreter. In a conversation at a friend's apartment in New York, Mora unraveled a complex set of artistic and political memories.

"I always felt that the Rosenbergs were victims of a social system and a political position—a system under which we were all living. But I didn't believe that United States justice could be so warped. I didn't think it would get to the point of the execution of two ordinary people."

As Mora remembers, "The case wasn't known in Mexico. And the Mexican press was a paid press. And the news was that they were going to judge them spies. I felt it necessary to do something publicly."

Despite the fact the in August 1950 Mexican agents cooperated with U.S. officials by kidnapping Rosenberg codefendant Morton Sobell and depositing him at the Texas border, Mexico was at the time a haven for radicals seeking refuge from the witch hunts. Many writers, artists, and activists had taken up Mexican residence, among them screenwriter Albert Maltz. Maltz was one of the Hollywood Ten, a group of blacklisted writers and directors sentenced to prison for contempt of Congress after refusing to name names at House Un-American Activities Committee hearings.

"One of the people who came to talk to us about the Rosenbergs was Albert," recalled Elizabeth Catlett, "Albert and Margaret Maltz. And it was after they visited that Pancho [Mora] decided to do the poster."

"I wanted the best way to present the Rosenbergs. What I thought would give the most impact was death," Mora recounted. "Pulling the switch coming out of the sleeve with the dollar sign on it. And another hand stopping it. And finally two victims sitting in the two chairs [fig. 5]. This is the idea I thought would be the most striking for the people in Mexico. I didn't do it as a superficial thing… and I wasn't bothered about the consequences. I didn't think about that… I think that an artist conscious of himself as an artist is an artist conscious for the whole world. My idea was in some way to help the defense of the Rosenbergs, to avoid the assassinations. And I did it with all my strength and all my character. What came out was that poster. That's my position as a revolutionary artist and I'm not ashamed of it. On the contrary, I'm very proud of it."

Mora also took an active interest in the life of his Rosenberg poster, hunting up a printer and finding the right people in the union that pasted posters up in the city. Some didn't want to because of the pressure that would have been exerted on them not to put up the posters. They generally pasted bullfighting and entertainment posters, rarely anything remotely political.

"I was very anxious to see what would happen," Mora remembered. "By the next day it was pasted all over Mexico City. Thousands of them! It was 1952 and this was the first poster on the Rosenberg case in Mexico, and people saw it and read it. It was a great success as far as the *Taller* was

concerned—success for the collectivity of the *Taller*. We were out on the streets again, presenting a new problem."

Ralph Fasanella says he is a little obsessed with the Rosenberg case. His staccato speech, often delivered as sentence fragments requiring skillful concentration to comprehend, reveals a passionate man committed to social justice. In his mid-seventies now, he is a self-taught painter, described as one of America's premier primitive artists. In his work there is no easy resting place for the eye, each square inch of a canvas packed with a dizzying array of people, buildings, signs, neon lights, religious icons, automobiles—the stuff of pulsing urban life.

Over a marathon six-hour meeting at his studio and home in Ardsley, New York, punctuated by several meals, Fasanella, and his gracious wife and business manager Eva, talked about his life and art. As a union organizer in the Thirties, Fasanella began suffering from arthritis in his hands. Warned that unless he started using them his problems would increase, he took up drawing, at first doodling at meetings as a form of physical therapy.

Beginning in the shop where he worked, Fasanella collected money for the Rosenberg-Sobell defense effort and became deeply involved in the case. "I'd go up to people and say, 'You remember Tom Mooney, Sacco and Vanzetti? The Rosenbergs are being framed on the same basis!' With that approach I collected $32 in the whole shop. Now that may not seem like a lot of money now, but then it was. People pitchin' in a quarter, a half-dollar. A lot of people understood what was happening."

What is intriguing about the Rosenberg paintings, Fasanella says, is how the political climate affected them."After I got through, no one would touch 'em. No galleries. Not even the union halls would show them. That was in '63, '64. Now the New York State Historical Society up in Cooperstown has one on exhibit and one of them was travelling in a show in Germany." A year after the couple

was executed, Fasanella completed his first Rosenberg paintings. In 1963, he did two more. "The Rosenbergs came out a lot in my paintings," Fasanella said. "Somehow I think the symbol of the Rosenbergs is a symbol for expressing myself."

Fasanella, whose flood of emotions swirl in and out between the eddies of the art world and the political world, reaches high water with a rare, unemotional description of the McCarthy period. "It was the freezing of America. The McCarthy period's censorship is still at work. The killing of the Rosenbergs really did the job, once and for all. When I painted those paintings it brought me back to that period. The restrictions of the period. The fear of painting, too. You were constantly on the verge of being in trouble. Maybe others were free, but you could feel it… but in this place [his home and studio], we never showed those paintings. It's only in the last ten years that we pulled them out. We wouldn't show nobody. We'd run upstairs and put them in the back, so no one was even looking at these paintings. It's always been a problem, but it's not just my problem, it's everybody's. And, as far as I'm concerned, it still remains."

Rupert Garcia cut his political and artistic teeth during the San Francisco State College student strike in 1968. First as an organizer, later as an artist making posters, he was in the middle of the campus protest. Garcia saw no distinction between his work as an artist and as an organizer, and felt a sense of fulfillment that the two interests could be neatly joined.

He didn't come to politics from an intellectual's perspective. As a Chicano living in California during a politically tumultuous period, Garcia made connections between his community and others, most notably the civil rights and antiwar movements.

"I was a painter with a capital 'P,' until the strike occurred at State," he recalled, sitting in his Oakland, California studio. "I discontinued making easel paintings because the notion of making a painting on an easel was meaningless in the context of all that

Fig. 5. Mexicans learned about the case through posters like this one created by Taller de Grafica Popular. Francisco Mora, *Help Stop This Crime*, 1952, woodcut, 23½ x 15¾" (detail).

was occurring at the college. It made no sense. So what else do you do if you're a picture-maker? You make posters. That's what I did. That's why I learned silkscreening. I didn't learn it in a classroom, I learned it as a consequence of the conflict on campus. I went on to become a screen printer for eight years."

Garcia, a compact man with a wide smile and abundant energy, became aware of the Rosenberg-Sobell case in 1969 when he had gone to hear recently-freed Rosenberg codefendant Morton Sobell speak in Berkeley. But it was ten years before he did his portraits. Seeing the Rosenbergs on the cover of *The New Republic*, Garcia was moved. "They struck me for what they represented, but they also struck me in terms of aesthet-

ics—the sensibility of their faces imposing on my space.

"The intention to make the picture is multi-faceted," Garcia recalled. "Part of it is as a person who is very concerned with what he sees in the world. And part of it was to honor them, to pay homage to them and provide a reminder of what they had gone through. That's why I think the portraits just ooze off the page into our present time zone. They speak to the issues of their time zone and ours, in that there is a continuation of folks who are still being entrapped. People are still being duped, scapegoated. What happens is our eyes are taken off the real enemy and just a few folks are fingered as a symbol of the problem so we put them in jail and the problem goes away."

Garcia's point of view on the impact

art can have in fostering social change is one not often articulated. Can art make a change? I ask him. "Yes," he said, "it can make a change in *me*. It can change *me*, make *me* feel better and want to continue to be a better person. If it can work for me, perhaps it can work for other people."

For novelists like E. L. Doctorow, Robert Coover, and Tema Nason and playwright Donald Freed, the Rosenberg case served as inspiration for major works. Doctorow's 1971 novel, *The Book of Daniel*, and Coover's *The Public Burning* in 1977, made powerful statements about American politics, culture, and justice. Tema Nason, whose autobiographical novel *Ethel* is expected to be published shortly, gives a fully-formed identity to Ethel

Rosenberg and offers readers a chance to speculate about who she really was.

Doctorow says his novel is not really about the Rosenbergs. Their arrest for conspiring to pass atomic secrets to the Soviet Union was just the jumping-off point for his gritty look at family, the radicals of the Forties and Fifties and the New Left. The children in the novel are fictional, their stories not at all based on the lives of Michael and Robby Meeropol.

For Coover, the line between reality and surreality is easily crossed by anyone—cabinet members, Betty Crocker, Uncle Sam. His 563 pages of political madcap provoke both chortles and chills. Richard Nixon narrates, the execution is set in Times Square in New York, and President Eisenhower and J. Edgar Hoover, among others, parade through the book's pages much the way they behaved during the witch hunts, only sillier and more frightening.

In *Ethel* Nason offers a fictional autobiography whose power lies in its voice, a plausible self-portrait of Ethel Greenglass Rosenberg—singer, organizer, daughter, wife, mother, and independent woman.

The Rosenbergs have made numerous cameo appearances in fiction, poetry and drama. Deena Metzger's play *Dreams Against the State*, David Evanier's short story, *The Prince of Progressive Humanity*, and the novels *Anne's Youth* by Frances Gladstone, and *You Must Remember This*, by Joyce Carol Oates are just a few recent examples.

As for music, more than a few folk songs have been written. In the mid-Seventies, Bob Dylan wrote the as yet unreleased hard driving rocker, *Julius and Ethel*. Among the lyrics is the line, "Eisenhower was president/Senator Joe was King/Long as you didn't say nothin'/You could say anything." Also, at least two cantatas have been composed. One, by Leonard Lehrman, is based on the Rosenbergs' *Death House Letters*.

Robert Eaton's 1987 play about the atom bomb, *Out with a Bang*, features the Rosenbergs in its history of the

bomb from Hiroshima to the present. Recent Off Broadway plays have also made references to the couple and the case.

For the writer Sylvia Plath, however, the Rosenberg case carried an extra charge. As writer, she had chosen to open her disturbing 1963 novel *The Bell Jar* like this:

"It was a queer sultry summer, the summer they electrocuted the Rosenbergs... The idea of being electrocuted makes me sick and that's all there was to read about in the papers— goggle-eyed headlines staring up at me from every street corner and at the fusty, peanut-smelling mouth of every subway...."

But the case and its implications spilled over into her private life as well.

Eisenhower was President / Senator Joe was King / Long as you didn't say nothin' / you could say anything. — Bob Dylan

Chosen as a Guest Editor at *Mademoiselle* in the summer of 1953, she had kept an extensive diary. Only the following entry has survived, written on the morning of the executions.

NEW YORK *June 19, 1953*. All right, so the headlines blare the two of them [the Rosenbergs] are going to be killed at eleven o'clock tonight. So I am sick at the stomach. I remember the journalist's report, sickeningly factual, of the electrocution of a condemned man, of the unconcealed fascination of the faces of the onlookers, of the details, the shocking physical facts about the death, the scream, the smoke, the bare honest unemotional reporting that gripped the guts because of the things it didn't say.

The tall beautiful catlike girl who wore an original hat to work every day rose to one elbow from where she had been napping on the divan in the conference room, yawned, and said with beautiful bored nastiness: "I'm so glad they are

going to die." She gazed vaguely and very smugly around the room, closed her enormous green eyes, and went back to sleep.

The phones are ringing as usual, and the people planning to leave for the country over the long weekend, and everybody is lackadaisical and rather glad and nobody very much thinks about how big a human life is, with all the nerves and sinews and reactions and responses that it took centuries and centuries to evolve.

They were going to kill people with those atomic secrets. It is good for them to die. So that we can have the priority of killing people with those atomic secrets which are so very jealously and specially and inhumanly ours.

There is no yelling, no horror, no great rebellion. That's the appalling thing. The execution will take place tonight; it's too bad that it could not be televised...so much more realistic and beneficial than the run-of-the-mill crime program. Two real people being executed. No matter. The largest emotional reaction over the United States will be a rather large, democratic, infinitely bored and casual and complacent yawn.

Years went by before playwright Donald Freed crafted the Rosenberg case into a play. Sticking close to actual events, he relied heavily on the trial transcript, seeing in it a "theater of cruelty" which needed little embellishment. The author of several plays, novels, screenplays, and nonfiction works, Freed's play *Inquest* ran in 1970 on Broadway where it was well received despite intimidation by the FBI.

Walter and Miriam Schneir's 1965 book, *Invitation to an Inquest*, revived Freed's earlier fascination with the story, he told me during a visit to his home in Los Angeles. Freed said the image of the "show trial" is theater itself, a "theatre of fact, of cruelty, in the philosophical sense that it forces an audience to choose."

The Rosenberg-Sobell case was part of an almost collective unconsciousness of a whole segment of the population, Freed said. Before reading John Wexley's book, *The Judgment of Julius and Ethel Rosenberg* (the first full-scale study of the case, written in 1955), Freed knew nothing about the story or about its politics. Wexley's book became a primer for Freed, or, as he called it, "an initiation."

"Whatever sentiments or empathy or predilection I might have had for appreciating the unequal struggle between the powerful and powerless, a very modern, American historical stamp was put on those feelings by the Wexley book," Freed recalled. His political awareness now having awakened, Freed followed the heroic political campaign waged by Helen Sobell in her efforts to free her husband, Morton, and to clear the Rosenbergs.

By the time the Schneirs' book was published, the body of information was so extensive and organized that it was easy to dramatize. "At least the structure was there," Freed remembered, "the diagram of the case. All of that work had been done."

The play was tried out first at the Cleveland Playhouse. It was 1969 and, after almost twenty years, Morton Sobell had just been released from prison. "Sobell came down for opening night. There was great excitement. There was a discussion with the audience after the performance, as there was every night in Cleveland. Spirited and intense. Sid Peck and others from Cleveland involved in the indictments, the political trials of the late Sixties were there, and so a natural kind of link was established."

The audience felt the passion of the political action, Freed said, gesticulating with his pipe from time to time for emphasis. The Playhouse was full, and media attention was not confined to the entertainment pages of the paper. Op-ed pieces appeared on the editorial pages of the *Cleveland Plain Dealer*. Stories spilled over onto the news pages.

"The cast was a mix of professional and amateur actors, but all played with great passion and all had made themselves knowledgeable about the case. Later, in New York, the cast became personally involved, too," Freed recalled, ruefully, "and were subsequently spied on by the FBI."

"It was director Larry Terrant's first directorial assignment there. And there was no budget to speak of. So it was crude, unpolished, and enormously moving. In New York, however, it was polished, high tech (more than 100 slide carousels were used), it had marvelous artisans and artists involved, a world-famous director (Alan Schneider), and brilliant actors. And it had an improved script, definitely from Cleveland, and it was cold, cold as ice, really. The producers and the cast were intimidated. And the dirty tricks of the FBI involved using the wife of a well-known gossip columnist to contact some of the actors. Roy Cohn was involved. The New York reviews were wonderful (two favorable ones in *The New York Times*), but the producers were so anxious that they didn't take advantage of the reviews at

> The myth of the government is the atom-bomb spy ring; the official myth is called history.

all. Clive Barnes, then critic for the *Times*, was censored, the one and only time in his career. A paragraph was cut from his review. In fact, in the FBI files I have, our secret police tried to stop the *Times* from even covering the play."

Though Freed's work often begins with events in the news— his plays and books have dealt with the Black Panthers, Richard Nixon, the CIA's role in the coup in Chile—the mythic, as much as political events, is what captures his attention. *Inquest* also captured the attention of the FBI, an arguable criterion for its political reality. On the other hand, Freed's introductory remarks in the published script, as well as elements of the play cut from production—the gods of the 20th century, a prologue of Freud, Nietzsche, and Marx— attest to its mythic exploration.

As an artist, Freed sees his job as taking the headlines and transforming the stories from what they are, a mix of journalistic gossip, and exposing them as stories of power or "fairy tales of

power." Presenting these fairy tales before the crucible of public imagination reduces them to lower orders of abstraction. By so doing, Freed believes, "they begin to speed up the historical transition from gossip, lies, rumors, fantasies, nightmares, and other sources of mythology. From history, which is the self-serving record of power, over into mythology, which is the disguised popular version of events which have reached every home in the land.

"It isn't any great leap to bring into play myth and politics, myth and the newspaper. Because events happening and unfolding in our lifetimes are potentially myths as much as they are history. Without the intervention of the artist, the myth becomes infantile. So that John Kennedy is still alive on a Greek island. That's the myth of the public if left to itself. Kennedy alive, a vegetable, in Greece. The myth of the government, the state, is the Warren Commission Report."

As Freed describes it, between these two choices there is nothing left but a nervous breakdown. The same choices hold true for the Rosenberg case. The myth of the government is the atom-bomb spy ring; the official myth called history. The unofficial myth, the people's myth, is still evolving, struggling for existence. A project such as this is part of that struggle.

Says Freed, "The Warren Commission Report will never change. It's freeze-dried. That's history." The Rosenberg case *is* changing. It's alive." The books, articles, art, film, and public debates are all a part of a living organism, an unfolding myth. "It's a product of ongoing intervention."

What I didn't realize, when I undertook this project five years ago, was that as much as I was trying to understand the connections between art and politics and why the Rosenberg-Sobell case continues to haunt the artistic imagination, I was also trying to understand who *I* was, where *I* came from. While the recent spate of books about the cultural and political aspirations of the Sixties generation—

my generation—continues to help me fit together pieces of that critical time in my life, I am drawn back even further.

I was only three years old when the Rosenbergs were electrocuted at Sing Sing. Growing up in a middle-class Jewish home near Springfield, Massachusetts, I was worlds away from the dark stain spreading over the Fifties. For me those years flew by faster than Stevie Nissenbaum and I could pedal our bikes to Friendly's. Faster than the Elvis Presley 78's could spin on my brother, Stuart's, phonograph. Time only slowed down at *Bobe* and *Zayde* Okun's mysterious old house, which though thousands of miles from their native Russia, still retained the smells, tastes, and sounds of the old Yiddish world.

The incongruous combination of prosperity and persecution, pride and paranoia, which held the country in a vise from the end of World War II until the waning days of the Eisenhower presidency, has a hold on me still. Could we really have been so crazy?

There is another troubling question. From the beginning of this project, the Jewish aspect of the Rosenberg story has nipped at my consciousness. I understand why many Jews in the Fifties didn't publicly protest the undercurrent of anti-Semitism washing over the Rosenbergs and Morton Sobell. After all, the Holocaust was too fresh a memory and, I suppose, many Jews didn't want to draw undue attention to themselves. But even as I write, thirty-

eight years after the arrests, no comprehensive investigation has ever adequately addressed these questions:

If they had not been Jews, would the Rosenbergs have been executed?

In a city with the largest Jewish population in the world, why were there no Jews on the jury?

And conversely, why were a Jewish judge and Jewish prosecutor appointed to conduct the trial?

(A chilling tributary in the flood of anti-Communist sentiment seeking to drown the Rosenbergs was a CIA plan, addressed in the exhibition by Margia Kramer, to use the couple to convince Jews to get out of the Communist movement in exchange for their freedom.)

Beyond the obvious dramatic dimensions of a story whose elements pit brother against sister, accusations of espionage, and a mighty government ritualistically murdering two of its lowly citizens, perhaps there is another reason why so many artists and writers were drawn to create art about the case: Even if they might consciously deny it, maybe it is the artists who were atoning for the rest of us, since as a nation we carry the Rosenbergs's blood on our hands.

I don't know. The blacklist and witch hunts effectively broke any remnant of a leftist political movement in the country, severing the connection between the activists of the Thirties and Forties with those of the Sixties. The art world, too, reflected that break. It has taken a long time for it to be reestab-

lished, an activity, which like a surgeon reattaching a severed limb, must be done slowly and with painstaking determination. What role the exhibition and this book will play in that process remains to be seen.

The artist Dennis Adams, who is 40, may not feel similarly, but his works of public art—bus shelters with large, curiously cropped photographs of the Rosenbergs, Roy Cohn and Joe McCarthy and Bertolt Brecht, among others—raise questions about America's historical amnesia. They have been the subject of much debate since they first appeared in and around New York City in the mid-Eighties. If waiting bus passengers know who the figures are, they stop and think; if they don't know, they may ask themselves who these strange people from a bygone era, are imposing on their space with large, questioning eyes?

Adams says some people think he is haunted by images of the Fifties, a charge he doesn't dismiss. "Although I've used more contemporary images… the Fifties were… in a very personal way the first political images I remember.… I think a lot of people are interested in knowing the political climate they're born into. Because the political climate is being filtered through the voice of the mother and the father and the family life. And, as you get older, you want to come to terms with that history."

For me, this book and exhibition are an attempt to do just that.

THE UNITED STATES VS. ROSENBERGS AND SOBELL:

A Capsule View

WALTER SCHNEIR
AND MIRIAM SCHNEIR

"On August 6, 1945, a split atom sent waves of destruction circling out over Hiroshima—an explosion whose implications still batter against the institutions of our time. On June 19, 1953, two people, charged with having transmitted secrets of this destruction to a foreign power, were executed after judgment by their fellow citizens."

Thus the *Columbia Law Review* began a critique of what it called "the outstanding 'political' trial of this generation."

The awesome enormity of the crime for which Julius and Ethel Rosenberg were condemned was made clear by Judge Irving R. Kaufman when he pronounced the death sentence on April 5, 1951.

"... by your betrayal," he told the Rosenbergs, "you have undoubtedly altered the course of history to the disadvantage of our country."

Two coconspirators in the case, Morton Sobell and David Greenglass, received prison terms of thirty and fifteen years respectively.

So ended a trial whose implications, like those of the split atom, "still batter against the institutions of our time."

For fourteen days in New York City's federal courthouse at Foley Square, the drama of United States vs. Rosenbergs and Sobell held the stage, pitting brother against sister, friend

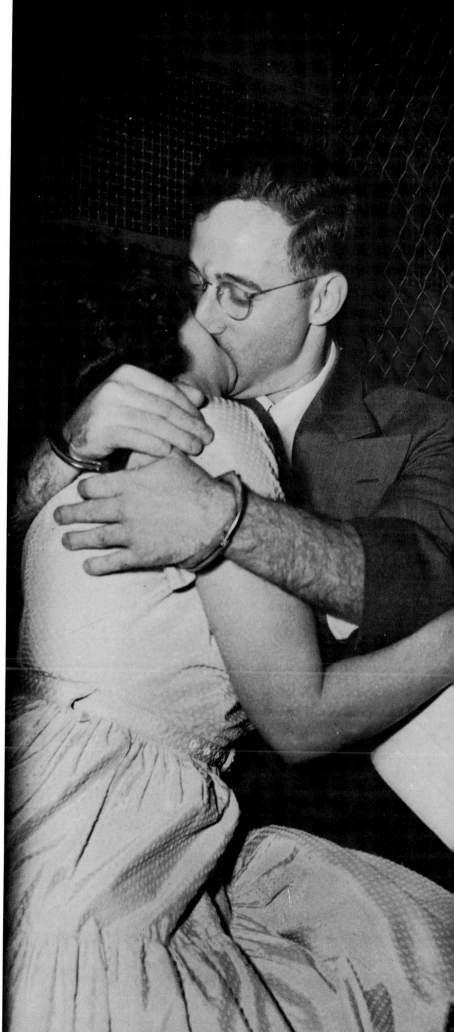

Fig. 6. Julius and Ethel Rosenberg embrace following their August 23, 1950 arraignment in Federal Court in New York. (Wide World Photos.)

against friend. The charge was conspiracy to commit espionage; the defendants were all alleged to have been participants in a plot aimed at obtaining national defense information for the benefit of the Soviet Union.

But the crux of the matter was the accusation that the Rosenbergs—in the language of the government prosecutor—had stolen "through David Greenglass this one weapon, that might well hold the key to the survival of this nation and means the peace of the world, the atomic bomb." The motive for this crime was said to be ideological: Communism.

In the face of deeply incriminating testimony, the accused husband and wife had repeatedly denied any involvement in the conspiracy. Morton Sobell (whose alleged espionage role was not related to the atomic bomb) also claimed his innocence.

Testifying against Julius and Ethel Rosenberg was Ethel's younger brother, David Greenglass, who pleaded guilty and appeared as the principal prosecution witness. David, a machinist who had been stationed at Los Alamos as an enlisted man during World War II, told the court how he divulged the secrets of the atom bomb at the request of his brother-in-law and sister. His wife, Ruth, confirmed her husband's story and added to it.

Chief prosecution witness against Morton Sobell was Max Elitcher, Sobell's boyhood chum, neighbor, and co-worker, who provided the only testimony linking his former friend to the espionage conspiracy.

Finally, the dramatis personae included the curious little Philadelphia chemist, Harry Gold (already under sentence of thirty years), who had skyrocketed to sudden notoriety some ten months before when FBI Director J. Edgar Hoover revealed him as the confessed American accomplice of British spy Klaus Fuchs. A man who appeared to have tiptoed through life with downcast eyes, Gold shed his cocoon of self-effacement on the witness stand and told his story in robust tones, frquently jabbing his right forefinger at the jurors to make a point. About him, the federal prosecutor

had said: "Harry Gold, who furnished the absolute corroboration of the testimony of the Greenglasses, forged the necessary link in the chain that points indisputably to the guilt of the Rosenbergs."

All seven of these individuals were alleged, either during the trial or in press reports, to have been sympathetic to or active in radical left-wing politics. All seven were Jews (as were the judge and two of the main prosecuting attorneys in the case, Irving H. Saypol and Roy M. Cohn).

Julius and Ethel Rosenberg, David and Ruth Greenglass, Morton Sobell and Max Elitcher were all in their late twenties or early thirties, married, and the parents of young children. The Rosenbergs and the Greenglasses were related and had lived in the

> "The Sacco-Vanzetti case united the liberals; the Rosenberg case divided them."

same New York City Lower East Side neighborhood all their lives. The Rosenberg, Sobell, and Elitcher families were acquainted socially; Julius, Morton, and Max had been classmates at the College of the City of New York, where they studied engineering. In a sense, the outsider in this group was Harry Gold, a forty-year old bachelor, who—except for an alleged espionage meeting with the Greenglasses—did not claim to have known or met any of the other principals.*

The day after Judge Kaufman sentenced the Rosenbergs to death, a brief item in a *New York Post* column suggested that the government was prepared to barter the lives of the condemned couple for information. Soon the choice facing the Rosenbergs was widely known and publicly discussed. The refusal of the prisoners

---

*Similarly, prosectuion witness Elizabeth Bentley never had met any of those against whom she testified.

to proffer a *mea culpa* was frequently in the press as conclusive evidence of their political fanaticism, disregard for their children, and an overwhelming wish to become Marxist martyrs. The apparent use of a death sentence for coercion was generally accepted with out criticism.

In the United States, a small but persistent minority, its ranks buttressed by the presence of a few scientific notables, was accutely troubled by the case. In part, this response was conditioned by the distrust some people felt for any trial with wide political implications conducted in an atmosphere of hostility and tension. The constant questioning of the Rosenbergs as to their political ideas, opinions, reading habits, and affiliations made the trial seem suspect.

Students of history were well aware that, in times of stress, any judicial system may fail. Juries may be wrong and judges biased; the innocent may be convicted. Hearing the Rosenbergs' repeated assertions of innocence, some were reminded painfully of the injustices visited on Dreyfus, on Mooney and Billings, on Sacco and Vanzetti.

But a claim of innocence is no proof of innocence, though such claims, persisted in over a very long time and even under extreme duress, may make us uneasy. And knowledge of previous miscarriages of justice can at best serve as a warning of caution, nothing more.

Nor did a reading of the trial record provide any positive answer for most people as to the guilt or innocence of the Rosenbergs, though many who studied the trial record came away with gnawing uncertainties as to the validity of the verdict. In the United States, some Rosenberg partisans undoubtedly were completely convinced of the innocence of the pair; others believed that there was more than a reasonable doubt as to their guilt. A third point of view was that the Rosenbergs were probably guilty of "something," but that the importance of their crime had been greatly exaggerated for political purposes.

Not surprisingly, many of the comparatively small band who sought clemency for the Rosenbergs—particularly members of the clergy—completely bypassed the thorny issue of guilt or innocence, concentrating their efforts instead on the severity of the sentence.

In particular, one unique aspect of the Rosenberg case served to discourage support for the couple: All previous cases that American liberals and radicals had assailed as judicial errors or outright frameups had been tried in state courts; the Rosenbergs were tried by the Federal judiciary. To cry frameup here was a far more serious matter; it was, in effect, to accuse high officials of the United States government itself of perpetrating a vicious hoax.

Such an accusation would not be an easy one to make under any circumstances. But in 1952 and 1953, the tide of McCarthyism was at its crest. The far left was no longer a force in American politics; the ranks of the liberals were badly split—former New Deal supporters were shaken and confused by the barrage of congressional charges regarding Communists in government. After the conviction of Alger Hiss in early 1950, many American liberals vowed total abstinence from any further dalliance with the radical left; while some few were seduced from their resolves by the Rosenberg case, most reacted to the affair by hurriedly snapping shut their political chastity belts and tossing away the keys.

Later, sociologists David Riesman and Nathan Glazer commented aptly in the *Partisan Review*: "The Sacco-Vanzetti case united the liberals; the Rosenberg case divided them."

If the campaign for the Rosenbergs achieved only modest mass appeal in the United States and practically no support from the press, in many other nations the case became a *cause célèbre* with impressive popular backing. Undoubtedly, Communist parties played a considerable role in this protest movement. What nettled and bewildered knowledgeable Americans, however, was the inexplicable depth and extent of pro-Rosenberg sentiment among non-Communists

Fig. 7. Morton Sobell (left) and a U.S. deputy marshal, en route from City Prison to his trial with the Rosenbergs at Federal Court, March 6, 1951. (UPI/Bettmann News Photo).

abroad, particularly in Western Europe.

Far more than in the United States, many influential Europeans—often after studying the facts of the case and reading the trial record—were convinced of the Rosenbergs' innocence. Their statements on the case shaped the views of millions. In France, the campaign to save the doomed couple produced an astonishing unanimity among all factions of that nation's polychrome political spectrum. The Rosenberg case was, in fact, the single issue about which dis-

putatious French citizens had been able to unite since the war.

For the vast majority of Americans, the worldwide outcry over the Rosenbergs was puzzling, even infuriating. For had not the Rosenbergs been tried and convicted in an American court of law? Was not the case officially closed when the jury brought in its verdict and the reviewing courts let that verdict stand? Some of the most distinguished newspapers had editorially congratulated Judge Kaufman after the sentencing. Why then this frenzied effort on behalf of two spies who had outrageously betrayed their country and showed no signs of contrition?

In fine, the only mystery about the case for most Americans was a general bafflement about the great clamor being raised by millions over the fate of the Rosenbergs. Both the press and public opinion in the United States generally ascribed this uproar to the abysmal duplicity on the part of Rosenberg partisans who willfully distorted the truth. At the very least, supporters of the couple were said to be the foolish dupes of Communist Machiavellianism. In Europe, however, the Rosenberg case was seen by many as a dispiriting symptom of the deterioration of traditional democratic freedom in the United States.

As the movement for clemency grew, the Rosenbergs' refusal to admit their guilt and cooperate with the government became the central issue in determining their life or death. For twenty-six months, the colloquy between the government and the Rosenbergs proved futilely repetitious. Confess or die, said the government. And, from their death-house cells, the prisoners replied: We are innocent. Toward the end, the macabre spectacle was watched by a vast audience. Surely this was one of the strangest tests of will ever staged in an international arena by a great and powerful nation and two of its more obscure citizens.

Those who had bet that the two would break lost their gamble. The Rosenbergs died in the electric chair at Sing Sing Prison, still asserting their innocence. They were the only Americans in United States history ever executed for espionage by judgment of a civil court. Also a first for the federal judiciary was the double execution of a husband and wife. Before the electrocution of Ethel Rosenberg, the last woman put to death by the United States government was Mary Surratt, condemned nearly ninety years before for alleged complicity in the assassination of Abraham Lincoln.

Of the principal prosecution witnesses, neither Ruth Greenglass, nor Max Elitcher, nor Harry Gold was indicted in the case. (Gold served the sentence received at an earlier trial for his espionage activities with Klaus Fuchs. He was paroled in 1966 and died in 1972.) David Greenglass was freed in 1960 after serving ten years of his fifteen-year term.

Like the Rosenbergs, Morton Sobell could certainly have mitigated his punishment by confession and cooperation. During his long imprisonment (which included more than five years in Alcatraz) he could probably have gained his freedom in this way at any time. After eighteen years and five months behind bars, he was released on January 14, 1969. He continues to affirm his innocence.

UNKNOWN SECRETS
Art and the Rosenberg Era

NINA FELSHIN

Those who cannot remember the past are condemned to repeat it.
George Santayana

Remember, there was once a Congress in which they had a committee that would investigate even one of their own members if it was believed that that person had Communist involvement or communist leanings. Well, they've done away with those committees. That shows the success of what the Soviets were able to do to this country with making it unfashionable to be anti-Communist.

Ronald Reagan
Interview in the
Washington Times
September 30, 1987

Some social observers, including many artists, see in the America of the Eighties an attempt to rework the America of the Fifties. The Eighties have been a decade whose fascination with the Fifties is reflected by the nostalgic borrowing of that decade's stylistic conventions by some and a critical examination of its darker side by others. Many of the nation's most influential leaders who came to political maturity during the Fifties apparently long for its return, politically and culturally. Most notable among them is the man whose presidency dominated the decade, Ronald Reagan.

In the exhibition *Unknown Secrets: Art and the Rosenberg Era,* it is not the America of John Cheever's affluent, segregated suburbs that is the focus of attention, at least not directly. The focus, instead, is on discovering a deeper meaning to the Fifties, a meaning that can best be uncovered by digging beneath the decade's formica veneer.

Within this context the present exhibition was born. It is somehow fitting that

its two-and-a-half-year national tour would begin in 1988, the thirty-fifth anniversary of the execution of Julius and Ethel Rosenberg.

Originally conceived as a historical exhibition featuring works produced during or not long after the Rosenberg era, it evolved into a more ambitious project. To help broaden the range of media and ideas and insure a contemporary examination of the era, 27 artists, some not born or only children at the time of the trial, were invited to create new works specifically for the exhibition. Research also revealed a third group—contemporary artists who in the last ten years have independently created work about the event. Two artists in the exhibition, Rudolf Baranik and Leon Marcus, are represented by works from the Fifties and the Eighties. In all, the exhibition includes sixty works—60 percent contemporary and 40 percent historical.

The invited artists were given five articles emphasizing different aspects of the case, and a bibliography. Prompted by the fact that the majority of the selected historical works tended to be fairly literal, the contemporary artists were encouraged to explore broader parameters established for the exhibition. In addition to the Rosenberg-Sobell case, the artists could address the political climate that produced the event, the McCarthy Era and the Cold War, and the surrounding cast of characters, including Dwight D. Eisenhower, J. Edgar Hoover, and Ronald Reagan.

Another possible subject for consideration was the "Jewish question." Besides the Rosenbergs and codefendant Morton Sobell, their accusers, David and Ruth Greenglass and Harry Gold, were also Jewish, as was the sole witness against Sobell, Max Elitcher. More to the point, perhaps, is

the fact that trial Judge Irving R. Kaufman, prosecutor Irving Saypol, and assistant prosecutor Roy Cohn were all Jewish. Numerous critics have speculated that their appointment was intended to deflect accusations of anti-Semitism. Whatever the reason, it offered insufficient protection from the charge since the jury was devoid of Jews, despite New York City having the largest Jewish population of any city in the world.

More recent events offered additional source material. The Pollard and Walker family espionage episodes were cited as additional ways to explore moral and political questions about the Fifties and the Eighties. Finally, artists were advised that their references to actual events could be specific, even documentary, or they could be evocative and metaphorical, provided they weren't so obscure that viewers wouldn't make the connection.

The result was an extraordinarily broad range of works created for the exhibition. Within this range certain groupings emerged. Among these are: comparisons between the Fifties and the Eighties (Marina Gutierrez, Margia Kramer, Greg Sholette), the Rosenbergs as symbols of the "other" (Kim Abeles, Robert Arneson, Karen Atkinson, Adrian Piper, Deborah Small), the family (Doug Ashford, Terry Berkowitz), anti-Semitism (Luis Camnitzer, Alex Grey, Kramer, Lorie Novak, Piper), the Cold War at home and abroad (Sue Coe, Gutierrez, Kramer, Juan Sanchez, Sholette, Small), the media (Chris Bratton, Kramer, Antonio Muntadas, Saul Ostrow, Martha Rosler, Patty Wallace), justice (Jerry Kearns, Ostrow, Wordsworth), memory (Dennis Adams, Camnitzer, Novak, Kenneth Shorr, David Wojnarowicz), the Fifties (Gary Bachman, Bratton, Rosler), and public spectacle (Paul Marcus, Archie Rand).

The criteria in selecting the artists was not style, technique, or medium, but a fresh approach to extra-aesthetic content.

The earlier works employ predictable traditional media and methods—oil paint on canvas and various graphic techniques, such as woodcut, lithography, silkscreen, and drawing. The contemporary works utilize a broad range of nontraditional and hybrid media, including found objects collaged and manipulated photographs, phototext, plexiglass and mirrored glass, videotape, audiotape and radio.

Much of the recent work uses appropriated photographic images—a practice that developed after the Fifties and the historical work in the exhibition. In addition to these recycled still photographs, archival film footage and audio recordings are incorporated into several current works. Interestingly, none of the artists of the Fifties turned to photographic and film images of their day when creating work that addressed the Rosenberg case.

These differences reflect an aspect of the evolution of issue-oriented art in the second half of the 20th century. Another major difference relates to how content or meaning is communicated. With the earlier works, what you see is pretty much what you get. The verbal discourse that is needed to unlock many recent works is not required by the historical ones; styles are based in realism, and their messages are direct. Much of the contemporary work, with its texts and subtexts, multiple references, collage and montage, reveals itself more slowly. For a contemporary audience, whose sensibilities have been shaped by conceptual art and postmodernism, this work is often more challenging and, when successful, also more rewarding.

The almost complete absence of realism among the contemporary works should not obscure the fact that this approach continues to be used by socially concerned artists. Indeed, works such as Sue Coe's *Needs of the State* (plate no. 21) and Paul Marcus's *The Greatest Show on Earth* (plate no.

9) demonstrate that tradition's continuing strength and resiliency.

Interestingly, the creation of the earlier works coincided with the heyday of Abstract Expressionism. In the context of *Unknown Secrets,* it is worth citing some fascinating, albeit controversial, accounts published during the past fifteen years which suggest that the U.S. government used Abstract Expressionism as a weapon in the cultural cold war.[1]

In one article, artist-critic Eva Cockcroft documented how the Museum of Modern Art (MoMA) provided the first line of defense through its international programs of the Fifties.[2] The role or, in effect, the exploitation of Abstract Expressionism is implicit in the introduction to the catalogue *The New American Painting (1958)* by MoMA's director, Alfred Barr:

One often hears Existentialist echoes in their (Abstract Expressionists') words,

> ## The U.S. government used Abstract Expressionism as a weapon in the cultural cold war.

but their "anxiety," their commitment, their "dreadful freedom" concern their work primarily. They defiantly reject the conventional values of the society which surrounds them, but they are not political engagés even though their paintings have been praised and condemned as symbolic demonstrations of freedom in a world in which freedom connotes a political attitude.[3]

The New American Painting, a landmark exhibition of Abstract Expressionist painting, toured Europe in 1958-59 under the auspicies of MoMA's International Council, established in 1956 to administer the Museum's four-year-old international program. Through such programs, MoMA, in effect, represented the U.S. government abroad for the better part of the Fifties.

It is an amusing irony that Rudolf Baranik's abstract painting, *Banners,*

1953 (plate no. 14), which includes partially discernible words commemorating the Rosenbergs, was selected for *Recent Works by Young Americans,* a nationally travelling exhibition (1954-56) organized by MoMA's Department of Circulating Exhibitions.

One work in *Unknown Secrets,* Greg Sholette's *Men: Making History, Making Art: 1954,* 1987 (plate no. 18) acknowledges this revisionist view of recent history by juxtaposing images of the 1954 CIA-backed coup in Guatemala, the Army-McCarthy hearings, and a Hans Namuth portrait of Jackson Pollock at work. Sholette says that he hopes the work will trigger a mental connection between these three events of the Fifties and parallel ones of the Eighties, "specifically in our use of Third World proxy armed forces to patrol our 'borders,' the almost desperate need to identify with a virile male leader, and an upsurge of a very subjective, individualistic art."[4]

Besides Sholette, two other artists employ images of the Fifties to suggest parallels in the Eighties. In *Remembering the Rosenbergs,* 1987 (plate no. 22) Marina Gutierrez deploys uniforms representative of the military-industrial complex on a blue field which are surrounded by symbols of its power—the American flag and the bomb. Dangling like trophies from the bottom of the painting are cut-outs of six countries—Greece, Korea, Iran, Guatemala, Lebanon, and Cuba—all of which were Cold War targets of U.S. intervention. In the center of the painting stand Ethel and Julius Rosenberg represented as martyrs and surrounded by symbols of American power. The uniforms that stand in for men suggest that, while the names may change, the structure—and gender—of the system remains the same. "Then and now," says Gutierrez, "secret intervention leaves bloody imprints on their target countries . . . Julius and Ethel are replaced by new names, Puerto Ricans and Palestinians. The continuous fallout from cold/hot wars, police actions and low intensity conflicts."[5] Like Sholette, Gutierrez does not make direct references to the Eighties in the work itself, letting the comparison occur in the viewer's mind.

Not so for Margia Kramer. In a ten-minute tape, which is one component of her video installation *Covert Operations,* 1987-88 (plate no. 40), Kramer juxtaposes footage of the Army-McCarthy hearings with footage of the Iran-Contra hearings. The tape specifically compares the two decades' startlingly different applications of the Fifth Amendment—that section in the Bill of Rights which is designed to protect citizens against self-incrimination. During the Fifties, witnesses pleading the Fifth were branded communists; at the Iran-contra hearings in 1987, they were heralded as patriots.

A number of works are concerned with the notion of the "other"—the state of being different from the white, Protestant, middle-class majority. Although their approaches vary enormously, Kim Abeles, Robert Arneson, Karen Atkinson, Luis Camnitzer, Alex Grey, Kramer, Adrian Piper, and Deborah Small use the Rosenberg case to examine various aspects of the idea that, as Abeles observes, "anyone who appears unlike oneself is suspect."

Adrian Piper's statement about *Xenophobia I: Anti-Semitism,* 1987 (plate no. 48) can serve as a concise summary of the concerns addressed in this group of works. "*Xenophobia I: Anti-Semitism,*" Piper says, "explores Fear of the Other and the way it distorts our perception of other people whom we regard as strange, unfamiliar or threatening . . . The Rosenberg case focused inward the fears of Communist contamination and infiltration generated by the Cold War and the Army-McCarthy hearings. We used the Rosenbergs to transform our fear of an alien other invading us from the outside into fear of one another, alienating ourselves from the suspected invader within us: the idea of sharing, trust, and mutual solidarity." The cracked mirror surface of Piper's work, with photographic images of Ethel shortly before sentencing and Julius being escorted to jail, "challenges us to scrutinize ourselves in the act of xenophobic rejection," says Piper, thus implicating all of us in their fate.

Kim Abeles's multi-layered *Other (In Memory of Ethel and Julius Rosenberg),* 1987 (plate no. 35) demonstrates her ongoing practice of combining commonplace objects to create sculpture that is poetically and conceptually evocative. The passport photos of people of color, primarily Latins—people who are "different" and often unwelcome in the United States—are symbols, just as the Rosenbergs are, of the"other." The passport photos are affixed to a Fifties-style desk/chair, which has been transformed into a highly evocative object. As a Fifties school desk, it symbolizes the site of some of our earliest lessons about "otherness." In addition, its vertical members, covered with the photos, resemble prison bars, while its burnt arms and copper coils suggest the electric chair. The typewriter, suspended from the opening in the seat of the chair, symbolizes the power of language to create and to destroy.

> A number of artists use the Rosenberg case to examine the idea that anyone who appears unlike oneself is suspect.

Beyond this evocative level, there exists a possible reading that is more specifically tied to the Rosenberg case. The sculpture's components could seem to symbolize certain aspects: the typewriter representing Ethel's alleged complicity, the passport photos alluding to allegations of the couple's planned flight, and the suggestion of a hidden compartment beneath the chair recalling charges of a "secrets" hiding place.

The language of the witch hunt is the subject of Deborah Small's work, *Witch Hunt,* 1987 (plate no. 28). Small says she compiled "names gathered from the Rosenberg era's witch hunters who attempted to use the 20th-century witch hunt as a tool for social and thought control. These names—*red, parlor pink, commie scum, dupe, agitator,* etc.—did not serve to define an individual's ideology, but rather acted as an excuse to call them before HUAC, to question their loyalty and their public and private affiliations, to coerce them into naming names, to dismiss them from their jobs, to censor them, and in the Rosenberg case, with the witch hunt hysteria at full pitch, to execute them."

Witch Hunt is a large sculptural construction of shelves and blocks installed against a wall. Blocks, as the dictionary reminds us, can refer to "the piece of wood on which a person condemned to be beheaded lays his neck for execution." The names of the witch hunt are painted on small blocks arranged on each shelf. The structure's supporting blocks display painted images of witches and devils from the 16th- and 17th-centuries. Beside them are images signifying communism: portraits of Marx, Lenin, and Trotsky, a hammer and sickle, and details from Soviet revolutionary posters. Other support blocks contain blacklists—lists of "subversives" or organizations, the Hollywood Ten, and portions of *Red Channels* and the *Hollywood Blacklist.*

Whereas Small examines the Rosenbergs' execution within the historical context of the witch hunt, Karen Atkinson places their death within the tradition of the inquisition. An inquisition, in Atkinson's definition, is "an official investigation, esp. one of a political or religious nature, characterized by lack of regard for individual rights, prejudice on the part of the examiners and recklessly cruel punishments. Despite their retrospectively ludicrous aspects, inquisitions are curtain raisers for massacres," Atkinson says. "America does not parade heretics through the streets in *sanbenhitos* (inquisition garments), rarely submits them to physical torture if their skins are white, and never burns them alive except in remote areas like Korea, Vietnam and Latin America. (Inquisitions also) appeal to headline writers."

In her large, multi-part wall installation, *Era After Era,* 1987 (plate no. 29) this definition can be read on the spines of the books. On the large red pedestal that serves as the book shelf, a United States map is superimposed on a map of the world. This map is interspersed with photographic images of events or symbols associated with inquisitions, or actions which can be labeled as such, placed in the appropriate geographic locations. A photograph of the Rosenbergs shares the U.S. and world map with images of the Salem witch hunts, the Ku Klux Klan cross burnings, lynchings in the south, the Holocaust, Hiroshima/Nagasaki, torture in Latin America, and Vietnam.

Luis Camnitzer, Alex Grey, Margia Kramer and Lorie Novak, like Adrian Piper, focus on anti-Semitism as a component of the Rosenberg story. Camnitzer's *The Rosenberg Project*, 1987 (plate no. 34) is a haunting object that hovers between Hitler's Germany and Sing Sing prison. For Camnitzer, it symbolized his personal experience:

"I was one year old when my family left Germany escaping Nazism," he says. "I always felt that it was because of the death of six million other Jews that I was allowed to stay alive, thus defining my life simultaneously as particularly precious, and highly dispensable. Once ideology matured in me, the natural question arose if I also could die twice, once for background and once for thinking. It is the question of multiple deaths which I felt keenly symbolized in the Rosenbergs, the accidental escape of the first to be caught up and synthesized in the second, completing a vicious labyrinthine circle as only Borges could design in fiction and only macabre madness is able to design in reality."

Margia Kramer's *Covert Operations*, 1987-88 (plate no. 40), consists of a folding screen located in front of a video monitor. The folding screen, a form of domestic furniture that simultaneously conceals and reveals, functions for Kramer both sculpturally and metaphorically. The videotape, previously described, is visible through inset panels on the folding screen made of transparent film. Printed on the film is a phototext of an extraordinary CIA memorandum from 1953, released to the Rosenbergs' sons through the Freedom of Information Act. The memo, from an unidentified CIA operative to the FBI, outlines a program in which the Rosenbergs's "role of victims to anti-Semitism" would be exploited in a campaign of psychological warfare.

The proposal called for "A concerted effort to convince Julius and Ethel Rosenberg, convicted atom spies now under sentence of death, that the Soviet regime they serve is persecuting and ultimately bent on exterminating the Jews under its sovereignty. The action desired of the Rosenbergs is that they appeal to Jews in all countries to get out of the communist movement and seek to destroy it. In return, death sentence would be commuted."

The plan sought to have the Rosenbergs themselves precipitate the destruction of the "Soviet propaganda machine" that made them "heroes . . . and martyrs to American anti-Semitism." The memo writer believed the ideal emissaries to approach the Rosenbergs should be "highly intelligent rabbis, representing reformed [sic] Judaism, with a radical background or sympathetic understanding of radicalism and with psychiatric knowledge. Such men," the memo

> With the rise of television as the central medium of mass culture, a national security state has arisen.

added, "can be found." While this plan was never successfully implemented, it suggests the level of paranoia that prevailed in Washington.

Lorie Novak, who was born a year after the executions, nevertheless, like Camnitzer, places herself at the intersection between "Auschwitz" and "The Rosenbergs." In one of her two photographs in this exhibition, *Past Lives* (plate no. 31), 1987, composed of overlapping projected images of a group of Klaus Barbie's young victims, Ethel, and Lorie as a young child with her mother, Novak movingly draws attention to the grievous consequences for children of two of anti-semitism's darkest moments.

One of the most tragic aspects of the Rosenberg story was the orphaning of their two young sons, who were ten and six at the time of the executions. In a decade when the nuclear family

was synonymous with the American way of life, it is not surprising that, in accepting the consequences of refusing to compromise, the Rosenbergs reinforced their status as "other." When sentencing them to death Judge Kaufman said, "The defendants Julius and Ethel Rosenberg . . . were conscious they were sacrificing their own children . . . Love for their cause dominated their lives—it was even greater than their love for their children." The Rosenbergs's prison correspondence and the recollections of those who knew them stand in sharp contrast to Judge Kaufman's assertions.

Two other works in *Unknown Secrets* address the issue of family— Doug Ashford's *April 6, 1951. Room 110, The Federal Court N.Y., N.Y. and Nine of the Jurors*, 1987 (plate no. 25), and Terry Berkowitz's *The Children's Hour*, 1987 (plate no. 26). Interestingly, though, neither work deals directly with the impact of the case on the children. Nonetheless, that the arrests, trial, and executions triggered several other approaches vis-á-vis the family suggests the degree to which that institution serves as a kind of subtext of the entire event.

Berkowitz's richly layered *The Children's Hour* focuses on the relationship between Ethel Rosenberg and her brother David Greenglass. It represents, for Berkowitz, "a paradigm for betrayal." The central element of the work is a children's dining set, a table and two chairs. The table top is laminated with newspaper articles related to the case. Placed on the table are two round mirrors on which sit bowls of raspberry Jell-o. (These allude to the government's allegation that two halves of a torn Jell-o box served as an identification code between David Greenglass and Harry Gold.) The chair that has been knocked over has a red imprint of a child's hand.

Completing the piece is the soundtrack. While sitting in the child's chair and scanning the articles on the table top, including their own reflections in the mirrored plates, viewers can listen to a brief, haunting audiotape. The sounds of children singing are heard against a background of playground noises and reporter Bob Considine's eyewitness account of the executions.

Doug Ashford's *April 6, 1951. Room 110, The Federal Court, N.Y., N.Y. and Nine of the Jurors* consists of ten photographs with superimposed drawings. Nine of the photographs are head shots of Rosenberg trial jurors taken from a video monitor. The tenth is an image of the courtroom in which the Rosenbergs were tried, upon which is superimposed a children's book drawing of a prototypical American family. Fragments of this drawing are superimposed on the images of the jurors.

By manipulating these appropriated images Ashford draws a comparison between two parallel narratives. "One is a historical story," he says, "the trial and execution of Julius and Ethel Rosenberg. The other is a more continuous one—the ongoing narrative of the American family." The work examines the intersection between the family and trial by jury—both considered positive symbols of "our way of life"—and "questions how at a certain moment, these two institutions worked toward a mutual distortion." By asking us to consider this distortion vis-á-vis the jurors, Ashford is also asking us to consider its ramifications for the Rosenbergs.

The distortion of justice is explored in Saul Ostrow's *Balancing Justice (Idealism and the Media Will Make You Blind)*, 1987 (plate no. 46), and Wordsworth's *Untitled: (Homage to Ethel, Julius and Morton)*, 1987 (plate no. 2). Wordsworth, an anonymous group of artists, offer an image of Justice behind bars in a straightforward representation of what happens "when Justice is bent and altered to serve the interests" of the powerful, rather than the interests of "human dignity."

The central image in Ostrow's work is that of a scale. A globe of the world, pierced with a knife, rests in one tray. In the other is a Brancusi sculpture of a head. Cold War pursuits are weighed against consideration of the individual. A sheet of plexiglass is propped up by a radio, which should cause the scales to be off balance. However, the balance beam gives the scales the ap-

pearance of equilibrium. The radio, tuned to an all-news station symbolizes how we obtain information. Its constant drone suggests passivity, while its structural function serves as a metaphor for the media's claim to balanced reporting of the news. Ostrow's work implies that the media have the power—which they fully exercised during the hysterical atmosphere of the Rosenberg years—to substitute the appearance of justice for justice itself.

Another work that focuses on the media is Chris Bratton's *Quiz Show*, 1988 (plate no. 57). Like Ostrow's work, there is no specific visual or verbal reference to the Rosenbergs. But both pieces suggest that certain media phenomena introduced after World War II and entrenched during the Fifties are now permanent fixtures of our way of life.

Bratton's *Quiz Show* combines two related subjects. As Bratton explains, " . . . coincidental with the rise of television as the central medium of mass culture . . . a national security state has arisen which has, at the center of its operations, surveillance." According to Bratton, "Surveillance and the mass media play on the process of seeing and being seen."

Quiz Show consists of a 1950s Zenith television set, which Bratton describes as an "exaggerated and slightly altered version of a Charles Eames design." A videotape plays continuously while the TV set revolves on a motorized base. The tape mixes archival footage of a Fifties quiz show, "The $64,000 Question," and Bratton's interview with a former FBI agent. The footage of the quiz show serves as a backdrop for the agent's talking head.

The expected correlation between the interviewer's spoken questions—which also crawl across the screen as text—and the agent's answers occasionally occurs, but just as often it is thwarted, resulting in nonsequiturs. The videotape proceeds, Bratton explains, with "questions posed and questions answered, with varying degrees of correspondence between interrogation and reply."

Choosing "The $64,000 Question,"

which turned out to be rigged, can be viewed as a subtle reference to the Rosenbergs' trial, which was influenced by unethical ex-parte discussions between the judge and the government. The era, according to Bratton, was a time when television became "the critical conveyance of consumer culture" which was shaped primarily by program sponsors for whom news and documentary took a back seat to entertainment.

The art in this exhibition raises disturbing questions about the Rosenberg-Sobell case and America of the 1950s. As a complement to the existing books, articles, films, poetry, plays, and music, it provides further evidence that the issues raised by the case are still alive.

Whether we remember it or not, the Rosenberg case remains a part of our national consciousness. Its meaning for our era is not at all elusive. As Robert Coover, author of the novel *The Public Burning*, has written, "We have wretched memories, pathetically brief attention spans. Facts blur, vanish, return scrambled. All we seem to hang on to are the patterned condensations we call stories."

Perhaps *Unknown Secrets* can help us hang on to a little more than that.

NOTES
1. See, for example, Max Kozloff, "New American Painting During the Cold War," *Artforum*, XI:9(May 1973), pp. 43-54; Eva Cockcroft, "Abstract Expressionism, Weapon of the Cold War," *Artforum*, XII:10(Summer 1974), pp. 39-41; Serge Guilbaut, *How New York Stole the Idea of Modern Art*(Chicago 1983).
2. Cockcroft, op. cit.
3. Quoted in Cockcroft, p. 41.
4. Artist's statement. The subjective, individualistic art to which Sholette alludes is neo-expressionism, critically dominant in the first half of the Eighties, now in eclipse.

Unless otherwise indicated, all artists' quotations are from statements written for the exhibition.

UNKNOWN SECRETS:
ART AND THE
ROSENBERG ERA

Pablo Picasso, *Untitled,* 1952 (Plate 1).

Wordsworth, *Untitled: Homage to Ethel, Julius and Morton*, 1987 (Plate 2).

Arnold Mesches, *The Judge,* 1956 (Plate 3).

Arnold Mesches, *The Funeral #2,* 1955 (Plate 4).

Mort Dimondstein, *Priming the Witness,* 1955 (Plate 5).

Angel Bracho and Celia Calderon,
We Have Not Forgotten the Rosenbergs, 1954
(Plate 6).

Francisco Mora, *Help Stop This Crime,* 1952 (Plate 7).

Fred Ellis, *Cold War Warrior,* 1952 (Plate 8).

Paul Marcus, *The Greatest Show on Earth,* 1987 (Plate 9).

Hugo Gellert, *Embraced by Posterity*, 1953 (Plate 10).

Hugo Gellert, *Morton Sobell*, 1954 (Plate 11).

Rockwell Kent, *Book Burners,* 1951 (Plate 12).

Rockwell Kent,
*The Judgment of Julius and
Ethel Rosenberg,* 1955
(Plate 13).

Rudolf Baranik, *Banners*, 1953 (Plate 14).

PAT - RI - CIDE (pa/tri sīd) The act of killing (obsl.) one's father; a term used during the human physical annihilation era, ending in the 22nd Century. By extension, from the middle of the 21st Century, the killing (obsl.) of a father even if not by his offspring.

MAT - RI - CIDE (ma/tri sīd) The act of killing (obsl.) one's mother; a term used during the human physical annihilation era, ending in the 22nd Century. By extension, from the middle of the 21st Century, the killing (obsl.) of a mother, even if not by her offspring.

Late 21st Century dictionaries cite as an example of Patricide and Matricide the killing by the State authorities (archaic) by electrocution (obsl.) of two citizens, Julius and Ethel Rosenberg, father and mother of two small sons. This especially brutal act took place in the middle of the 20th Century in the late North American Empire. The barbaric act was protested by enlightened strata all over the world and served as one of the catalysts for the ending of violence as a human practice.

Dictionary of the English language, 24 Century. Excerpted by Rudolf Baranik

Rudolf Baranik, *Dictionary of the 24th Century (excerpt)*, 1987 (Plate 15).

Arnold Mesches, *The Kiss,* 1954 (Plate 16).

Gary Bachman, *The Eye Never Sees What Flies Into It,* 1984, (Plate 17).

Greg Sholette, *Men: Making History, Making Art: 1954*, 1987 (Plate 18).

Jerry Kearns, *Capitol Punishment*, 1987 (Plate 19).

Alice Neel, *Eisenhower, McCarthy and Dulles,* 1953 (Plate 20).

Sue Coe, *Needs of the State*, 1987 (Plate 21).

Marina Gutierrez, *Remembering the Rosenbergs* 1987 (Plate 22).

David Wojnarowicz, *The Anatomy and Architecture of June 19, 1953 (for the Rosenbergs)*, 1987 (Plate 23).

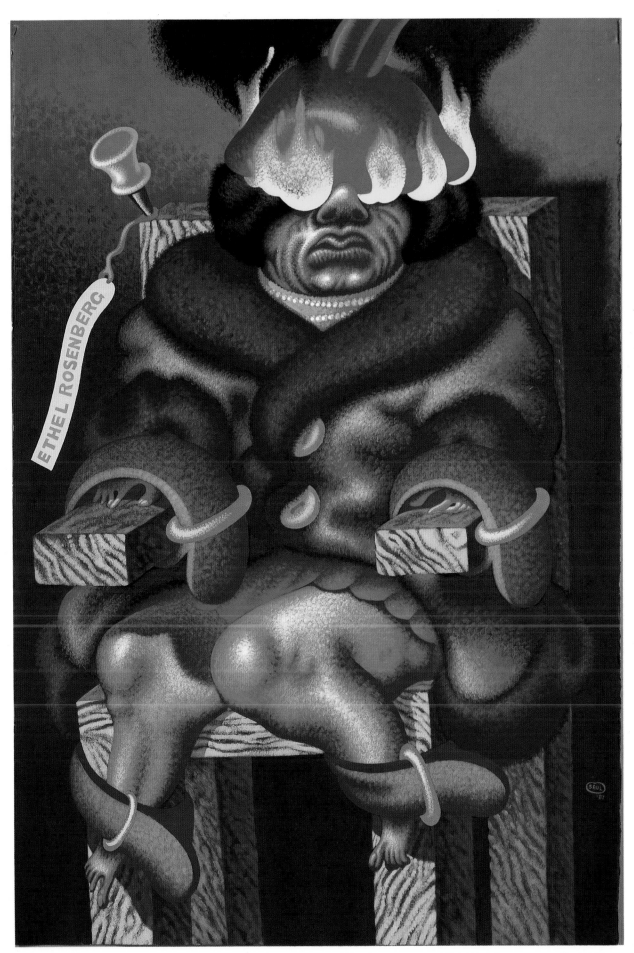

Peter Saul, *Ethel Rosenberg in Electric Chair*, 1987 (Plate 24).

Doug Ashford, *April 6, 1951. Room 110, The Federal Court, N.Y., N.Y. and Nine of the Jurors*, 1987 (detail) (Plate 25).

Terry Berkowitz, *The Children's Hour*, 1987 (detail) (Plate 26).

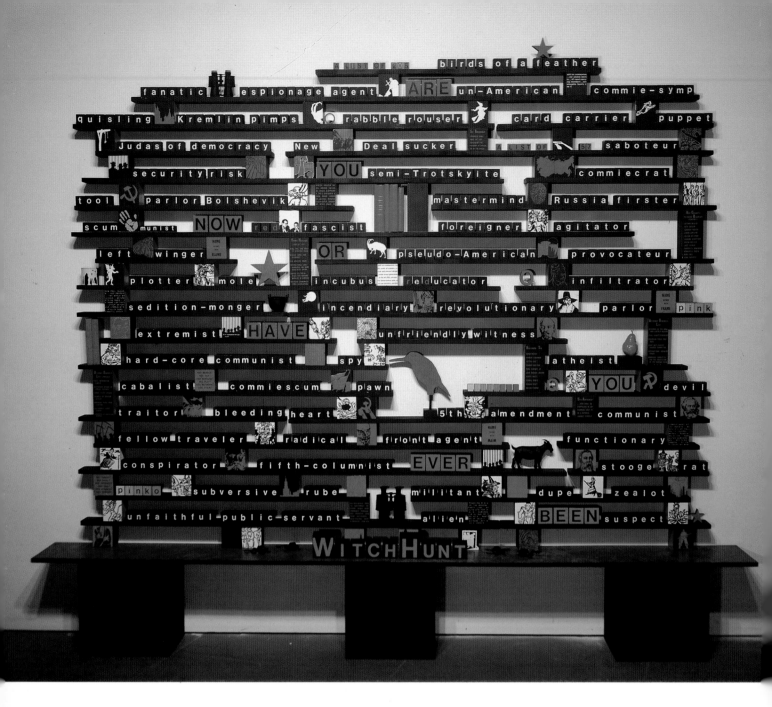

Deborah Small, *Witch Hunt*, 1987 (Plate 28).

Karen Atkinson, *Era After Era*, 1987 (Plate 29).

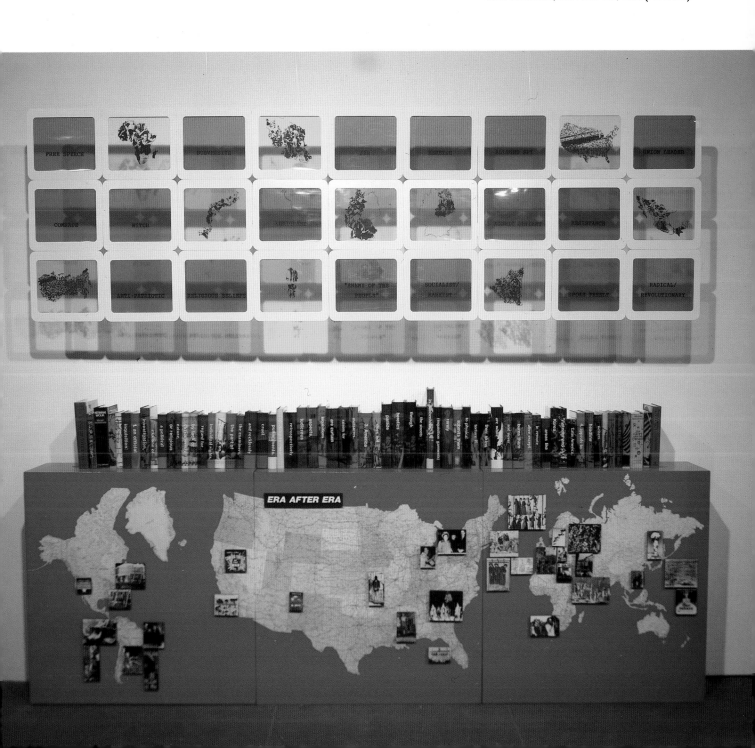

Leon Marcus, *Roy Judas Cohn (Blessed be Thy Holy Name)*, 1986 (Plate 30).

Lorie Novak, *Past Lives*, 1987 (Plate 31).

Robert Arneson, *2 Fried Commie Jew Spies*, 1987 (Plate 32).

Fernand Léger, *Liberty, Peace, Solidarity*, 1952 (Plate 33)

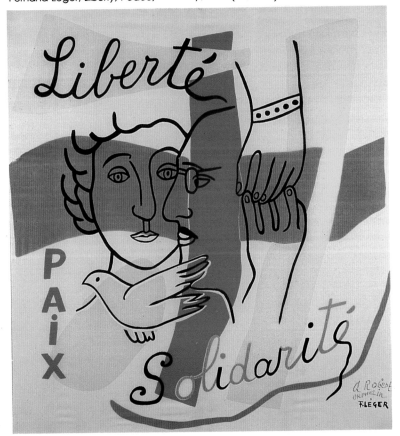

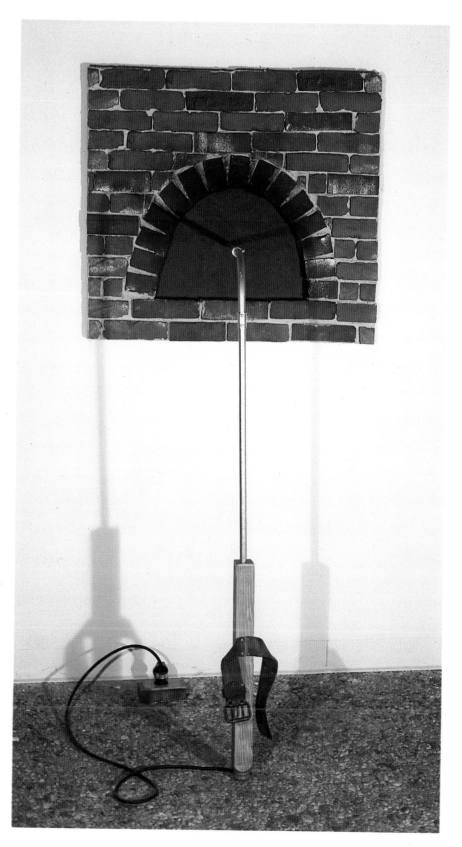

Luis Camnitzer, *The Rosenberg Project*, 1986 (Plate 34).

Kim Ableles, *Other (In Memory of Ethel and Julius Rosenberg)*, 1987 (Plate 35).

Juan Sanchez, *The Rosenbergs: Framed Conspiracy*, 1987 (Plate 36).

Patty Wallace, *Spy vs. Spy/Tic Tac Toe*, 1986 (Plate 37).

Archie Rand, *Pendulum*, 1987 (Plate 38).

Ralph Fasanella, *McCarthy Press*, 1963 (Plate 39).

Margia Kramer, *Covert Operations,* 1987-88 (Plate 40).

Rupert Garcia, *Julius Rosenberg,* 1980 (Plate 41).

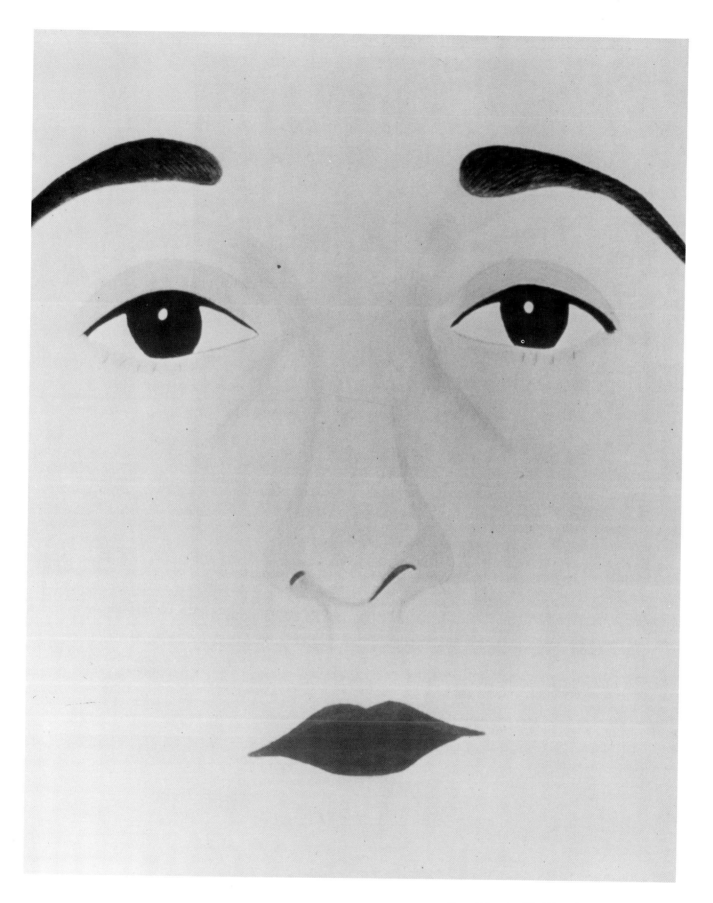

Rupert Garcia, *Ethel Rosenberg*, 1980 (plate 42).

Louis Monza, *The Couple that Paid,* 1953 (Plate 43).

Leon Marcus,
Through the Keyhole, 1954
(Plate 44).

On June 16, 1953, President Eisenhower wrote to his son John, serving in Korea:

To address myself...to the Rosenberg case for a minute. I must say that it goes against the grain to avoid interfering in the case where a woman is to receive capital punishment. Over against this, however, must be placed one or two facts that have greater significance. The first of these is that in this instance it is the woman who is the strong and recalcitrant character, the man is the weak one. She has obviously been the leader in everything they did in the spy ring. The second thing is that if there would be any commuting of the woman's sentence without the man's then from here on the Soviets would simply recruit their spies from among women.

Detail

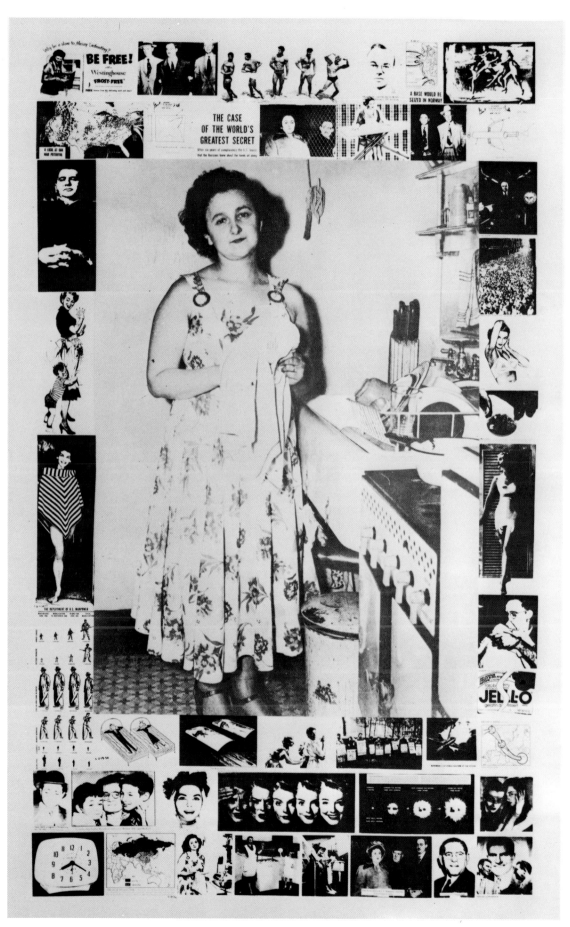

Martha Rosler, *Unknown Secrets,* 1988, detail (Plate 45).

Saul Ostrow, *Balancing Justice (Idealism and the Media Will Make You Blind)*, 1987 (Plate 46).

Kenneth Shorr,
Commemorative Governmental Portraits, 1987, detail
(Plate 47).

A SERIES OF OFFICIAL PORTRAITS WERE PRODUCED CELEBRATING
THE GOVERNMENT'S TRIUMPHANT PROSECUTION OF THE ROSENBERGS.
THESE COMMEMORATIVE PORTRAITS OFTEN EQUIPPED WITH ETERNAL
FLAMES APPEARED BRIEFLY IN VARIOUS GOVERNMENT BUILDINGS
DURING THE MID-1950's. HASTILY CONSTRUCTED AND POORLY
PROTECTED, THE PORTRAITS BEGAN TO FESTER AND ROT. SOME
WERE ATTACKED BY VANDALS. ALL WERE REMOVED IN 1957 FOR
RESTORATION. GOVERNMENT SCIENTISTS LABORED DESPERATELY,
EXHAUSTING THE MOST DARING FORMS OF RESTORATION. ALL
PROVED HOPELESS. THUS, THE PORTRAITS WERE DEPOSITED
IN THE GOVERNMENT ARCHIVES. NOW, THIRTY YEARS AFTER
THEIR REMOVAL, THEY ARE ON PUBLIC DISPLAY.

Detail

Adrian Piper, *Xenophobia: Anti-Semitism,* 1987 (Plate 48).

Antonio Muntadas, *6/19/53*, 1987-88 (details) (Plate 49).

Dennis Adams, Bus Shelter I, 1983 (Plate 50).

Dennis Adams, *Bus Shelter II*, 1986 (Plate 51).

Anthony Toney, *Procession,* 1954 (Plate 52).

Victor Arnautoff, *In Memoriam,* 1953 (Plate 53).

Adelyne Cross-Eriksson,
American Justice
(Save the Rosenberg Couple), 1953
(Plate 54).

Cook Glassgold,
Ethel and Julius Rosenberg: The Atom Spy Hoax, 1979
(Plate 55).

Ralph Fasanella, *McCarthy Era-Gray Day*, 1963 (Plate 56).

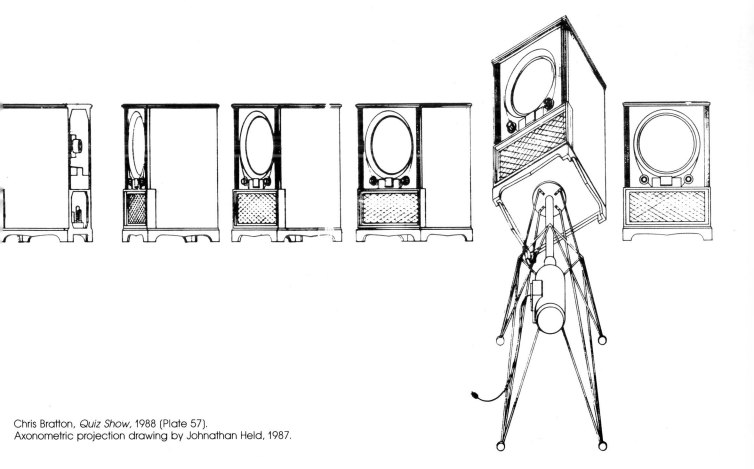

Chris Bratton, *Quiz Show*, 1988 (Plate 57).
Axonometric projection drawing by Johnathan Held, 1987.

Fig. 8. Ben Shahn, *Bartolomeo Vanzetti and Nicola Sacco* from the Sacco-Vanzetti series of twenty-three paintings (1931-32), tempera on paper over composition board 10½ x 14½". Collection, The Museum of Modern Art, New York. Gift of Abby Aldrich Rockefeller.

THE ROSENBERGS AND POSTWAR SOCIAL PROTEST ART

PETER SELZ

"Then I got to thinking about the Sacco-Vanzetti case... Ever since I could remember I'd wished that I'd been lucky enough to be alive at a great time—when something big was going on, like the Crucifixion. And suddenly I realized that it was. I was living through another crucifixion. Here was something to paint!"

Ben Shahn had studied painting in New York and Paris. He had worked as a photographer with Walker Evans and as a fresco painter with Jean Charlot, but it was only in 1932 that he found his true vocation when encountering the narrative subject of the Sacco-Vanzetti case. In a spurt of energy he created two large panels and twenty-three gouaches dealing with the injustices of the trial, the execution, and the worldwide demonstrations that ensued as its consequence.[1]

Ever since the Rosenbergs and Sobell were executed in 1953, their case has been studied, debated, and reassessed, but no posthumous pardon has as yet been granted. This exhibiton and book are part of a much needed thirty-fifth anniversary reappraisal. It is also a testament to the powerful union that can be forged between art and political issues.

Even if the Rosenbergs had, until now, not found a Ben Shahn to commemorate their fate, a good deal of powerful protest art has occurred in their (and our) behalf. I vividly recall arriving in Paris in June 1953 and hearing large groups of protesters chanting, "Eisenhower Assassin!" and seeing many posters of the General-President with his well-known broad smile, showing sixteen teeth, each of them in the shape of an electric chair. This poster was the work of Louis Mittelberg, chief cartoonist for *L'Humanité*.

Many of the leading European artists, especially men of the left such as Pablo Picasso and Fernand Léger in France, and Renato Guttuso in Italy, made prints, drawings, and posters, calling as Léger did in his silkscreen, for *Liberty, Peace and Solidarity*.

The strongest painting done at the time was by the young Dutch artist

Karel Appel. In *The Condemned*, (Fig. 9) two figures were painted with a wild and vehement brush in thick impasto and glaring colors, expressing a mixture of anger and despair.

A good many American painters also responded, taking up different aspects of the case. Of particular interest today are the works by Arnold Mesches, his monstrous and terrifying *The Judge*, the awesome *The Funeral* and the casein drawing, *The Kiss*, which evokes an irredeemable sense of tragedy. Although communicating on a plane of greater seriousness, Mesches predicted some of the current pictorial formulations.

In the 1950's, however, artists in the United States had turned principally toward abstraction as their own modernist protest against outworn forms of the past. They placed primary importance on "an adventure into an unknown world, which can be explored only by those willing to take risks," as Adolph Gottlieb and Mark Rothko wrote to *The New York Times* in 1943.[2] Art—certainly mainstream art—was transformed from figurative painting of both the American scene and of social-political realism toward subjective abstraction. By and large an art that was political in subject matter was eschewed.

Avant-garde art and politics, which had often been comrades-in-arms in the modern world, were clearly separated. This attitude was clearly expressed in an important statement by Robert Motherwell and Harold Rosenberg, who announced that "Whoever genuinely believes he knows how to save humanity from catastrophe has a job before him which is certainly not a part-time one."[3] (Nor one which is the exclusive job of males.) In the postwar period of deep crisis, this new stance was "in a sense a political apoliticism."[4]

But attitude, patronage, fashion are all in continuous process of change and so are the form and content of art. In the Eighties, to which a large part of this exhibition is dedicated, narrative art is again very much part of the picture, a picture which has also once more permitted art with political content. And many of these

artists would agree with Bertolt Brecht that culture and consciousness can be challenged only with new forms of art, because the audience will not be shocked out of its passivity with traditional forms of the past. In order to be truly effective, political art must subvert and deconstruct the codes of the establishment.

It seems to me that a number of the artists in *Unknown Secrets* have been successful in addressing the Rosenbergs with a personal and authentic statement in painting and sculpture. In response to the call for work for this exhibiton, a large number of pieces were created in a multiplicity of styles and media.

Peter Saul, known for his stridently fierce cartoonlike images condemning the Vietnam War, came forth with a painful and violent painting of Ethel Rosenberg strapped in the electric chair, her head in flames, painted in shrieking acrylics—a scream of despair.

Like Saul, Robert Arneson has his roots in the "bad taste" art of the Sixties. First in his ceramics and also in his later politically-engaged bronzes and paintings, Arneson operates sardonically in a world between black humor and tragedy. For the Rosenberg exhibition he depicted the couple as two disembodied bronze heads, giving Julius Rosenberg a small American flag "earring" inscribed with the message "I Like Ike." Always a man of irreverence, Arneson has inscribed the words *2 Fried Commie Jew Spies* across their foreheads.

It is *Truth* in the electric chair at the center of Sue Coe's monumental painting. With the Rosenbergs on either side, blinding beams of light are directed at her—or are they the rays of death emanating from the shower heads of the concentration camps? Steps ascend to her tribunal in the upper regions (Truman, Eisenhower, McCarthy, Nixon, Judge Kaufman, among others), while historical, cultural, and political figures, dressed in black, are standing below. [They include Lillian Hellman, Picasso, Einstein, Dalton Trumbo, and U.S. Communist party leader Gus Hall.] The painted

Fig. 9. Karel Appel, *The Condemned*, 1953, oil on canvas, 56⅛ x 43¼". Collection Van Abbemuseum, The Netherlands.

nightmare bears the telling device: *Needs of the State.*

Jerry Kearns appropriates the cool art of indifference from Pop for his wild and combative political pictures. He is represented here with an acrylic of a postcard reproduction of the White House, which is somewhat off-color registration. Above the presidential mansion is the inscription: "The man who threw the switch that ended the Rosenbergs's lives was Joseph Francel. His fee was $150 for each execution." What price justice?

The current popular nostalgia for the Fifties notwithstanding, there are perilous resemblances between the repressive controls of that decade and the more sophisticated brainwashing techniques of the administration of President Ronald Reagan. But the pluralistic art world of the Eighties permits a great deal more art that is political in its nature and committed in its engagement. Departures from orthodoxy have become prevalent. Much of the work of the 1980's is narrative as well as descriptive and even prescriptive in nature. Artists are once more using the tools at their command to comment on U.S. military and financial involvements in Central America, South Africa, and the Middle East, among other places, as well as on the final act of auto-destruction.

Works of art may not alter the sociopolitical system, they may not prevent catastrophe, but they can be instruments that ask questions of moment—they can cause us to ponder and reflect. In an age in which communication has become dominated by disinformation, authentic art of personal vision can, and perhaps must, be a moral act.

Notes
1. Ben Shahn, quoted in James Thrall Soby, *Ben Shahn* (New York, 1963), p. 11.
2. Adolph Gottlieb and Mark Rothko, letter to *The New York Times,* June 7, 1943.
3. Robert Motherwell and Harold Rosenberg, opening statement for *Possibilities* (New York), No. 1 (Winter 1947/48), p. 1.
4. Serge Guilbaut, *How New York Stole the Idea of Modern Art* (Chicago, 1983), p. 2.

Fig. 10. Lee Jaffe, *Eclipse: Portrait of Julius and Ethel Rosenberg,* 1983, gold, silver aluminum leaf, copper wire, oil on canvas, 129 x 153". Collection Saatchi Museum, London.

THE CRUCIBLE AND THE EXECUTION
A Memoir

ARTHUR MILLER

Toward sunset on the West Side Highway, the mindless traffic monster stretching itself downtown toward Brooklyn, where I was heading my Ford station wagon, although where I was coming from is lost in my mind's dust. Well, not quite—it was probably from the Martin Beck Theater, where, now that I think about it, *The Crucible* was playing. Yes, and that is probably why I had forgotten what was supposed to happen on this day, or rather this evening at sunset. I had been so busy redirecting the play to cut expenses and keep it from closing, and had eliminated the sets entirely to reduce the number of stagehands. That is undoubtedly why I had forgotten what was supposed to happen at sundown. A bit more than thirty years ago now.

But I may also have dropped it out of my mind because I did not believe it would really take place; something or someone would intervene at the last minute and stop it, call it a bad dream and let us all go back to the reality of the past twenty New Deal years. But coming at me over my car radio now was a voice—it could have been Robert Trout on CBS, who had the mix of solemnity and conversational airiness that the occasion would have asked for—saying that all appeals had been exhausted with the failure of the Supreme Court or any of its Justices to order a stay of execution, and now there would be only President Eisenhower—I may as well mention that he looked remarkably like my father—who had the power to stop it, at least for a while. And I recall shifting course around the dogleg at, I think, Twenty-third Street and feeling confident that Eisenhower, whom I knew to be a non-fanatic, would at the last moment decide that it really wasn't necessary to kill this pair and that we should give ourselves time to think it over again.

I remember noticing, not without some resentment, that none of the drivers in the cars on both sides of me were doing anything unusual, although some must have been listening to the same broadcast. Their faces had the usual vacant looks of people caught in traffic, the look of having their feet massaged. And all this gave me a feeling of loneliness, although God knows many of them may have been as concerned as I. Nevertheless, I was frightened to be so alone with the rapidly falling sun, an aloneness that extended out to my right to the Pacific Ocean and south past my shoes to the Gulf. I could not be sure the Rosenbergs were not guilty of having passed atom bomb information to the Russians, but I had no doubt the atmosphere in the press and the courtroom would have made almost impossible a more lenient verdict than death. Because of *them,* so it was made to seem, we had lost our monopoly over the greatest weapon in history to the worst tyranny in history.

The sheer heat of the anti-Communist feeling in the country should have warned a cool judge away from, not toward, the death penalty, and when you have a brother as one of the main supports of the prosecution's case against his sister's husband, you have got to take some long thoughts before believing him. There is no hatred on the earth, no resentment as coruscating as that between related people, as all civil wars display.

Robert Trout—if indeed it was Trout—kept breaking into the program to describe frantic phone calls from a Rosenberg lawyer to this or that Supreme Court justice. Appeals from foreign governments, demonstrations in Paris, but my bets were on Eisenhower, who, as I have noted, looked a lot like my father. And the orange light in the sky was turning a very pale blue. Or so I recall it.

I was struggling in my car with what I did and didn't believe, with one eye on the color of the changing sky. I knew nothing of espionage, but they seemed like such unlikely spies, so naive in their left-rote statements that if I were a Russian I would worry about which idealistic fantasy would catch and sweep them out of my control next week. And, in the subsequent thirty years, a number of Soviet spies, Americans, have been sent to jail, but interestingly I cannot recall one who was idealistically pro-Soviet; they were practical people who wanted large amounts of money fast, plus in some cases a little healthy vengeance on their employers.

Money played no part in the Rosenbergs's lives, it seemed; only passions did. And I had shared some of them, like the rational promise of socialism, the end of Jew-hate, which was a hope that took a long time dying. I could easily visualize them, though, children of East European and Russian people—shawls over their heads, the men bearded—whose pogrom-ridden lives had turned them toward the great Russian Revolution as the prayer's answer. And this, after all, was only a very few years after Jews in Poland had tried to flee eastward toward Russia when the Nazis came, not to the West; a very few years since, as

General MacArthur had rhetorically announced, civilization hung "on worthy banners of the courageous Russian Army."

So I drove downtown knowing all this and I had to wonder if it was possible, after all, that the sad-faced couple had in fact expressed their attachment to the Soviets by passing some dread atom secret; one had to try to believe anything in order to test one's disbelief in it. And around Fourteenth Street, as I recall, I thought of Dr. Harold Urey, who had been one of the makers of the bomb, and his repeated flat statements that the informer who claimed to have sketched an atomic-bomb diagram for Julius was a mere mechanic incapable of selecting and amalgamating such decisive secrets.

If Urey was right, or almost right, or just about right, then surely they had to wait a bit longer before they executed this couple, and I could just picture Eisenhower, who was no fool about technology, saying let us wait until we get this Urey business ironed out, let us examine his objections, which after all, suggest something fradulent somewhere in this case, or something like error.

By around Twelfth Street Robert Trout, if indeed it was he, was reporting that the press people were forming a vigil at the prison. And a rabbi was standing by, as I recall, to usher the Rosenbergs into heaven after the United States government killed them. I do not remember anymore whether it was he or another man of the cloth who dared to say—and such were the times that it took real stomach to say such a thing—that this was Sabbath eve and that it was a very bad thing to kill two Jews tonight. It would be, perhaps, like executing a Christian on Sunday. This recollection forces me to correct myself—the defense attorney had asked that in view of the imminent Sabbath the execution be delayed until Monday. Instead, it was advanced several hours to make sure to avoid the setting of the sun. They were to be killed more quickly than planned to avoid any shadow of bad taste.

Not that I, nearing the sloping descent to the Canal Street exit, thought there was bigotry involved, nor at least in the usual sense. What I did fearfully regret was that Jews were so prominent in the prosecution of the case, people like Roy Cohn and Irving Saypol, not to mention the judge, Irving Kaufman. I was now on Canal Street, moving inch by inch in very heavy traffic toward the Manhattan Bridge, and I knew the anxiety in myself, to be candid about it, the worry and the chill of unquiet that there had been so many Jews so noticeable in the left over the past decades. So I could understand the perhaps special need Jews could have, their very complicated desire to show that they too were patriotic Americans. And once they felt this way I was afraid they

would take it out on the Rosenbergs for making Jews look bad.

This was one of my strongest hopes in Eisenhower, actually; he was not Jewish and perhaps would feel secure enough to say let's wait, let's hold this up for a few exploratory days or weeks.

Now I could see the bottom of the ramps of the Manhattan Bridge. The sky had only a tinge of the sun's yellow anymore.

CBS said they were switching to Sing Sing prison altogether rather than continue to pick up sporadic bulletins. A hushed voice, as though from a sickroom, described the waiting reporters and officials, the telephoning to the Supreme Court. What were people like me to believe? I was left with a powerful impression that one of the

Rosenbergs's chief accusers, Harry Gold, was crazy. Certainly he had altered and added to his story from week to week under FBI suggestion, or so it seemed. Why not clear all this up? Where was Eisenhower? Where was anybody who did not have career interest in an execution, or an ideological passion to hunt these two down? Where was justice, cool and dispassionate?

We were only eight or so years past the discovery of the mounds of dead in Dachau, Bergen-Belsen, Auschwitz, and other marks of Cain on the forehead of our century. They could not merely be two spies being executed but two Jews. It was not possible to avoid this in the second half of the 20th century; not even with the best will in the world could the prejudicial

Fig. 11.   Thousands of supporters gather on Seventeenth Street in New York on the eve of the Rosenberg's's June 19, 1953 executions. The city prevented the crowd from holding their vigil in nearby Union Square. (UPI/Bettmann News Photo.)

stain be totally avoided—no, not even if it were undeserved. Such were the times.

As I have always remembered it, my Ford's front wheels touched the ramp of the bridge, and rising higher I could see that there was no longer any sunlight in the sky, which was deep blue. It was night. But actually it was a little earlier in the day when the sun was still up that the announcer said that the Rosenbergs had just been executed.

I suppose that the dimming of lights in the prison accounts for the setting of the sun in my memory of the news. But I am sure of one thing—oddly, I wanted to believe they were guilty, although it was beyond me to agree they should have died. I still could not believe the prosecution's story about a diagram when Harold Urey did not believe it; I could not forget the in-laws' testimony; but I wanted to believe that there was absolutely conclusive evidence which I had never heard of.

I was alone in the traffic crossing the bridge; the other drivers still seemed to be having their feet massaged. But maybe I did too.

That evening, so I was later told, the audience stood up at *The Crucible* to observe a minute of silence at the end of the play, which indeed finishes with an execution, and the actors told me there was no applause at this performance.

The years would confuse matters, people thinking I had written the play about the Rosenbergs instead of two and a half years before their names were even in the papers.*

And the years would also not let the case rest. According to the new, revised account of the trial by Walter and Miriam Schneir, it appears that General Leslie Groves, who headed the wartime Manhattan Project, had said a year after the executions that the information the Rosenbergs were accused of having given to the Russians would have been of only minor value in any attempt to make a bomb. This statement never saw daylight until recently, when the Freedom of Information Act made the revelation possible. Yet the justification for the death sentence was precisely that it was the greatest crime in history. I wish I could say this statement of Groves's comes as a shocking surprise.

In fact, it was more or less my conjecture as my car rolled into Brooklyn, and I know I was never so alone in Brooklyn in my life. Because I was scared. And now, thirty years later, with Jews trying to flee Russia, that moral shambles, it is simply too terrible to contemplate two people choosing to die rather than speak a word against the Future, which quite possibly was how they saw the Soviet Union at the time.

Who knows what they would have thought now, had they not been killed? Had statements like General Groves's not been suppressed maybe a genuine debate would have thrown light on the case. What was all the hurry? That was what I wondered then and still do.

And it has occurred to me that the greatest crime in history was quite different; but when God discovered the first man-killer among men He did not execute Cain, even for slaying his own brother. But I suppose that is what it takes to be God.

*EDITOR'S NOTE
Indeed, the years *would* confuse matters. In Miller's 1987 autobiography, *Timebends, A Life* (Grove Press), he devotes several pages to *The Crucible*, describing in detail his initial research visit to the Salem (Massachusetts) Historical Society. It was in April 1952, nearly two years after the Rosenbergs had been arrested, and a little more than a year before their executions.

NOT SO HAPPY DAYS:
The Politics and Culture of the 1950's

PAUL VON BLUM

Americans are fond of simple historical generalizations, especially those pegged to specific decades. Sweeping comments about the Fifties, Sixties, Seventies, and Eighties abound in the media and in public and private discourse. I see this phenomenon regularly in daily conversations and especially in my work as a university teacher. Although many of my students freely acknowledge a lack of specific knowledge, they nevertheless reveal a series of media-inspired images of the recent past. Colleagues throughout the country report similar experiences about their own students' willingness to accept simple, grandiose judgments about the complexities of social, political, cultural, and emotional life.

Examples are legion. Thus, the Seventies and Eighties have been "Me" decades, in apparent response to the social activism of the 1960's. And that turbulent time, to quote a recent student comment in a course on the history of social protest, consisted of "riots, long hair, and free love." It was scarcely the first time that I found the civil rights, student, and anti-war

movements characterized so simply and definitively. Comments like that are common far beyond college campuses in the United States. I hear them regularly on radio talk shows, in supermarkets and shopping centers, in airport waiting areas, and elsewhere. Increasingly, I find myself discouraged about superficial attitudes that contain just enough truth to discourage deeper inquiry.

Probably no period in recent history is subject to such deep historical misperceptions as is the Fifties. An astonishingly large percentage of people today have a vision of postwar America as a time of widespread economic prosperity, political stability, cultural openness, and even experimentation—the rock 'n' roll revolution with Elvis Presley, after all, came to prominence during the Fifties. There is, I think, a romanticized notion that we had a kindly grandfather in the White House, that we enjoyed an abundance of cars, television, and other material pleasures, and that Americans were in general well off and not involved in war after the end of the Korean conflict. A "Happy Days"

mentality exists today, generated and fortified by the mass media. It obviously has a strong emotional appeal.

This positive vision has also been given more intellectual form in recent years. Conservative writers and scholars have argued that the Fifties were indeed an era of good times for most Americans. They contend that peace and prosperity were the hallmark of the period and that artistic and other creative accomplishments placed America at the forefront throughout the world. Perhaps the most important academic expression of this perspective is Jeffrey Hart's book *When the Going Was Good.* An English professor at Dartmouth, Hart provides the most comprehensive apologia for the early cold-war epoch. His book is an elegant and sophisticated tribute to the 1950's nostalgia that has existed throughout the Reagan presidency of the Eighties: "Let us, then, return to the world of the 1950's, and try to see it clearly, see it in its whole significance, as a remarkable and often beautiful, and very important period in American life.[1]

Interestingly, the recent cheerfulness about the Fifties has supplanted an earlier set of simplistic generalizations about that time. I recall vividly how people used to perceive the Fifties as a time of apathy and dull conformity. It was the age of the "organization man," of people who uncritically adapted to whatever institutional demands were made upon them. According to this view, the Fifties were also a time of massive political apathy and inaction. One had the impression that nothing of political significance really happened until the election of John Fitzgerald Kennedy, in November 1960.

Neither of these over-generalizations about the Fifties is helpful, although both contain elements of truth. The new nostalgia conceals many of the dark realities of the time and encourages people to avoid learning and thinking about realities that placed American democracy in precarious danger.

The vision of a nonpolitical America similarly deflects attention from the actual events of the Fifties. The era from the end of World War II to the Kennedy presidency—the *actual* "Fifties" that transcends arbitrary chronological definitions—was actually highly politicized, albeit in ways that fundamentally contradict the glowing view of Professor Hart.

It is important, thirty-five years after the execution of Julius and Ethel Rosenberg, to come to grips with the fearsome political and cultural ambience of that entire era Although there are numerous scholarly and experiential accounts of the severe political oppression and cultural orthodoxy of cold-war America, there is a constant need in a largely ahistorical society to provide a more accurate and realistic perspective than is typically available from the electronic media. Students and others would do well to learn more about the ways that a society can create a huge gap between its democratic principles and its daily practices.

What, then, was the political and cultural ambience of the early cold-war era? The image of a kindly, benevolent Dwight Eisenhower presiding over an affluent America may be emotionally gratifying, but it is also profoundly inaccurate. To be sure, "Ike" in retrospect appears far more benign than many of his more malevolent successors like Richard Nixon, Lyndon Johnson, and Ronald Reagan. During his presidency, Eisenhower demonstrated a pragmatic conservatism that made him anathema in certain extreme right-wing circles. As Richard Hofstadter has accurately noted, he recognized the "irreversability of the historical process that has brought us from simple agrarian conditions to the complex conditions of modern urban life and corporate organization."[2]

Notwithstanding Eisenhower's understanding of some modern social realities, his administration was characterized by a deeper conservatism that both fostered and reinforced the underlying political repression of the cold-war period. A closer view of the Eisenhower administration reveals his enthusiastic support of traditional social, economic, and political values and practices that advance the interests of affluent white men at the expense of most other groups in American society. Like that of Ronald Reagan, his cabinet consisted predominately of this class, including ultrareactionaries like George Humphrey and Ezra Taft Benson. His selection as vice-presidential candidate of Richard Nixon, who had come to national prominence as a result of his red-baiting campaigns in California and his key role as a member of the House Un-American Activities Committee, reveals at best a cynical political opportunism and at worst a conscious decision to exploit the hysteria of the era.

President Eisenhower likewise was unmoved by any vision of racial justice. Despite some pleasant rhetoric and specific action in enforcing judicial desegregation orders, he revealed little personal commitment to changing the pervasive racial injustice throughout the United States. Physical and emotional violence against black citizens evoked no passion in Eisenhower. The successes of the civil rights efforts of the Sixties owe nothing to the Republican president of the Fifties.

Perhaps most important, Eisenhower was a major actor in the anti-Communist hysteria of the era. His differences with Senator Joseph McCarthy were more matters of political opportunism and fear than substance. Like President Harry Truman before him, Eisenhower encouraged the security investigations and purges that cast a pall over the political life of the nation. His domestic policies mirrored those of McCarthy save for the personal grandstanding of the junior senator from Wisconsin. In 1954, for example, Eisenhower proposed in his State of the Union address to deprive Communists of U.S. citizenship. Most ominously, the president declined to intervene in the Rosenberg case, refusing to consider even the human implications of a death sentence for a couple with two small children. To perceive him as a friendly grandfather presiding over a time of happy days, under these circumstances, is nothing short of bizarre.

A clearer sense of the political ambience of that time also requires a similarly harsh judgment about Eisenhower's immediate predecessor, President Truman. He was substantially responsible for setting the tone for the cold war. His "Truman Doctrine" established the policy of opposing Communist "aggression." It formalized the hostility between the United States and the Soviet Union following the defeat of the Axis powers in World War II. This conflict, in turn, became the backdrop for the repressive domestic events that would, eventually, be collectively known as McCarthyism.

Harry Truman's conduct of the cold war set the stage for the domestic hysteria that was to dominate for more than a decade. Seeking to counter and defuse Republican claims to primacy in the anti-Communist crusade, President Truman initiated a series of internal policies that would be intensified a few years hence. Loyalty programs, the Attorney General's list of subversive organizations, and criminal indictments of Communist leaders were all part of the political culture of the late Forties. These policies, which flew in the face of both constitutional guarantees and the values of a free society, hardly made the early Fifties a time of "happy days."

Such formal mechanisms of political repression created a climate of tremendous fear throughout the United States. Cold-war rhetoric combined with an internal zest for anti-communism throughout virtually every social institution. In his monumental study *The Great Fear*, David Caute chronicles the ambience of the era. His more accurate picture stands in stark contrast to the recent, more positive image of the Fifties. His account details how "the wealthiest, most secure nation in the world was sweat-drenched in fear."[3]

Throughout the entire country, people worried about their past political activities, including youthful efforts during the Depression that might be construed as sympathetic to the Communist Party. Thousands sought to dispel suspicion by denouncing present and former colleagues. Loyalty oaths were required in schools, colleges, government agencies, and even private companies. The FBI increased surveillance of real and imagined political radicals. Many aging immigrants with suspect backgrounds were subjected to harassment and even deportation by Immigration officials, the 1950's version of the infamous Palmer Raids of 1919–21. Individuals were dismissed from jobs in every setting in the country because of their past or present political indiscretions.

Senator McCarthy was a comparatively late entry into the witch-hunting zeal of the times. A cynical and malevolent opportunist, he seized on the mounting fear to advance his personal political standing. His unique gift for manipulating the mass media for his own ends enabled him to occupy center stage for several years.[4] But the reality is that "McCarthyism" was a more pervasive phenomenon than the specific activities of Joe McCarthy himself.

The "great fear" was equally manifest in the intellectual life of the nation. Books and magazines were removed from stores and libraries and even some personal collections in private homes. Foreign mail was carefully scrutinized for subversive influences. Books by writers and paintings by artists with left-wing associations were no longer acceptable. Teachers at all levels became extremely cautious in their classroom and private discourse. Self-censorship in all fields became a ubiquitous reality in America. In short, a powerful chill on the free expression of ideas hovered over the political landscape.

Compounding the problem was the timid response of individuals and institutions that might have mobilized effective opposition to the mounting hysteria. With some conspicuous exceptions, universities, the mass media, professional associations, trade unions, and religious groups retreated in the face of the repressive onslaught, in many instances sacrificing their own "suspect" personnel in order to maintain their own status, privilege, and political "correctness." The cowardice of those who should have known better, in fact, is among the saddest stories during the not so happy days of the Fifties.

One telling way to understand the pervasive fear and irrationality of that time is to relate specific incidents that serve, in retrospect, as valuable if unnerving historical source material. In a recent university class, for example, I related some personal recollections from my childhood during the Fifties. In 1954 or so, I remember standing with my aunt and a neighbor in her backyard in Philadelphia. All three of us were jarred by the screech of a siren nearby—a sound that we clearly recognized as that of a fire engine or ambulance. When I asked about what might be happening, the neighbor replied that the police were probably hunting Communists. Her remarks were not spoken in jest; indeed, they were presented with both sincerity and apprehension. It was obvious that this suburban housewife had a genuine notion that communists were present nearby and that the authorities were involved in a dramatic and fully legitimate search for them. I have carried the memories of this incident for more than thirty years and have come to see it as the embodiment of the social pathology of the entire era.

In another childhood example, I recall my sixth-grade teacher who daily proclaimed his faith in the wisdom of Senator McCarthy to his class of impressionable children. Along with the Pledge of Allegiance and other ritualistic tokens of patriotic devotion, my teacher informed us that only Senator McCarthy stood between our families and our very way of life and Communist tyranny. He regularly implored us to watch for Communist influences at home and in the community. He mentioned that certain newspapers and magazines were very dangerous and that we should be vigilant in our selection of reading materials. Seemingly unaware of the irony, he regaled us with stories about how Soviet teachers distorted the truth and kept their students uninformed. It was brainwashing, pure and simple, and it was not unique. It was part of the deeper political culture of those fearsome times. And today's citizens, most especially its students and other young people, should be keenly aware that it happened.

There are, to be sure, many thousands of similar anecdotes that reveal the spirit of the times. Equally important to note is that these political realities—realities that far transcend the vicissitudes of elections and other formalities of American government—had tremendously devastating human consequences. In the dark ambience of McCarthyism, careers were ruined, family life was frequently and negatively altered.

Loyalty probes, FBI harassment, institutional cowardice, and ubiquitous fear and irrationality thus dominated the political life of the nation for more than a decade in the mid-20th century. These realities dramatically belie the happy-days nostalgia, in both its popular and scholarly containers, of the "fabulous Fifties." Politics pervades the entirety of social life, and the early cold-war period was an especially vivid example of the pernicious influences of the "great fear." The cultural life of the nation, in particular, was deeply and tragically affected by the climate of suspicion and repression of that time. It is thus valuable to take a glimpse at some of the cultural consequences as a vital backdrop for looking at the present exhibition of art of the Rosenberg era.

A dramatic example involves the effects on the film industry in the United States. Hollywood producers were perhaps even more intimidated by the loyalty investigations than other industries. Partly, this was the result of having produced some films sympathetic to the Soviet Union, an American ally during World War II. Furthermore, there were many liberals and leftists, including persons with past and present Communist Party connections, working in the film industry. Their presence, clearly, made Hollywood a prime target for congressional investigators.

In 1947, the House Committee on Un-American Activities conducted an inquiry—"vendetta" would be an appropriate term here—regarding the men who came to be known as the Hollywood Ten. Persecuted for refusing to disclose their political associations, these screenwriters and many others in the Hollywood community suffered blacklisting, imprisonment, and long-term emotional harm during this unfortunate era. The ubiquitous call to "name names" placed individuals in tremendous jeopardy and caused some to turn informer, either against their personal inclinations or as opportunistic ways to save or advance their careers. More fundamentally, these investigations, often accurately characterized as witch hunts, cast a pall over the entire industry that would deeply affect the nature of the films that were produced throughout much of the Fifties. It was, as Lillian Hellman eloquently proclaimed, scoundrel time in America.[5]

In their paranoia, industry leaders in Hollywood attempted to adapt to what they saw as the new national mood of repression. For more than a decade, every movie that was produced, no matter how innocuous, was made in the shadow of the anti-Communism of the era. It was subject to the influence of the House Committee on Un-American Activities, which operationally determined who could write, who could act (and who could not), which subjects were appropriate (and which were not), and even how the plots should be resolved.[6] Virtually all shades of liberal thought were stifled from the late Forties through the mid-to-late Fifties. Indeed, anything that might be perceived as controversial was suspect. Moreover, the human cost

was profound, for hundreds of lives and careers were shattered, frequently beyond repair.

An atmosphere of creative orthodoxy prevailed, limiting artistic freedom and depriving Americans of a vital source of information and ideas. Hollywood not only reflected the dominant hysteria, but also reinforced it. The motion picture industry has been a major instrument of mass communications for much of the 20th century. Its reinforcement of McCarthyism thus added another unsavory element to the cultural and political ethos of that era.

Indeed, as if to deflect attention from its favorable treatment of Russians during the war, and more basically to establish its own political reliability, Hollywood produced a series of overtly anti-Communist features in the late Forties and early Fifties. Movies such as "I Married a Communist," "Iron Curtain," "Big Jim McClain," "I Was a Communist for the FBI," and "Red Danube" were, to be sure, poorly made, embarrassing affairs designed merely to curry political favor. There is no evidence that they had any significant specific effects on mass audiences. Nevertheless, they serve as valuable source material for a deeper understanding of the social pathology of those times.

In recent years, I have shown one of these films, "The Red Menace," to some of my classes. Artistically and historically, the film is preposterous. Undergraduates laugh at the vulgar caricatures of the major figures. They find the plot absurd and generally resent the simplistic political message and foolish sexual stereotypes. Its value, however, lies in its very existence as a visual reminder of what could happen in a society that abandons its democratic values and practices. What the students see is a film that manifests the worst of the fear and intellectual dishonesty of that era. That the film was even produced and distributed is revealing. When I explain the context, it becomes easier to understand why my aunt's neighbor thought that a siren meant that the police were searching for Communists

and why my sixth grade teacher attempted to brainwash his students with monstrous misinterpretations and outright lies.

It is equally instructive to examine the world of art during the Fifties. The conventional wisdom is that it was then that America became the art capital of the Western world. For this was the era of abstract expressionism, the school of "action painting" that allegedly was the first authentically American art that could rival the finest European modernism. This notion has been expressed so often in the past forty years that it is uncritically accepted in many art-historical and critical circles. Most major books on modern art history promote this view aggressively and effectively. It has become an article of faith, and both politically progressive and conservative scholars are among the most vigorous protagonists for this artistic development.

It is intriguing to examine one of these conservative voices in a broader inquiry about the cultural life of that period. Jeffrey Hart, the Dartmouth professor responsible for promoting the cheerful view of the Fifties, writes favorably and extensively about the advent of abstract expressionism:

They... made the first real advance since the Twenties in artistic consciousness. In the Fifties, the Cedar Tavern was to art what the Dome and the Select had been in the Paris of the Twenties. At the Cedar, you ran into Jackson Pollock, Willem de Kooning, Mark Rothko, and their younger colleagues... During the Fifties, the most exciting creative ideas and the most intense artistic energies were being generated within a few blocks of the Cedar Tavern. The radical modernism of the New York School of the Fifties has to be understood against the background of the 1930's, when the modernist movement launched by Picasso, Braque, and others was virtually suspended. From about 1930 until the mid-Forties, the propagandistic style known as Social Realism dominated the art world... Painters like Ben Shahn and William Gropper, now almost forgotten, were for a time considered major fi-

Fig. 12.   Jack Levine, *Witches' Sabaath*, 1963, oil on canvas, 96 x 84". (Courtesy Benton Foundation.)

gures. This style of painting celebrated the People, who were always depicted as having thick wrists and necks and abnormally small brain cavities. Diego Rivera and José Clemente Orozco were imposing their garish cartoons on public buildings. And then, poof!—with the end of the war, all of this Popular Front art disappeared... [E]veryone had more than enough of peasants and Okies and blacks...[7]

Hart's commentary is an intriguing fusion of avant-garde ideology and conservative disdain for the tradition of socially conscious art. His view, save perhaps for his sardonic dismissal of ethnic and working-class groups, resonates as well in the liberal intellectual community. But that vision, in fact, is yet another contemporary version of the happy-days mentality that inhibits a closer understanding of the political darkness of the cold-war period.

Abstract-expressionist painting, without doubt, made significant formal advances in art. Artists like Pollock, de Kooning, Rothko, Motherwell, Frankenthaler, Gottlieb, and Reinhardt were talented, creative individuals who produced some exciting, visually complex works. But these efforts, like all cultural products, must be understood in context of the political and social realities of the time. It is important to understand why a pattern of engaging but nonrepresentational art came to prominence at a particular moment in American history. It is equally important to understand why an older tradition of social commentary in art would be savagely disparaged at the same time.

Eva Cockcroft has addressed part of this issue boldly and perceptively. In her article entitled "Abstract Expressionism: Weapon of the Cold War," she argues that the new American avant garde served the ideological needs of the powerful in this society.[8] More recently, Serge Guilbaut's brilliant study of abstract expressionism and the cold war has shown how this new artistic movement was a "political apoliticism" that easily adapted to the dominant ideology of the era. It is no coincidence that the artistic forms

most favored by the political and cultural elites should offer no commentary, no critique of the harrowing political realities of loyalty probes, congressional investigations, and, indeed, the very assumptions and conduct of the cold war.

It also takes little imagination to discover why artistic social criticism should be out of official favor at the same time. Like their counterparts in film, music, literature, and other creative enterprises, left-leaning visual artists found themselves stigmatized during the early cold-war period. Doors to museums and galleries suddenly closed as political repression and the new orthodoxy of abstract expressionism consolidated its hold on America. Many socially conscious artists too were harassed by Congressional and other investigators for their politcal thoughts and associations and even for the content of their work.

There were numerous local incidents of artistic censorship, further eroding the nation's traditional commitment to the free expression of ideas. In July 1949, for example, the American Legion in San Francisco sought removal of Anton Refregier's Post Office murals in that city on the grounds that they were "communist art." The Legion found a sympathetic ear from Congressman Richard Nixon.

I realize that some very objectionable art, of a subversive nature, has been allowed to go into Federal buildings... I believe a committee of Congress should make a thorough investigation of this type of art in Government buildings with a view to obtaining removal of all that is found to be inconsistent with American ideals and principles.[10]

There were all too many additional examples. The great Mexican muralists Rivera, Orozco, and Siqueiros, whose work had transformed Mexico into a world center of modern art, had been similarly influential in the United States in the Thirties and Forties. Each of these artists had produced major murals in American cities. By the Fifties, however, these highly proclaimed efforts had come under familiar political attack.

In Detroit in 1952, a former mayor led a campaign to remove Rivera's murals at the Institute of the Arts because they were alleged to be Communist propaganda as well as "blasphemous and decadent."[11] Although this censorship attempt failed, it once again revealed the chilling spirit of the times in early cold-war America. A comparable attempt, however, succeeded the following year in New York City. In response to considerable pressure, authorities at the New School for Social Research covered one panel of a four-panel mural by Orozco, because it contained images of Soviet leaders painted in 1930 that were no longer acceptable less than a quarter-century later.[12]

Despite the repressive political climate, many socially conscious artists continued to create works that combined technical skill with trenchant social commentary. The works in the present exhibition exemplify the resilience of an ancient tradition of socially engaged artists who use their talents to call attention to oppression and social injustice.

Socially conscious art in America, though in reputational eclipse because of the political and cultural darkness of McCarthyism, still remained a vibrant creative force. Artists Ben Shahn, William Gropper, Jack Levine, Jacob Lawrence, Leonard Baskin, Raphael Soyer, and many others, produced paintings and prints about a myriad of social and political topics. Shahn, Baskin, and Levine, in fact, used their art to directly address the insidious consequences of political repression in America.

Jack Levine's painting Witches Sabbath (fig. 12) is an example of a masterful work from that troubled era. His effort is a bitter view of the congressional witch hunts that despoiled the American political landscape. The Ku Klux Klan regalia in the background sets the tone, especially in light of the witches' sabbaths in European history. In the center is Senator Joseph McCarthy himself, and to his right is his unsavory cohort and Rosenberg assistant prosecutor Roy Cohn. The typewriter belongs to an uncritical reporter—

Fig. 13,14,15. Judy Baca, *The Great Wall of Los Angeles*, 1983, Farewell to Rosie the Riveter,
Development of Suburbia, Red Scare and McCarthyism. Details from a mural
depicting a history of Greater Los Angeles.

fooled by the fraudulent "evidence" on McCarthy's table—and alludes to the press role in creating an equally uncritical public. The painting's visual distortion emphasizes the murky nature of the entire proceedings.

Works like this have inspired many contemporary social artists to use their own work to come to grips with the American past, including the tragic political repression of the Fifties. The social activism of the Sixties and early Seventies catalyzed a new and exciting body of socially critical art. Like their predecessors, today's representatives of that tradition have addressed a vast complex of social and political topics. From protesting American involvement in Vietnam and Nicaragua to supporting the struggles of blacks, Latinos, women, and gays, progressive artists have often been at the forefront of modern movements for social change.

Some have also sought, three decades later, to use their art to counter the happy-days nostalgia of the Fifties. Perhaps the most impressive recent example can be found in the longest mural in the world, the "Great Wall" in the San Fernando Valley in Los Angeles. Working under the direction of muralist Judy Baca, teenagers have painted a monumental "people's history" that views American life from a more realistic, unromantic perspective.

The panels dealing with the Fifties are especially perceptive. In one section, entitled "Farewell to Rosie Riveter," (Fig 13) viewers can see how the end of World War II also constituted the end of a temporary period of sexual equality. Having fulfilled their patriotic duty in substituting for men in the nation's factories, women were supposed to slip quietly back to their prescribed pattern of passivity and subservience. The lure of television would serve as a pleasant palliative, muting any residual resistance born of their wartime autonomy in the workplace. The expression of anxiety on the woman's face, however, reveals the essentially reactionary character of that postwar development.

The next panel, "Development of Suburbia" (Fig 14) similarly reveals a bleaker reality than that portrayed in the nostalgic versions of some contemporary television programs. The prosperity and comfort for white families fleeing the cities in the 1950's is juxtaposed against the influx of poor minority groups into American urban centers. The human consequences of the social and economic distress of these groups, portrayed effectively here, generally receives scant attention in the mass media.

The central panel dealing with the Fifties in the Great Wall deals, appropriately, with McCarthyism. Called "The Red Scare and McCarthyism" (Fig 15), this section powerfully depicts the pernicious influence of the congressional probes of that era. A menacing McCarthy hovers over the most highly publicized victims in Southern California, the Hollywood Ten. A useless typewriter is a graphic symbol of the powerlessness of thousands in the presence of the finger-pointing witch hunters who temporarily occupied center

> One reason for this exhibition is to ensure that there will never be another Rosenberg case.

stage in American political life.

Still other panels detail further features of the unsavory character of that time. One panel chronicles the police harassment in Los Angeles of gay men in a bar—an all-too-ubiquitous reality that has survived in this land long after the eclipse of McCarthyism. In another panel, civil-rights figures Rosa Parks and Martin Luther King appear, as if to illustrate the slow but inevitable ascent from the domestic repression of the early cold war. Significantly, the dominant figure in this panel is Paul Robeson, whose brilliant accomplishments in athletics, film, drama and music would now be fully recognized had it not been for his savage persecution during the bleakest days of the Fifties.

Cumulatively, this section of the

Great Wall serves as a visual corrective to the misleading and widespread happy-days image of that time in contemporary America. Its existence, however, raises a more fundamental question: Why, after all, should we concern ourselves now about an unfortunate era long since gone?

As noted earlier, there are many accounts of the terror and oppression of McCarthyism. One could properly, however, draw an analogy to the Holocaust, where there are even more accounts in print, in art, and on film about the grotesque destruction of millions of innocent Jews and other minorities. The blunt reality is that Americans are a largely ahistorical people, easily inclined to ignore the deeper lessons of the past even when they are familiar with many of the salient facts. As with the Holocaust, it is crucial to reiterate constantly that there are some historical events that we simply cannot allow to recur. Indeed, one of the reasons for an exhibition of Rosenberg-era art works is precisely to ensure that there will never be another Rosenberg case in this country. *Never.*

Four decades ago, Albert Camus wrote a novel about a plague in the Algerian port city of Oran. Although he used the metaphor of the bubonic plague, his real intention was to highlight the moral and political plagues that regularly despoil human life. In the novel, the forces of resistance finally overcome the disease that has devastated the city and its population. Based on Camus's own experiences in the French Resistance, *The Plague* is a powerful reminder that people must be ever vigilant in keeping the forces of evil and destruction in check.

At the conclusion of the story, the relieved citizens of Oran celebrate as they prepare for their return to normal life. In contrast, the chief protagonist of the novel, Dr. Bernard Rieux, expresses his personal apprehensions. His words underscore the compelling moral and historical need for a Rosenberg exhibition:

And, indeed, as he listened to the cries of joy rising from the town, Rieux remembered that such joy is always imperiled. He knew what those jubilant crowds did not know but could have learned from books: that the plague bacillus never dies or disappears for good, that it can lie dormant for years and years in furniture and linen-chests; that it bides its time in bedrooms, cellars, trunks, and bookshelves; and that perhaps the day would come, when for the bane and enlightening of men, it would rouse up its rats again and send them forth to die in a happy city.[14]

Notes

1. Jeffrey Hart, *When the Going Was Good* (New York, 1982), p. 17.

2. Richard Hofstadter, *The Paranoid Style in American Politics* (New York), 1964, p. 96.

3. David Caute, *The Great Fear* (New York, 1978), p. 11.

4. See Edwin Bayley, *Joe McCarthy and the Press,* for a good account.

The literature on McCarthy and McCarthyism, of course, is enormous.

5. There is a vast literature on the Hollywood blacklist. Many of the principals have written personal recollections. See, for example, Dalton Trumbo's *Additional Dialogue,* Alvah Bessie's *Inquisition in Eden,* and Lillian Hellman's *Scoundrel Time.* Good examples of analytic treatments include Victor Navasky, *Naming Names,* Robert Vaughn, *Only Victims,* and Larry Ceplair and Steven Englund, *The Inquisiton in Hollywood.* The film by Martin Ritt, "The Front," starring Woody Allen, also provides an interesting view of the squalid days of the blacklist.

6. Peter Biskind, *Seeing is Believing* (New York: Pantheon, 1983), p. 5. This book is a valuable source for a more comprehensive treatment of how the films of the 1950's reflected ways that a complex set of ideologies contended for public allegiance.

7. Hart, *op. cit.,* pp. 218–219.

8. *Artforum,* Volume 12 (June 1974).

9. Serge Guilbaut, *How New York Stole the Idea of Modern Art* (Chicago, 1983). This book is a sophisticated effort that subjects art history to some rigorous methods of real history.

10. Jan Clapp, *Art Censorship* (Metuchen, N.J.: Scarecrow Press, 1972), p. 283.

11. *Ibid.*

12. *Ibid.*

13. See Paul Von Blum, *The Art of Social Conscience* (New York, 1976) and *The Critical Vision* (Boston, 1980) for extended treatments of socially conscious art in Europe, Mexico, and the United States.

14. Albert Camus, *The Plague* (New York, 1948), p. 278.

For Ethel Rosenberg
Adrienne Rich

Although she didn't write the poem
"For Ethel Rosenberg" until 1980,
Adrienne Rich had felt its pull for a
long time. "Sometimes a political
event can take place in your lifetime
and you can be at the time very
apolitical as I was then," she says.
"...yet that event becomes part of you,
lying in wait for you ever after, until
you can integrate it. Not just integrate
its meaning into your life, but to
integrate your personal life into history.
I didn't do research to write this poem.
If I had it would have been a very
different kind of poem. All I did was to
try and remember, to imagine, and
then, to ask questions."   —R.O.

Convicted, with her husband,
of "conspiracy to commit
espionage"; killed in the
electric chair June 19, 1953

1.
Europe 1953:
throughout my random sleepwalk
the words

scratched on walls, on pavements
painted over railway arches
Liberez les Rosenberg!

Escaping from home I found
home everywhere:
the Jewish question, Communism

marriage itself
question of loyalty
or punishment

my Jewish father writing me
letters of seventeen pages
finely inscribed harangues

questions of loyalty
and punishment
One week before my wedding

that couple gets the chair
the volts grapple her, don't
kill her fast enough

Liberez les Rosenberg!
I hadn't realized
our family arguments were so important

Fig. 16.   Theo Balden, *Ethel Rosenberg*, 1958, wood, 47". Collection the Museum der
Stadt Güstrow, German Democratic Republic. (Photo: Christian Krausharr.)

my narrow understanding
of crime   of punishment
no language for this torment

mystery of that marriage
always both faces
on every front page in the world

Something so shocking   so
unfathomable
it must be pushed aside

2.
She sank however into my soul   A weight of sadness
I hardly can register how deep
her memory has sunk   that wife and mother

like so many
who seemed to get nothing out of any of it
except her children

Fig. 17. James Whitmore, George Grizzard, and Anne Jackson played the parts of defense attorney Emanuel Bloch and Julius and Ethel Rosenberg, in Donald Freed's 1970 Broadway play, *Inquest*. (Photo: Orlando Guerra.)

THE VOICE OF FREUD. Men have brought their powers of subduing the forces of nature to such a pitch that by using them they could now very easily exterminate one another to the last man. They know this—hence arise their current unrest, their dejection, their mood of apprehension.

The VOICE OF MARX. If we set out to discover the impelling forces which stand behind historical figures, and constitute the true final impulses of history, we cannot consider so much the motive of single individuals, as those which set in motion great masses and entire nations.

(*In slow motion, the atom bomb media resumes. Through the flames, the TIME CHAMBER OF THE 1950's begins to bleed into visibility. First comes the popular cultural axis: early television laugh tracks vie with the cries of the bomb victims; a song like* Cry *canceling the sirens; sports heroes; the big mouths of expensive cars and Milton Berle and Walter Winchell, etc. Next comes the political axis: the brutal comedy routine shares space with Joseph McCarthy; the political imagery of the American Cold War is established before the last layers of the media—the "Atom Spy Ring" case, itself—is firmly imprinted. A dating*

process is evolved from the rash of masthead headlines. The fall-out of sights and sounds slows and drops until only frozen images remain on the various screens.)

THE SCREEN. EVERY WORD YOU WILL HEAR OR SEE ON THIS STAGE IS A DOCUMENTED QUOTATION OR RE-CONSTRUCTION FROM EVENTS

(*A capsule of J. Edgar Hoover appears.*)

The VOICE OF J. EDGAR HOOVER. The twentieth century has witnessed the intrusion into its body fabric of a highly malignant cancer—a cancer which threatens to destroy Judaic-Christian civilization.

(*On the screen the "spy ring capsule." The head of* KLAUS FUCHS *covers the screen. Headlines tell the story of his arrest. On one screen the diagram of the Spy Ring begins. This is a cancer-like network. The "Communist Cancer," of the Hoover world-view, is in the paranoid style.*)

VOICE OF KLAUS FUCHS. There are other crimes which I have committed, other than the ones with which I'm charged. When I asked my counsel to put certain facts before you, I did so in order to atone for these crimes. They are not crimes in the eyes of the law.

VOICE OF J. EDGAR HOOVER. Communist man is a brute, ideologically trained . . . he is immune to the emotions of pity, sorrow or remorse. He is truly an alarming monster, human in physical form, but in practice a cynically godless and immoral machine. ((*A capsule of JOSEPH McCARTHY.*)

VOICE OF JOSEPH McCARTHY. I have here in my hand a list of two hundred and five that were known to the Secretary of State as being members of the Communist Party.

VOICE OF J. EDGAR HOOVER. The secret of the atomic bomb has been stolen. Find the thieves! In all the history of the F.B.I., there never was a more important problem than this one, never another case where we felt under such pressure. The unknown man simply has to be found.

(*On the screen: film of DAVID GREENGLASS being taken into custody. Headlines and the diagram of the Ring tell the story. Film of JULIUS AND ETHEL ROSENBERG being arrested. Headlines for the arrest of the ROSENBERGS appear on the screen. On opposite corners, in tight spotlight, stand JULIUS and ETHEL ROSENBERG.*)

JULIUS ROSENBERG. Hello, my love. You are so close at hand and yet your being in a different corridor separated by so much steel, locked away from my sight and beyond my hearing range, the frustration is terrific. Tonight I was able to hear your voice when a few of the high notes of one of your arias was faintly audible . . . Physically I am fairly comfortable and already in the routine of things . . . I read about six newspapers a day, play chess on a numbered board by remote control with another inmate and I am reading "The Old Country" by Sholem Aleichem.

ETHEL ROSENBERG. Dearest Julie. There has been a fine intermittent rain all afternoon . . . every so often the rain lets up and I kneel down to a crevice in the concrete . . . In this crevice an apple seed which I have planted and have watered patiently . . .

JULIUS ROSENBERG. (*Overlapping.*) . . . is sprouting bravely. All my love, darling. Your own, Ethel.

(EMANUEL BLOCH *appears in a pool of light.*)

EMANUEL BLOCH. In the middle of dinner, the phone rang; a man I had never met named Julius Rosenberg asked if I could see him. We took a little walk, it was a nice night, and I said to him, "Mr. Rosenberg, I don't think you have anything to worry about." I figured it was probably something minor, like a loyalty oath case; I handled a lot of them at that time. So I am the defense. (*Shakes his head and sighs.*) I had no idea of what was waiting for me. They were arrested in August of 1950 and executed in June of 1953—in between was the trial. That's all I know. (*Pause.*) I was the defense, but I can't tell you what really hap-

pened to those two human beings. Let me put it to you this way—the future determines the past.

(*Over all the screens and scrims the diagram of FUCHS to GOLD to GREENGLASS to the ROSENBERGS spreads and duplicates itself like a cancer or octopus over the ROSENBERG memorabilia. In the darkness the juror selection drum begins to glow and spin.*)

FIRST AGENT. Mrs. Rosenberg, you'll have to come with us—you're under arrest.

SECOND AGENT. (*Showing identification.*) Federal Bureau of Investigation. Special Agents.

ETHEL ROSENBERG. What? Do you have a warrant?

FIRST AGENT. We don't need one. Let's go upstairs.

ETHEL ROSENBERG. But I just left the grand jury up there. I was called up to testify, that's all. My children are waiting for me. I have a three year old.

SECOND AGENT. Let's go.

ETHEL ROSENBERG. Why are you doing this—I came down here today of my own free will. My children are expecting me. (*They walk into another area*). Listen, I have to phone my neighbor. She's watching the children for me.

FIRST AGENT. All right. Go ahead.

ETHEL ROSENBERG. (*Searches through her purse for a coin to place in the pay phone. The FIRST AGENT offers her a coin.*) No, I have my own. (*Deposits the coin, dials the number.*) Hello. Listen, don't show any alarm. Are the boys there? Listen, after I testified, as I'm walking out, two F.B.I. agents meet me and they're holding me here. I'm calling Mr. Bloch and I'll have him call you. Meanwhile, take the children over to my mother's. And listen, let me talk to Michael for a minute. (*Pause*). Hello, Michael. Are you helping take care of Robby? Listen, dear, Mommy has to stay downtown a while. What? Michael, do you remember what happened to Daddy?

Well, dear—(*tries to block out the scream from the other end.*)

(*THE SCREEN: This headline appears and remains until the end of the Act. The media is now beginning to throb with GOLD-related thematic imagery. The comics and cartoons return.*)

NEW YORK TIMES:
ATOM BOMB SHELTERS FOR CITY
AT COST OF $450,000,000 URGED

IRVING SAYPOL. Who was your Soviet superior at this time?

HARRY GOLD. Anatoli Yakovlev.

IRVING SAYPOL. Now in May of 1945, did you have a meeting with Yakovlev?

HARRY GOLD. Yes, I did.

IRVING SAYPOL. Now, will you tell the jury what happened on this occasion?

HARRY GOLD. Yakovlev told me that he wanted me to go to Albuquerque, New Mexico. Yakovlev then gave me a sheet of paper; it was onionskin paper, and on it was typed the following: First the name "Greenglass," just "Greenglass." Then a number "High Street"; all that I can recall about the number is that the last figure—it was a low number and the last figure, the second figure was 0 and the last figure was either 5, 7, or 9; and then underneath that was "Albuquerque, New Mexico." The last thing that was on the paper was "Recognition signal. I come from Julius." In addition to this, Yakovlev gave me a piece of cardboard which appeared to have been cut from a packaged food of some sort. It was cut in an odd shape and Yakvolev told me that the man Greenglass, whom I would meet in Albuquerque, would have the matching piece of cardboard.

IRVING SAYPOL. Now will you tell the jury about your last contact with Yakovlev?

HARRY GOLD. Yakovlev called me and said he would meet me at the Earl Theatre in the Bronx at 8 o'clock that night. At exactly eight o'clock I was in the upstairs lounge of the Earl Theatre.

IRVING SAYPOL. What happened there?

HARRY GOLD. There I was accosted by a man. The man who met me was not Yakovlev. He was tall, about six feet two, had blond hair and a very determined feature. He walked with a catlike stride, almost on the balls of his feet. (GOLD *leaves the courtroom. He poses and whispers.*) I first got involved in spying through Tom Black of Jersey City. He was a fantastic man. He coiled a pet blacksnake around his neck and he had a trained crow that he used to pitch marbles to. I got involved in order to get Black off my neck about joining the Communist Party. I didn't want to. I didn't like them—they were a bunch of wacked-up bohemians. First I created a wife I did not have. Then there had to be children to go along with the wife, and they had to grow old—it's a wonder steam didn't come out of my ears sometimes. When I went on a mission for the Russians, I immediately turned a switch in my mind and when I was done I turned the switch again and I was once again Harry Gold—just a chemist. Then there was Steve Swartz. A virtual giant; long arms, big feet . . . (*All the time axes, from political to personal, are building.*) I recall him distinctly. He was at least six foot—possibly six foot one, and had an extremely savage face, tough-looking face, a plug-ugly.

FBI AGENT. Didn't you have some recognition sign between the two of you?

HARRY GOLD. Yes, we did. I believe that it involved the name of a man and was something on the order of Bob sent me or Benny sent me or John sent me or something like that.

FBI AGENT. Then, in this case you would have had to say, "Julius sent me, huh?"

HARRY GOLD. Who's Julius?

ETHEL ROSENBERG. Manny, what are we supposed to do?

EMANUEL BLOCH. We bring it all out. We tell them what it was like being a poor Jew, growing up in New York, as

Fig. 18.   The stage set for *Inquest* employed multiple screens, slide projectors, and archival film footage. (Photo: Orlando Guerra.)

you two did. *There are no Jews on this jury!* There are three million Jews in this town, and I can't get a Jew on the jury.

ETHEL ROSENBERG. But we get Saypol and Kaufman.

EMANUEL BLOCH. Kaufman is murder. If I let myself go, I'll go to jail for contempt. I'm telling you.

ETHEL ROSENBERG. Manny!

EMANUEL BLOCH. He's ready to cite me right now. So, you go on the stand, we opne up your whole lives—

ETHEL ROSENBERG. Oh, Manny!

EMANUEL BLOCH. Why you believe in some kind of socialism, social justice, whatever. Then, if they start redbaiting, at least we can call their bluff

JULIUS ROSENBERG. Wait a minute—not so fast.

EMANUEL BLOCH. I'm even seriously considering bringing your psychiatrist on.

ETHEL ROSENBERG. No, I'm sorry, that's out, Manny. But I think maybe Manny's right. With the Fifth Amendment, we're damned if we do, and we're damned if we don't.

JULIUS ROSENBERG. Wait, I thought we had to destroy their evidence, phony as it is—the watches, the console table, the Jell-o box, for God's sake!—but, if we do as you say, if we don't take the Fifth Amendment, if we

answer just one question they can ask anything—

ETHEL ROSENBERG. But the jury might be convinced if we—

JULIUS ROSENBERG. Honey, please let's let Manny go over this.

ETHEL ROSENBERG. All right, I'm sorry.

JULIUS ROSENBERG. Please. We've got to deal with their evidence. Now, how do we do that? The jury believes what—

EMANUEL BLOCH. All right. Look, Julie, the point is if I had anyone to help me—if I had any money for investigation or real research—we could go your way. Maybe we could get Einstein on the stand, I don't know. The thing you've got to recognize is that we're alone! The Left—your own family, Ethel, for God's sake! We're alone. The country's hysterical. I just don't know which way to go. You wouldn't believe what's going on outside. People who knew you—friends—are taking photographs from over the years and flushing them down the toilet! People are getting passports, no one wants to testify.

JULIUS ROSENBERG. Look, Manny, I'm afraid of it. If we don't take the Fifth Amendment, the FBI is going to bring in professional informers to testify that we were Communists. Who is the jury going to believe? Us or the FBI? But if we take the Fifth, they can't pursue it. Can they?

EMANUEL BLOCH. No!

JULIUS ROSENBERG. And the worst of all is if I don't take it, they're going to try to drag every name of everybody I ever knew or worked with or went to school with out of me. Not just names—but real people, innocent people. They'll make twenty spy rings before they're through. What's the good of a privilege if we don't use it!

EMANUEL BLOCH. I'm so disgusted, I don't know. Maybe I'm kidding myself. I'm the wrong man for this case.

———

IRVING SAYPOL. The Court asked you this question: "Did you approve the communistic system in Russia over the capitalistic system in this country?" And you answered: "I am not expert on those things, Your Honor, and I did not make any such direct statement." Do you remember having testified that way?

JULIUS ROSENBERG. That's right.

IRVING SAYPOL. Well now, just a short while before you said that you felt "The Soviet government has improved the lot of the underdog there"; what did you mean by that?

JULIUS ROSENBERG. What I read in newspapers.

IRVING SAYPOL. And what did you read about the improvement of the lot of the underdog in Soviet Russia, as you read it in the newspapers?

JULIUS ROSENBERG. Well, that the worker there, as living standards were increased, his housing conditions were better than at times when he lived under the Czar. That is what I mean by increasing the lot of the "underdog."

IRVING SAYPOL. What newspapers did you read that in?

JULIUS ROSENBERG. Various newspapers.

IRVING SAYPOL. You mean *The Daily Worker*?

JULIUS ROSENBERG. On occasion; the *New York Times*.

IRVING SAYPOL. Any others?

JULIUS ROSENBERG. Yes.

IRVING SAYPOL. What others?

JULIUS ROSENBERG. The *Herald Tribune*, the *World Telegram*.

IRVING SAYPOL. The *Wall Street Journal*, perhaps?

JULIUS ROSENBERG. No, I don't read the *Wall Street Journal*.

IRVING SAYPOL. "Has made a lot of progress in eliminating illiteracy;" what did you know about that?

JULIUS ROSENBERG. They built schools.

IRVING SAYPOL. Where?

JULIUS ROSENBERG. From what I read.

IRVING SAYPOL. Where were the schools built?

JULIUS ROSENBERG. In the Russian cities.

IRVING SAYPOL. What cities?

JULIUS ROSENBERG. I don't know, sir.

IRVING SAYPOL. Where did you read that, same newspapers?

JULIUS ROSENBERG. Newspapers.

IRVING SAYPOL. "Has done a lot of reconstruction work"; what did you know about that?

JULIUS ROSENBERG. Well, there are a lot of reporters that go to Russia and report how the cities have been rebuilt, that were destroyed by the Nazis.

———

EMANUEL BLOCH. Where are your children now?

ETHEL ROSENBERG. They are at a temporary shelter in the Bronx.

EMANUEL BLOCH. Have you seen them since you were arrested?

ETHEL ROSENBERG. No, I have not.

(On the dark stage we hear only the VOICES OF THE CHILDREN, 1953.)

VOICE OF MICHAEL. Dear President Eisenhower: My mommy and daddy are in prison in New York. My brother is six years old. His name is Robby. Please let my mommy and daddy go and not let anything happen to them.

If they come Robby and I will be very happy. We will thank you very much. Yours truly, Michael Rosenberg.

EMANUEL BLOCH. Now, your brother, Dave, was the youngest in the family?

ETHEL ROSENBERG. That's right . . .

EMANUEL BLOCH. What was your relationship?

ETHEL ROSENBERG. Well, he was my baby brother.

EMANUEL BLOCH. Did you love him?

ETHEL ROSENBERG. I loved him very much.

JUDGE KAUFMAN. Did he sort of look up to you?

ETHEL ROSENBERG. Yes.

JUDGE KAUFMAN. And your husband? Before the arguments that were discussed here in court!

ETHEL ROSENBERG. He liked us both. He liked my husband.

JUDGE KAUFMAN. Sort of hero worship?

ETHEL ROSENBERG. Oh, by no stretch of the imagination could you say that was hero worship.

JUDGE KAUFMAN. You heard him so testify, did you not?

ETHEL ROSENBERG. Yes, I did.

EMANUEL BLOCH. And it is not correct, is it, that there was any hero worship between Julius and your brother or your brother and Julius?

ETHEL ROSENBERG. It is certainly not correct.

EMANUEL BLOCH. Please describe the last time you saw your sister-in-law, Ruth Greenglass.

ETHEL ROSENBERG. After my brother was arrested, I waited for her one day at my mother's. She had the baby and we began to walk, she and I, with the carriage around the block.

———

ETHEL ROSENBERG. My brother had been arrested. My husband had been arrested. I had been subpoenaed to come before the Grand Jury. It was not for me to state what I thought or didn't think the Government might or might not have in the way of accusation against me.

IRVING SAYPOL. What you are saying is that you were under no compulsion to confess your guilt in respect to this conspiracy?

ETHEL ROSENBERG. I had no guilt—

EMANUEL BLOCH. Just a moment, please.

JUDGE KAUFMAN. She has answered.

ETHEL ROSENBERG. I had no guilt to confess.

JUDGE KAUFMAN. But in your own interest I think you ought to think about it and give us some reason. (*Pause*).

IRVING SAYPOL. Were you asked this question and did you give this answer:

"Do I understand you are going to decline to answer all questions that I ask you?"

"No, no I won't decline to answer all questions. It depends on the questions." Did you say that?

ETHEL ROSENBERG. Yes, I did.

IRVING SAYPOL. When you said it depends on the questions, you meant it depends on whether or not the question and the answer you gave would tend to incriminate you, is that right?

ETHEL ROSENBERG. That is right.

IRVING SAYPOL. You testified here today in response to questions from your counsel that the first time you saw Harry Gold was in this courtroom, is that so?

ETHEL ROSENBERG. That is right.

IRVING SAYPOL. Do you remember having been asked this question and giving this answer:

"Have you ever met Harry Gold?"

"I decline to answer on the ground that this might intimidate me, incriminate me, I mean."

Did you give that testimony at the time?

ETHEL ROSENBERG. I gave that testimony.

JUDGE KAUFMAN. If you had answered at that time, for reasons best known to you, you felt it that that would incriminate you?

ETHEL ROSENBERG. If I used the privilege of self-incrimination at that time, I must have felt that perhaps there might be something that might incriminate me in answering.

IRVING SAYPOL. As a matter of fact, at that time you didn't know how much the FBI knew about you and so you weren't taking any chances, isn't that it?

EMANUEL BLOCH. I object.

JUDGE KAUFMAN. Overruled.

ETHEL ROSENBERG. When one uses the right of self-incrimination one does not mean that the big answer is yes and one does not mean that the answer is no. I made no denial. I made no assertion that I did know him. I simply refused to answer on the ground that the answer might incriminate me.

Fig. 19. "Ike disturbed the balance of the cosmos by his stroke-head deathshake, 'NO'"
Guido Zingerl, *In Memoriam: Ethel and Julius Rosenberg*, 1982, acrylic on chip-
board, 32⁹/₁₆ x 32⁹/₁₆".

Television Was A Baby Crawling Toward that Deathchamber

Allen Ginsberg

It is here, the long Awaited bleap-blast light that Speaks
one red tongue like Politician, but happy its own govt.

either we blow ourselves up now and die, like the old
tribe of man, arguing among neutrons, spit on India,
fuck Tibet, stick up America, clobber Moscow, die
Baltic, have your tuberculosis in Arabia, wink not in
Enkidu's reverie—

it's a long Train of Associations stopped for gas in the de-
sert & looking for drink of old time H_2O—

The President laughs in his Chair, and swivels his head on
his neck controlling fangs of Number—

bacteria come numberless, atoms count themselves
greatness in their pointy Empire—

Russian Neutrons spy on all Conspiracy—& Chinese yellow energy waves have ocean and Empyrean ready
against attack & future starvation—Korean prin-
cipalities of Photon are doubles in all but name—dif-
fering Wizards of Art of Electron divide as many as
tribes of Congo—Africa's a vast jail of Shadows—I
am not I,

my molecules are numbered, mirrored in all Me Robot
Seraphy parts, cock-creator navel-marked, Eye Seer
with delicate breasts, teeth & gullet to ingest the living dove-life

foreimage of the Self-Maw Death Is Now;—but there is
the Saintly Meat of the Heart—feeling to thee o Peter
and all my Lords—Decades American loves car-
rides and vow-sworn faces lain on my breast,—my
head on many more naked than my own sad hoping
flesh—

our feelings! come back to the heart—to the old blind
hoping Creator home in Mercy, beating everywhere
behind machine hand clothes-man Senator iron
powered or fishqueen fugitive-com'd lapel—

Here I am—Old Betty Boop whoopsing behind the skull-
microphone wondering what Idiot soap opera horror
show we broadcast by Mistake—full of communists
and frankenstein cops and

mature capitalists running the State Department and the
Daily News Editorial hypnotizing millions of legional-
eyed detectives to commit mass murder on the Invisible

under drear eyeglass Dulles to ASSASSINATE!
INVADE! STARVE OUT! SUPPLY INVISIBLE ARMS! GIVE
MONEY TO ORGANIZE DEATH FOR CUBAN REVOLU-
TION! BLOCKADE WHAT FRAIL MACHINERY!
MAKE EVIL PROPAGANDA OVER THE WORLD! ISOLATE

THE FAITHFUL'S SOUL! TAKE ALL RICHES BACK! BE
WORLDLY PRINCE AND POWER OVER THE UNBELIEV-
ABLE! MY GOD!
AMERICA WILL BE REFUSED ETERNITY BY HER OWN MAD
SON THE BOMB! MEN WORKING IN ELECTRICITY BE
U.S. SADISTS THEIR MAGIC PHANOPOEIAC THRU MASS
MEDIA THE NASTIEST IN THIS FIRST HISTORY!
EVIL SPELLS THRU THE DAILY NEWS! HORRIBLE MASOCH-
ISMS THUNK UP BY THE AMERICAN MEDICAL AS-
SOCIATION! DEATH TO JUNKIES THRU THE TREASURY
DEPARTMENT! TAXES ON YOUR HATE FOR THIS HERE
WAR!
LEGIONS OF DECENCY BLACKMAIL THY CINEMAL FATE!
CONSPIRACIES CONTROL ALL WHITE MAGICIANS! I
CAN'T TELL YOU MY SECRET STORY ON TV!

Old Bones in his penthouse on a skyscraper in Manhattan, laconic on two phones that rang thru the nets
of money over earth, as he barked his orders to For-
mosa for more spies, abhorred all Cuba sugar from
concourse with Stately stomachs—

That's when I began vomiting my paranoia when Old National Skullface the invisible sixheaded billionaire
began brainwashing my stomach with strange feel-
ers in the *Journal American*—the penis of billionaires
depositing professional semen in my ear, Fulton
Lewis *coming* with strychnine jizzum in his voice making an evil suggestion that entered my mouth.

while I was sitting there gaping in wild dubiety & astound
on my peaceful couch he said to all the taxidrivers
and schoolteachers in brokendown old Blakean
America

that Julius and Ethyl Rosenberg smelled bad & shd die,
he sent to kill them with personal electricity, his power
station is the spirit of generation leaving him thru his
asshole by Error, that very electric entered Ethyl's eye

and his tongue is the prick of a devil he don't even know,
a magic capitalist ghosting it on the lam after the
Everett Massacre—fucks a Newscaster in the mouth
every time he gets on the Microphone—

and those ghost jizzums started my stomach trouble with
capital punishment, Ike chose to make an Artificial
Death for them poor spies—if they were spying on
me? who cares?—Ike disturbed the balance of the
cosmos by his stroke-head deathshake, "NO"

It was a big electrocution in every paper and mass
media, Television was a baby crawling toward that
deathchamber

Editor's note: Excerpted from a 5,000 word poem.

Fig. 20. Deborah Kruger, *St. Ethel*, 1986, xerox, pastel, wallpaper, 20 x 16". (Photo: Steven Borns.)

ETHEL
A Novel About
Ethel Rosenberg
TEMA NASON

"Losing the Rosenbergs in 1953 was very painful. But losing my innocence about the American system of justice was painful, too," writes Tema Nason, author of the novel, *Ethel*, a fictional autobiography of Ethel Rosenberg. The wife of a young assistant professor in the early Fifties, Nason remembers vividly "the fear rampant in the academic community, the fear in our hearts that some petition we had signed, some meeting we'd attended years ago, would now be cited as un-American.... People avoided discussing politics at parties. Suddenly no one had an opinion about anything in the public sphere."

Coming across the Rosenbergs's "Death House Letters" in 1979, Nason says she was tremendously moved, seeing the couple as real people with everyday concerns. She was by then a writer and planning a novel about her generation, "how we grew up during the Depression, went off to war, and then saw all our hopes and ideas smashed." The Rosenbergs's murder, Nason says, "represented the executioner's axe blow, ending the Age of Innocence" for her and many other children of immigrants from Brooklyn who were idealistic, cynical "yet so trustingly naïve about America."

As a woman, Nason saw Ethel Rosenberg as the archetypical victim of the whole McCarthy period. Coming of age at a time when young women were denied higher education, expected to accept the socially-assigned role of wife and mother, Ethel was ultimately "condemned to death for behaving in an unwomanly way!" Nason says. "She was expected to 'cooperate' in order to live for her children. Either way she couldn't win."

All at once, a light went off in her head. *Why not tell her story?* In everything she had ever read, Ethel had always been lumped together with Julius with no pre-existence or identity apart from her role as his missus.

"She deserved a life of her own," Nason decided, hoping through research and imagination to find it. In effect, "I appointed myself her ghost writer, no pun intended."

From the outset, two questions puzzled her: Why hadn't Ethel settled for a prison sentence, essentially buying clemency as her brother, David, had done? As the mother of five children, Nason is convinced that her own initial reaction would have been to have compromised her ideals and chosen life, no matter what the terms.

The other question was: How could she have survived 22 months on Death Row, in solitary? Where did she get the strength to endure?

In the six years it took to write *Ethel*, Nason attempted to answer those questions—and many others—in a book she thinks Ethel Rosenberg might have written herself if she had had the chance.

"Sometimes," Nason said, "I felt as though she was holding my hand and guiding the pen. Other times, she took the pen in her own hand and wrote."—R.O.

APRIL 1951

I'm one of the World's Great Dreamers. Along with Marx, Moses, Lincoln… also God. It's only recently that I've discovered this important fact about myself. If they ever make up another list—like the Seven Wonders of the World—*then I should be on it.* Yes, definitely. I belong. Because when I get into that golden chariot, I ride the skies like a rainbow. Oh, the thrill and the beauty of it! But the funny thing, no, it's not so funny, I'm beginning to realize, it's really very odd, at the time I'm up there, I don't know that, it all seems so natural, so real…

…like here now in solitary—the Death House at Sing Sing—sometimes I feel as though it's all happening to me in a play, and I'm in the audience watching myself perform. Sometimes I'm so angry I shake—or is it fear?—and yet part of me sits back and watches it happen as though it's happening to someone else, a woman I once knew and haven't seen in years.

Yesterday we're sitting in the Visitor's room separated by that damn wire screen and we're discussing our brief to the U.S. Circuit Court of Appeals, and I say to Manny, that's Emanuel Bloch, our lawyer and best friend, the only lawyer in the whole of New York City with guts enough to take our case, Manny, I say to him, I'm trying to understand why I'm here.

"Traitors!" Judge Kaufman screams at us that day in court. I'll never forget it. "Gave away the secret of the atom bomb to the Russians. Responsible for 50,000 deaths in Korea, maybe more!"

Me a traitor? Ettie Greenglass from Seward Park High? Mata Hari *was* a traitor, that's who… She was so beautiful, Greta Garbo up there on the screen…

Right away Manny's impatient with me. "Ethel," he says in that indulgent, yet chastising voice he gets from his uncle, the rabbi. "I don't follow you. Why are you off on that tangent today when we have this appeal to discuss? When I saw Julie yesterday, he said to be sure to talk it over with you—there're only three days left to file." And he zips open his case and shuffles some papers like he's got to be doing something with his hands. He's upset. The paper shuffling I

recognize from the courtroom. But this time he's upset because this time I've dared to say to him what I've never dared to say out loud before, so I don't continue with what's on my mind. But I look at myself in this "shmate," and I ask myself, what am I dong here, Ethel Rosenberg in a striped prisoner's uniform when I should be home fixing dinner for Julie and the kids. How scared they must be! So little, so young to be away from us. *How did all this happen to me? How did I get from my kitchen here? What am I going to do?*

> Thirty-Sixth Street is packed with people— everywhere hands are reaching out for signs and leaflets.

MAY 1951

Since last August—though it hardly seems possible—I haven't heard my sons laugh… or touched them, nor even seen them. At first, we thought it would be better this way, that we'd be coming home soon, and they wouldn't have to come to prison to see us. What an impression it would make on young children! But now I know it's worse—there's a great big gaping hole in our lives. We have just got to see each other, no matter what, and I've asked Manny to get busy on this.

There are times here when I get positively frantic. Where are my babies? Why are they keeping me away from them? And I'm scared that something terrible has happened to them, and they're not telling me. I try to quiet myself by reciting the facts—Michael and Robby are safe, they're safe, I repeat to myself, you know that for a fact. And I've received two of Michael's letters, each word printed so carefully, even a drawing from Robby—two small kids and a big empty sky. But still a couple of days ago, I started to shake so badly thinking about them, that I had to ask Molly to come and stand there close by, right next to the bars and talk to me. "Say something, anything," I tell her, "just

keep talking to me so I can hear your voice." And she does. I can't remember all she says because she talks for quite a while, pats my hand through the bars until the shaking stops, and I fall exhausted on my cot. As I'm falling asleep, I remember she's telling me the story of Moses from the Bible and how Pharaoh's daughter found him, this little baby crying in the bullrushes, and brought him back to the palace and took care of him, and he was safe.

That heartpinching fear is creeping over me again… and slowly I'm discovering that *when you can't live with now, you can always lose yourself in the past…*

1935! A lot's happening in the world and finally I open my eyes. Twenty years old and I begin to see the world for what it is, and not just the stuff of my dreams. It's the year Italy invades Ethiopia and Senator Huey Long is assassinated. Celia says he was a fascist and the newspaper quotes him as once saying, "Sure, we'll have fascism in America, only it'll come wrapped in the American flag." Smart man!

I'm learning, but I'm a slow learner. As one of the World's Great Dreamers, there are some things I don't want to believe. *That people are people.* It's as simple as that, though it's hard for me to accept even now here in Sing Sing. But it's true. Yet something in me—the Dreamer?—doesn't want to believe it, the hard facts about people. For instance, why are so many liberals and Jews being intimidated by the Communist witch hunt? And how about the Party? Where are they in our hour of need? When the stakes are so high?

Although recalling my entrenched innocence and basic optimism— don't all dreamers have to be?—I must have believed even back then in 1935 that whatever I was involved in, the outcome was crucial to my future. But in those days, my future was spelled out in lights on marquees. Front page headlines I didn't anticipate.

And yet, I'm beginning to realize that everything that happens, each small decision you make, is nothing more than taking a step in a certain direction.

On August 27, 1935, we all go out on strike.

Murray asked me to get to strike headquarters—which is at Christ Church on West Thirty-Sixth—earlier than the others. "That way you can help me get things lined up."

"Sure, be glad to," I tell him, pleased to be asked.

He's already there when I rush in, breathless, but neatly dressed. "It's important," he'd told us, "we want the crowd to see you striking for a living wage, not begging for a handout."

Good old New York, hot and muggy as usual. A short thunderstorm the night before hasn't done a thing to cool it off, and I'm feeling a little nauseous, anyway. Mom contributed by giving me a big argument before I left the house. "Stay out of it," she butts in as I'm making last minute arrangements on the phone with Celia. "Don't get mixed up with these troublemakers. You'll get in trouble, too, you'll see." She keeps on yakking at me, finally I get out with her still going a mile a minute.

Among the first who show up? Robert, of course. Right away he's offering suggestions that won't work and getting on everyone's nerves. Murray gives him something to do that gets him out of the way.

Soon others start showing up. Lots of nervous giggles. This is it! The girls, that is, the men are punching each other on the shoulder, the hearty stuff. "Hey, Sam!" "Hey Abe!" "Howsa boy? Ready for a little action" "Yeah," rubbing his hands together eagerly, "but my wife, she ain't so happy about it."

In less than an hour, Thirty-Sixth Street is packed with people—I can't believe my eyes—hundreds and hundreds are gathering outside the church and more come pouring in every minute. Everywhere hands are reaching out for signs and leaflets as Murray repeats last minute instructions. "Just stay calm no matter what," he warns us, "otherwise, we're playing right into their hands. They'll try to provoke us so they can go for an injunction to stop the picketing. Whatever you do, don't lose your head. Remember, they'll do their damndest!—

"Also be prepared for the scabs and guards they'll bring in from Pinkerton's or Bergoff's… strikebusters! Bums hired for this lousy business right off the street, from the flophouses on the Bowery— they'll stop at nothing. They're the scum—prison records, manslaughter, armed robbery, nice things like that— and they're armed with clubs, blackjacks, knives," he's speaking slowly so it sinks in, "and guns… loaded. They're going to fight us with every weapon they've got. So watch out, everybody!"

"One more thing," he says and then gives us the bad news. "Our parade down Broadway this afternoon is cancelled."

"Ooh!" moans the crowd.

When he adds, "The police refused to give us a permit," the crowd boos long and loud. "They can't get away with this," some yell out.

He cups his hands like a microphone and yells back, "You're damn right! But that's how much influence the bosses have!" The crowd's getting angrier. He's getting to them. "But we're still not giving up, we're working on it, you can bet your life!" Now he has them cheering. For me, it's an indescribable feeling—to be part of all this and the real strength and fierce determination I read on all the faces around me.

As we head out to our shops, Murray suggests a song. "C'mon everyone, let's show 'em the kind of spirit we have. Ethel, you've got the voice, suppose you lead off?"

So I call out loud and clear, "Okay everybody, here goes—*On the line, on the line, come and picket on the picket line, we'll win our fight, our fight for the right, on the picket, picket line.*" We go marching down Thirty-Sixth Street swinging our arms and singing with gusto.

We get to National a few minutes before Loebel and Kantrowitz arrive with the rest of their *mishpokhe*. There's our picket line, over one hundred strong, confronting them with big signs ON STRIKE! NATIONAL UNFAIR TO WORKERS! LADIES APPAREL SHIPPING CLERKS UNION, LOCAL 19953, AFL. And we sock it to them right off, "We want a living wage, we want a living wage!" Kantrowitz chomping on his cigar looks mad enough to play Edward G. Robinson in *Little Caesar.* He's about to snarl something at us when Loebel looking slick like he just left the barber's chair, grabs his arms and hustles him inside.

In a few more minutes, Carl and Larry show up. Carl's got this ghoulish grin pinned on his face as he cuts through our line and Larry keeps his eyes glued to the sidewalk. The other foremen arrive soon after in squad formation. When Fannie goes through, I pretend not to see her. For now, it's better that way.

About a half hour later, Lobelia, her dark skin shining with the heat, shows up. She doesn't say a word, picks up a sign, and takes her place in the line. Later, we happen to meet at the coffee shop up the street.

"How ya' doing, Ethel?" she asks, warmer and friendlier than she's ever been.

"Excited—aren't you?"

She surprises me a second time. "Scared," she says, "but Ah'm here, ain't I?"

"Good for you."

"My husban'… he giv me a big argument this mornin'. He ain't workin' and he's scared what's gonna happen— fool tried to keep me from comin'…" and she points to a large bandage above her right eyebrow, "threw frying pan clear cross room—caught me heah—five stitches they put in at Harlem Hospital, but Ah'm here." She's hurting all right, but something's boiling up in her, and it's good to see it happening.

And that's how it's going, like a current of electricity that's passing between all of us. My mind's racing ahead with ideas. It's so wonderful to see people stirred into action.

Even in prison, it's possible to be happy. It surprises me, that I can feel this way. But today, it's true. Today is Friday, our day to see each other, Julie and me, and each time they bring him in, my heart jumps. Even with a wire screen and bars between us as he sits outside my cell, his lips and eyes and voice keep telling me, I love you, and that means everything to me, because I have to live on that ration, our one hour together, for a whole week. And towards the end of the week—on Wednesdays and Thursdays, Dark Wednesday and Black Thursday, that's how I've come to think of them—my supply starts running out and my spirits drop precipitously. Drained, empty, shriveled…that's me, but just saying those words affects my happy mood today, so I'll stop.

Instead I'm listening. In my head, I'm hearing the song I heard this morning during my walk outside in the 'courtyard.' I couldn't see the bird, there're no trees, only the bare concrete that separates the Death House from the high wired fence, so where it perches or how, I don't know. But I heard five notes, repeated at frequent intervals like this… duh… dah dah dah dah… and now I'm trying to figure it out. Is it C FFFF or C GGGG. Suddenly it's become important to know this one simple fact—F or G. But I have no piano to try them out on, no bird book to consult—so the notes keep sounding in my head—duh… dah dah dah dah like a living being in my head keeping me company with a cheerful refrain.

This morning I was wrestling with fear again while taking this walk. Inside—though you'd never know it—I'm cowering like a coward, a jellied mold in the shape of a woman. There are so many insurmountable obstacles to our freedom. They keep mounting until I feel like they'll burst right through my thick skull.

And then I hear that mysterious bird sing out "duh… dah dah dah dah!" reminding me to have hope. That's what I really live on—hope and our love for each other and our children. And my shoulders relax and I take a deep breath and go on walking. Maybe that is the answer, keep walking—and now I'm happy and getting ready to see Julie. I won't have to force a smile, it's there on my lips.

"Stay close," Julie says hanging onto my hand as we approach the Loyalist rally which is off to one side of the campus with signs and banners all around, "I don't want to lose you." He presses his arm against my shoulder as I look up at him.

"I don't want to lose you." And we smile at each other in the way you do when you've turned your heart over to someone else and you know it's in good hands. There's always a light far back in his eyes—they're a warm greyish-green—that moves forward when he smiles at me. Just that makes me feel good again and I can't believe that I'm

thinking the same thoughts that so many other girls have—Frieda, Blanche, girls at work—all words I found so ordinary, so mundane. This is the language of love? Even those songs on the radio— "The Touch of Your Lips" "I Only Have Eyes For You" "The Way You Look Tonight" "That Old Feeling" That's how you sound when you're in love? Me, I used to think of Shakespeare and *Romeo and Juliet,* and Byron, and Keats. Surely your tongue becomes more inventive. But no, those same words come to my own lips. I love him so much. I find myself noticing his hands when he gestures in moments of great seriousness—or the fit of his jacket, how mansize his shoulders look from the back—though sometimes I have to remind him to straighten up, he gets that Talmudic stoop. Basically, you know, Julie is a very serious

> Each time they bring him in, my heart jumps. Even with a wire screen and bars between us.

guy! Sometimes I wish he saw things with a little more humor, but given his political commitment, he can't kid about it, like I'll do sometimes. The funny contradictions in people that amuse me? Well, him they irritate.

It all becomes obvious a few days later when we're spending a Sunday afternoon in Central Park.

"Do you think so?" he asks after first telling me about his Hebrew School teacher, whom he admired so much, and how Mr. Sopher on the day of his graduation from the Downtown Talmud Torah—1931 it was—told him what a fine man he was becoming—but maybe a little too idealistic and sincere for this world? "I felt bad, even though I was valedictorian," he says thoughtfully.

Picture us sitting on the grass after wandering around the zoo eating peanuts and feeding them to the animals. Anyhow, I remember being fascinated by the giraffe. How lofty his expression—and those wonderful markings. I hadn't realized how tall he was, with such an overall view of the jungle.

He's better built for survival than the lion, I thought, or is it more important to stand your ground and fight?

Anyhow, Julie's stretched out on his back with his head in my lap and still talking. "Sopher thought I was taking the teachings of Isaiah and Jeremiah too literally…"He sounds uncertain. Usually he speaks with such conviction. "You know, Rashi also believed in them. He…"

"Who's he?" I interrupt.

"A very important Talmudic scholar, a rabbi who lived in the Middle Ages and wrote a very important commentary on the Torah. Even today, he's studied and quoted. In his writings, he tried to interpret the Torah in practical everyday terms. Like Isaiah and Jeremiah, he, too, believed in helping the underdog and fighting for social justice. Also that there's a reason and a purpose for everything that happens in men's lives and in the history of nations— even if we don't understand it at the time. And that justice will triumph— that's right out of Isaiah. I don't know, though, watching what's going on these days in the world, what good can come of it?"

"What's bothering you, Julie?"

"The guys in the YCL? Sometimes they get on my back. 'Forget all the Hebrew School crap!' Al, or that guy, William, you met the other day?—they'll sneer at me. Like they insist my views are very naïve, tainted by a narrow sectarianism, that I see things only as a Jew, rather than as a Marxist who's been handed a scientific method for analyzing history, you know, dialectical materialism. Not only that, but a systematic approach towards really building a better world. 'Forget this religious crap—you know what Marx said, that religion is the opiate of the people,' Al said to me the other night… sometimes I feel caught in the middle…"

"Listen," I tell him, "I want to read more of this stuff you're talking about— dialectical materialism, all of that."

"Good," he says, "I'll bring over some books tonight."

But after letting off a little more steam, he comes back to Mr. Sopher. "So tell me, do you think he's right about me?"

"Have you ever gone back to visit this

Mr. Sopher?" I ask. "Sounds like he meant a lot to you."

"No," he says with no expression, "what for?"

And yet all the years he spent going to *cheder* and *Talmud Torah* have left their mark on him. There's something of the prophet in Julie. In that sense, we're very different. I went there three times and disliked it, the whole atmosphere, the foreignness of it, and said to myself, eight years old I was—all this doesn't make sense to me, and never went back. But his soul, I believe, still yearns to connect with the teachings of those days, though in political discussions he'll quote Marx, not Isaiah.

APRIL 1952

As I see it now, nineteen forty-five was the crucial year for us... and for the world. So much is crowded in—Roosevelt dies, the war ends, and so much else happens—that I ask myself, how to sort it all out...

That January, people are optimistic again after a cold bleak December with long casualty lists from the Battle of the Bulge. The American troops are breaking through the German lines and pushing them back, so naturally our spirits are up, especially since the Russians have just swept into Warsaw, and the news from the Pacific is encouraging. Of course, Ma's main concern is that the war should be over before her Dovey gets sent overseas. That's her number one reason for winning the war. Bernie's overseas, too, but somehow she worries less about him.

In a letter we receive from Dovey before Thanksgiving, he writes that he's been assigned to a secret project with a return address care of a post office in Santa Fe, New Mexico. Also that his training as a machinist is turning out to be very valuable. So maybe they'll keep him there for the duration. When I mention this to Ma, she looks towards Heaven and says, "*Gottenu*, it should only happen!"

Anyhow, when Ruth goes out there for their anniversary, she comes back and says the same thing, that Dovey's on a very important secret assignment. More

than that she can't tell us. And she raises her eyebrows to accentuate just how important.

When he's home on leave they come over for dinner one night. Dovey really looks good. He's lost that jowly look and trimmed down to fit into his corporal's uniform, with a fresh shave, and a new peppy stride, not his usual slouch. The uniform, too, gives him an air of authority he's enjoying, you can see it, he's a lot more self-confident.

"So, how's it going?" Julie asks him, and taps his waistline. "You're looking very fit. You like it out there?"

"Fine, fine," he says, "Yeah, it's the good life, sun all the time, not like back here... I miss Ratner's and Marty's corned beef, though."

"So we'll send you pacakges," I say, "not corned beef, but salami'll travel." I can't help smiling at him, I'm so happy to see him, and looking so well. He's a good kid, that Dovey. After all Ma's worries, he's turning out okay.

"Ran into Benny," he says, "haven't seen him since I left for basic."

"What's he have to say?" Julie asks.

"Nothing much, except that most of the guys've been drafted. Jackie's overseas flying bombers... Arnold's gone... killed taking off from an airstrip in the Pacific." He looks scared.

"How come Benny's around?"

"Bad knee," he says. "You know how he is—always a guy who tried to get out of doing anything. Even in the YCL... big talker, but that's all."

As we're sitting there, i'm thinking that the console table Julie bought at Macy's really comes in handy when we have company like this. With the leaf down, the four of us can sit comfortably around it, not like before with that shaky card table.

"That was a wonderful meal, Ethel," Dovey says opening the top button of his pants. From the pocket of his khaki shirt, he takes out a long cigar, removes the band, nips it carefully with a clipper, and lights up. He's the picture of contentment.

So it was worth using up all our ration points to serve steak, and butter with the rolls, I'm thinking, also that the chocolate eclairs with whipped cream went over big.

Ruth brushes at the smoke and looks annoyed. She always looks annoyed when the four of us get together. Don't ask me why. Quite a change in her since they got married. Before that, sweet as honey.

I get up to put some water on for coffee.

"So what are you doing?" Julie asks him.

David smiles, "I can't tell you."

"What d'ya mean?"

"Just that, Julie, I can't tell you. *Top secret.*"

He puffs away and the room smells with the smoke.

"Pfuiey!" I say. "Boy, that cigar stinks. Hey, when did you take up cigars?"

"Why don't you lay off him?" Ruth snaps at me. "I'm sick of you picking on him!"

"Picking on him? What are you talking about? When?"

"Now." And she gets that mean look on her face like an angry cat.

So I say, "Hey David, you know I was only kidding."

"Yeah, but lay off. I'm not a kid anymore, Ethel. Sometimes you forget."

"I'm sorry."

He tips back the kitchen chair against the wall, inhales, and gives a good puff right in our faces. "*Top secret,*" he repeats. Then closes his mouth as though it's been sealed tight by orders.

Julie and I have to smile at each other, the way he hams it up. *Top Secret!* Because you can see he's dying to let us know how important the work is, you can just see it. Between puffs gradually, he drops hints, and more hints—"working on high explosives"... puff puff... "could end the war sooner"... puff puff... "super secret"... long puff... "You should only know the famous scientists who're working there!" This time he rolls his eyes and moves his head from side to side. He's so thrilled to be in on something like this, all hush hush, and yet he can't stand not to be able to talk about it to us, to brag a little, that's his nature. "*Los Alamos*" he says, "*Top secret.*" Why shouldn't he feel great! He's doing important work for the war effort, and for the first time in his life, Ma's not hanging over him—or Ruth either. Only in her letters can she tell him to change his socks

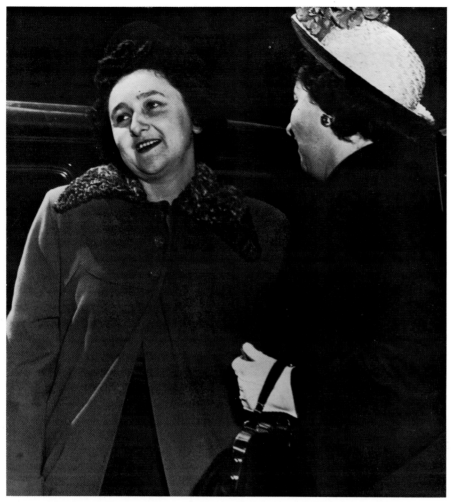

Fig. 21. "Mr. President, would you like to know what it's been like for me? This woman, Ethel Rosenberg, whom you describe as 'strong and recalcitrant'?"

night, and Dovey's the biggest talker... how he's going to do this and that after the war, oh, that brother of mine feels important for the first time in his life... we all agree that it'll be wonderful to live in a peaceful world again... And that if the Soviet Union and the U.S. go on being friendly allies, there's so much hope for the world *this time*... We talked, yes, but never the way Dovey and Ruth testified at the trial...

FEBRUARY 1953

Mr. President,

Would you like to know what it's really been like for me? This woman, Ethel Rosenberg, whom you describe as "strong and recalcitrant?"

I can still see it as though it's happening now, a scene I'm watching from the wings. It's a night like any other hot night in New York when it's too hot to breathe, and your thighs chafe from rubbing against each other so you keep applying talcum and thinking I've got to lose some weight. I'm in the kitchen getting dinner ready. Our kitchen that's small, cramped, and needs a good painting, apartment house beige I call it. Over in the far corner on the right as you walk in, there's a white chipped sink with a drainboard, and underneath, the pipes show. It's also where I keep the garbage can and the tin pail for mopping the floor. Next to it, a beige and black stove with space underneath for pots and pans, and the oven. Opposite the stove, right by the door, is a chipped white enamel table. We bought it from a private party in 1948 through an ad in the *Sunday Times* along with four kitchen chairs for fifteen dollars; they came down from twenty-five. What a funny expression—private party! Do you suppose with all the headlines, I'm now a public party? Anyhow they're a young couple in Brooklyn near the Brighton line station at Kings Highway and they're moving to a development in Syosset. Part of me envied them, moving out to Long Island. Nice for kids growing up. The chairs didn't match, but it doesn't matter, I told myself, it's a lot of bourgeois crap.

In our kitchen the refrigerator's oppo-

and wipe the snot off his nose! And he doesn't have to listen.

"Are the Russians in on it?" I'm thinking of the thousands who died at Stalingrad, and Pa's *shtetl* near the Polish border—how the Germans made them all march out into a field and then, one by one, shot them down. "I don't know," he says, "but I've heard a few guys speaking with an English accent."

"I hope so," says Julie. "Why shouldn't they be? We're all in this together... It would be the best thing for world peace."

Talked? Sure we talked—or rather, we *schmoozed*... the way you do when you sit around the table after dinner with the family, catching up with each other... little bits of news you forgot to put in letters about a cousin or a friend, discussing the war, how it's going, and our hopes for afterwards. We ask him

some questions—like what it's like out there—sure, like anybody would. Ruth breaks in to say she wants to come out there to be with him. "Could I live on the base?" she wants to know.

"No," he says, "only the top brass and scientists can have their families with them."

"So where could I stay?" she asks getting that whine in her voice.

"Probably Albuquerque," he says. "It's further away than Santa Fe but I hear housing isn't so tight."

He goes on to tell us that he's working in one of the experimental labs building models from blueprints the scientists bring him... "very close precision work... and I got a bastard for a foreman, he's riding me all the time." Which sounds like the old Dovey—always griping that someone's got it in for him.

Anyway, that's how we talked that

site the sink next to the wall, and for some crazy reason, the door opens from right to left instead of from left to right like a normal refrigerator. You can't imagine how inconvenient that is, Mr. President—every time you open the refrigerator door, you're caught between the refrigerator, the wall, and the door. Each time you take something out, you have to hold it in one hand, close the door with the other while getting out of the way of the door, put the package or jar down on the sink opposite and then go through the whole crazy business again for something else. Eight years we live in Knickerbocker Village. Well, for eight years I keep asking for another refrigerator, one that opens from left to right?—and for eight years, I get promises, … "it's on order"… "next week for sure"… "soon"… and "we'll check today why it hasn't come in"… and that night when the doorbell rings, I'm still boxed in by that damn refrigerator, can you believe it?—at the very moment there's this long insistent ring.

It's loud enough so I hear it over the radio which Michael has turned up to listen to *The Lone Ranger.* "Never mind, I'll get it!" I yell, grab the dish towel, and wipe my hands. Julie came home very tired so he's resting in the bedroom, and I don't want him disturbed.

I go into the hall, turn on the light, straighten my housedress, and after a moment, I open the door.

Two men in gabardine trench coats like Army officers, but wearing grey hats with dark bands and brims like in a gangster movie step inside one after the other, and close the door behind them. It's my home and they're inside it, and I don't say a word because my heart is pumping so hard.

Both men speak simultaneously, quickly, "Mrs. Rosenberg? We're from the FBI," and they both flash badges and quickly return them to the inside pocket of their matching jackets. Like a vaudeville team. One's tall, the other's short. "We'd like to talk with your husband."

What a crazy business, if you can believe it, my first thought when I see them? The apartment's a mess, what'll they think?

Even if Dovey hadn't already been arrested in June, and Julie called in for questioning once, two official looking men at our door would scare me. For that matter, any Jew. It's in our blood, that chilling fear. It always strikes out of nowhere. *What have I done?* Even when the police come around selling tickets for their Benevolent Association Dance, my heart used to jump… I'm rambling… I know it… a fault of mine whenever the needle inside jumps and I have to go back to something I'd rather forget… Part of me stays calm though… I can't let them see how frightened I am. They'll read it as guilt, and besides, for the children's sake… So I say, "Look, my husband's asleep… I'll have to wake him up."

The tall one who acts like he's in charge motions to me—*Go get him,* and then he barks at Michael, "Hey kid, turn that damn thing off!"

Michael turns around, looks at him indifferently, "Not yet… it's not over."

The FBI guy, without another word, walks over and flicks it off. Michael runs over and takes my hand. Robby's already clinging to my skirt, and holding them both so, I walk into the bedroom. Julie's out cold on Michael's bed, curled up like one of the kids. I shake him gently. He trembles… and wakens. "Wha… What?." He automatically reaches for his glasses and sits up.

"Julie… there're two men here from the FBI. They want to talk to you."

Running fingers through his hair, still groggy, he stumbles into the living room. "You're coming with us," says the tall guy. A clang of panic strikes me.

Robby runs into the bedroom and comes back dragging his chewed up security blanket and his thumb in his mouth. Michael asks the tall one, "What's happening?" The guy ignores him and tells Julie to empty all his pockets. I'm standing there like a dummy.

Julie ignores him and squats down so he's eye to eye with Michael. "Look Michael, they probably just want me to go downtown with them to answer some questions… maybe I'll have to stay overnight." Then he starts emptying his pockets, some change, keys, a scrap of paper with a customer's address, toothpicks, his wallet, soiled tissues.

"Okay, let's get moving," says the tall one.

The two men surround him and whip handcuffs on his wrists. Handcuffs! In shock he stares at the cold steel.

I make an instant decision. "Julie, I'm going with you… I'll come back here later. I'll ask Terry Grossman if the boys can stay with them."

The tall guy says, "Okay, why don't you use the phone, just keep it short."

As I go to use the phone, the short guy comes back from the bedroom with our Brownie reflex and my Timex.

"This is the only camera I could find," he says, "Pushed back on the upper shelf in their closet. Behind some blankets, closet's a mess. And look at this room," he exclaims with disgust, "toys, pieces from jigsaw puzzles, blocks, crayons, potato chips, crumbs all over the floor. What slobs! That's a Commie for you… they think they can make a better world for people like us! Oh, the watch was in the kitchen, on the drainboard… no jewel box."

As I'm dialing, the tall one's speaking. "Two agents are coming in after we leave. They'll do the whole job." Then he calls out to me, "Listen, perhaps you better tell your neighbor you want the kids to stay there tonight."

"Terry?" I say when she answers, "No, no, I'm okay. Yes, really… I just wanted to ask you a favor. Please tell me if it's okay, will you. Can Michael and Robby stay over with you tonight? Maybe you have a cot? I have one—it's in the hall closet… Well, they're taking Julie… to their… uh, office… yeah… for some questioning… I thought I'd go along… yeah, I'll be back but I'm not sure what time. You will? How can I thank you enough! Look, Robby sleeps with a small light on. Would you have one? No? So take it from the top of our bureau—you'll see it—it's a Mickey Mouse figure holding up a small bulb in his hand. Oh sure, things will go okay. *Thanks. I know you wish us well.*"

To continue, Mr. President,

The evening before the trial, I had this weird but exhilarating premonition that the case will be dismissed right off. That Manny's motion will be granted by Kaufman. Why not? The Law of the Land, the Constitution and the Bill of Rights will prevail. *I feel it, I just know it.* There I am, in my favorite chariot delivered to the door of the House of Detention by a liveried chauffeur and royally I climb in and take off.

So I issue an open invitation. "Hey everybody," I call out, "come by Rosenbergs's Delly!" Thats what they call my cell. I'm always loaded up wth food and I love to have company.

So we sing and tell jokes and laugh and I do imitations of a couple of the matrons who are off duty. There's one I swear must've worked in a concentration camp. I wind up reciting my final lines from *The Valiant* and even Jim's… "The coward dies a thousand deaths, the valiant dies but once"… Goose pimples break out on my arms and I feel a sudden chill like an icebag's plunked down in my gut. The excitement drains out of me like a drain unplugged by Drano.

The rest of the night I'm shivering constantly. The next morning getting dressed to go into court, I'm a wreck. My hands won't stop shaking. Finally I give up. Paula, from the next cell gently brushes my hair and even puts on some lipstick for me. "It'll be okay, baby, you'll see," she says. "Just hang on, you'll do fine." She keeps talking like that until I have to leave to get into the police van.

Outside, a tall thin woman in a worn winter coat and dark hat comes up to me, a loser in life—you can tell by the sour slump of her mouth—anyhow, she grabs my hand and gives it a hard squeeze. "Listen," she says, "You know what I wish for you?" I look at her. "They should send you right back to hell— that's where you dirty Commie traitors belong!" Already I'm public property.

Reporters and photographers are crowding around, asking questions, snapping pictures. That's the picture you've seen of me splashed across the front pages… my eyes looking back at you with no expression, my lips tightly locked. *You won't get anything out of me,* that's what one person told me it was like. Others, even some of the matrons, said to me, "That's a terrible picture of you, Ethel. It's not you, so unfriendly and cold, like a different woman." Still

that's the one that got printed in every newspaper all over the world, that people remember *as me*. My face frozen stiff. The whole time in court my hands are like ice, and my feet knock together under the table. I know that if I allow myself to feel anything, I'll go to pieces.

So what can I tell you about the trial? Don't believe the papers? But people do. Undoubtedly, Mr. President—you did, too. A good part of the time I was in shock—I saw myself, Ethel Rosenberg being transformed by the government and the press into a woman I didn't know, a woman whose steely lips wouldn't betray a word—held back the story the whole world was waiting breathlessly to hear. They were waiting for me, Ethel Rosenberg to speak. *Confess! Confess!* As if I had such a confession to make—about three slimy Jews ringing their oily hands in glee, two

> I saw myself, Ethel Rosenberg, being transformed by the government and press into a woman I didn't know.

Judases and one Delilah, ready to do in the United States, ready to sell it out to the Russians for a few lousy dollars, a camera, and a ladies' watch! They were pushing me, invent a story, coaching me, anything, but damn it, play your part! Don't run out on the show!

The trouble is—the script was being written for me, not by the one person who knew the real truth—namely, me!—but by those playwrights, those tremendous talents—you've heard of them?—Clifford Odets? Maxwell Anderson? Lillian Hellman? Arthur Miller? No, Saypol, Kaufman, and Cohn. You ever heard of them before the trial? Not me either. Not 'til the day I was arrested—then I began to know all about them, believe me.

How about putting them in a little skit for "Pins and Needles?" Set to music by Gilbert and Sullivan? Like?

Three little fink Jews are we,

Settling for Hell in e-ter-ni-ty
Better gold in our hands now
Than grave-en images when we're gone,
  Three little fink Jews are we.
Not bad, huh!

Yes, they were counting on me, all right, figuring they'd put the screws on me. Our two little sons left *af hefker*, lost, frightened, bewildered, no mother, no father, torn from us. And my own mother pleading with me, confess, Ettie, tell them the truth, whatever Dovey said, anything, *genug sheyn*. What truth, Ma, yours or mine? And my own kid brother's life at stake. Dovey that I carried in my arms when he was a baby. And Julie— Julie, my star-crossed lover. Oh Julie, my beloved, from whence did this plague descend upon us? These locusts? I never really understood what was happening… and where is our Moses?… Manny Bloch? No, Manny can't do it. He isn't the man for the job though he means well. I love him like a father. So how can I tell him this?

I never could have imagined all this, not even in my wildest dreams, not even if I am one of the world's Great Dreamers. Not this, never.

What a setup for an onstage confession right there in the courtroom! In time for the five-star extra. What real life drama! Can you imagine the applause when I would've finished? It would have been the longest, most dramatic scene in the history of the theatre and they wrote it just for me. Then they collect the royalties and I go to prison like a good girl with a fifteen-year sentence like Dovey. Watch, he'll be out in a flash! And I turned it down. That they never expected!

I must admit our senior yearbook predicted it. I would have been America's leading actress—not in 1950, but in 1951. They missed by only one year. Not bad when you're forecasting twenty years in advance. Could Gallup have done better?

But I let them down. I told the truth— and they didn't want to believe me. What a letdown! All that tremendous preparation—and me, I walk off the stage. Nothing more to say than what I'd said before, over and over and over again.We hadn't done anything. Talk?

Talk is cheap. It's the only thing left for poor people. What else do we have? Power? Money? Cars? An estate in the country? And for talk you go to the electric chair? Since when? In America? It says so in the Bill of Rights?

"She blew her lines!" says Roy Cohn to Saypol in the john afterwards. He's so mad he grabs his tie and rips it off. He's about to tear it up with his bare hands when he suddenly remembers he's got to go back into that courtroom and he doesn't have another one handy. "Damn her! Didn't you make it clear to her that she had to learn her part before Opening Night? Didn't I make it clear to you?"

Wait a minute, why is Cohn talking to Saypol this way? Who's the boss here anyway? Who's taking orders from who, I mean, whom?

So Saypol flushes and comes out, and he washes his hands, slowly, methodically, letting the water wash over them. He's quiet and his skin is white like paper. For him I wouldn't object to a concentration camp. Maybe he's worried what'll his wife say when he gets home. "Look Cohn," his voice quavers, but he tries to master it, "Don't talk to me that way."

"I'll talk to you anyway I like!" says Cohn, leering at his rat face in the mirror. With his manicured fingernail, he flecks a speck of egg off his tie, carefully knots it on again (would I like to pull it tight!) and stalks out letting the door slam on Saypol's foot. He slides his hand over his black slick hair and starts back into the courtroom.

"Let's go back in there," says Kaufman coming towards him grabbing his elbow. "I have to talk to you."

Inside he says, "Well, let's get it over with, boys. I wanted to tell you, I went to synagogue last night." That frog's mouth of his laughs self-consciously. "To check it out with Him." His aqueous eyes motion, upstairs. "It's O.K." he nods again to make sure they understand. Saypol and Cohn smile, a forced smile, granting him amnesty. Even they are offended by his arrogance. "We can go the limit, see." As he's saying this, he straightens his robes and pats his hair in place. With a satisfied smirk, he holds out his arm to Saypol. "Let's go!" His voice

carries the authority of the pretender to the throne.

The three henchmen link arms and march out.

That's a scene that never got reported in the papers, but I'll bet you my bottom dollar it happened.

"Manny," I asked him straight-out yesterday, "why'd you take so much crap from Kaufman and Saypol?"

"You wanna know the truth?"

"What else is there time for?"

"Because I could tell the bastards had their hearts set on a death sentence. Right from Day One. And I was willing to do anything, take anything from them—whatever I had to do—to avert that."

"You didn't tell us that?" What can I say to such a man?

"What was there to tell you? Would it have helped if I did?"

"Honestly speaking, Manny?" I look him straight in the eye. "No, it wouldn't have."

> "Manny," I asked him, "why'd you take so much crap from Kaufman and Saypol?"

"So." He spreads his hands helplessly. "You were right, of course. I should never have asked the court to impound David's sketches. Made them sound super important. I lost the case for you right there, you knew that at the time, I could see it from your expression, you were biting your lips not to say something."

He sits quiet for a few minutes. But not me, I got *shpilkes* in my whole body like someone injected Mexican jumping beans in my nervous system.

"Ettie, I never told you how alone I felt... the whole time... before the trial, during the trial... after... none of the scientists who knew anything about the bomb, who could have advised me... would come near me... everyone's so afraid for his own skin... I even tried writing to some of the big ones in Europe... Bohr, Meitner... no one answered. No

other lawyers to talk it over with, only my father... just the two of us... Recently I talked with one of the big scientists, I can't even tell you his name, he made me promise... anyhow, he's been wising me up... that the government's perpetrating a fake on us and the public. He says there's nothing David could have known that would amount to the 'secret of the atom bomb'... and yet I still can't get any of them publicly to testify to that. He explained to me, that once we dropped the bomb, every scientist in the world working in the field knew it was now possible to solve that problem—and if there was any 'secret'—the United States gave it away herself when we dropped the bomb on Japan. Go to the *Smyth Report*, this guy tells me, use it, it's all in there—the government's given away for free a lot more information on the bomb than David ever could have known and it was published shortly after the war. If the Russians wanted information, it's right in there... There's a lot I've messed up on, Ethel, I'm sorry..."

I'm thinking how lonely it's been for him... and all the time he's been trying, in his own way, to protect us from knowing the worst. Not possible, Manny, I'm thinking, it never is... just like we can't protect our kids no matter how hard we try. The world will still treat them as the Rosenberg sons. So will they have to pay the price, too? God, I don't want that to happen. Bad enough us. The only way we can help them is to give them pride in us, in who they are, not shame.

"The situation is changing though, isn't it? I mean, here are people like Einstein, and Urey—and even the Pope—who are appealing to Eisenhower for clemency. Even if he won't listen. And Julie tells me he heard on the radio that thousands of letters are pouring into the White House... ministers, rabbis, people from all over the world... wouldn't it be possible now to get a lawyer who specializes in these cases?"

He hesitates, then says, "Well there's a man by the name of John Finerty, I think, who helped Tom Mooney... I could try... also there's a law professor at the U. of Chicago, Malcolm Sharp, who wrote to me recently. He's interested..."

"Let's do it, Manny. Get in touch with them right away."

I'm like a different person when I go back to my cell. There's hope.

MARCH—APRIL
1953

Today Ma sent a delegation of one to do her dirty work. Bernie, my dearly beloved brother, shows up with a present for me, a box of stationery from Woolworth's. The funny thing is he looks so much like Pa—with the same straw hair that's faded into grey, but without Pa's smile and gentle eyes. And seeing him makes me sad. I miss Pa. Five years he's gone. I know he would have stood behind me, even if he wouldn't have openly opposed Ma. I guess he didn't have enough strength for that, but still he always managed to let me know he understood and was behind me, and *not* behind *her*. I think a lot about him these days. *I miss you, Pa.*

And what's dear Bernie supposed to tell me? He's been coached by her, I can tell, and he's not a very good actor; he hems and haws like he's trying to remember his line.

"Listen, Ethel," he says, "you're coming down to the finish line, so you better do something quick. Don't forget—June 18th!" Our fourteenth anniversary. As if I *could!* "Why won't you tell the government what you know? Ma said to tell

you. Why won't you listen to us, your family? Who else cares as much about what happens to you. You think, *his* family?"

My heart's on fire! "So you're at it again! My loving devoted family, interested only in what's good for me, right?"

I must be screaming though it doesn't seem that way to me because Bernie starts shushing me and trying to outtalk me.

"You want," he says, "they should make me leave? That's what you want? Then why don't you stop yelling?"

"Why don't you stop getting me so upset?"

"Who's trying to upset you? Such foolishness. We're only begging you to save your own life. Forget about Julie. He wants to die in the electric chair? That's his business! So let him. Who says you have to walk that last mile with him, too? Him? Or the Party?"

That's all he has to say. "Goddamit! That's one thing none of you are even willing to try to understand. Julie and I are telling the truth, and we're not lying, and we're not following Party orders. Can't you understand that? Once and for all?"

"But how about your children? Can't you give one thought to them? Do you remember how when Ma came to see you that first time, she asked you what to tell Michael, how that poor kid keeps asking her, 'Grandma, when is my mother coming home?' Not once, mind

you, but over and over again. And you said to her, 'Tell him I'll be home in two years.' Yes, that's what you told her to tell him, don't say different. And Ma's never repeated to you what Michael said when she gave him your answer, because she didn't want to hurt your feelings. But as soon as he heard those words, 'in two years,' he started to cry and carry on. You know how Michael gets and you know what he said? 'I hope she dies because of the harm she's causing me.' Those are your son's very words. So God help me! That's what you want? He should be hurt because of you?—left an orphan, him and Robby—mind you, not because you're hit by a car, die from double pneumonia. No, because you're more loyal to the Commies, those friends of yours, than to your own children. Dovey's smart, he knew enough to look out for himself and his family.

"Tell me, so what are *they* doing for you now that you're in here? They're raising money, getting you the best lawyers? No. Two years already here you sit and here you'll die if you don't think of yourself and your children first. But still they mean more to you than your own kids!"

"Get out of here! Get him out of here!" I'm roaring.

I'm still shaking.

THE ROSENBERGS IN FILM

Film treatments of the Rosenberg case have ranged from the documentary to the dramatic. The highly regarded 1974 ninety-minute film by Alvin H. Goldstein, *The Unquiet Death of Julius and Ethel Rosenberg* (updated in 1978 and 1983) (Fig. 22), is the definitive documentary examining the facts of the case. Conversations with many of the living principals, including Morton Sobell and lawyers for both sides, were augmented by archival footage, still photographs, and interviews with FBI agents, some of the jurors, and the Rosenbergs' sons, among others. The film, produced for public television, where it has been frequently aired over the years, was released on videocassette in 1987.

In 1975, French writer Alain Decaux teamed up with Stellio Lorenzi to transform Decaux's play, *Les Rosenbergs ne Doivent pas Mourir* (*The Rosenbergs Must Not Die*) (Fig. 23), into a five-hour docudrama. Since France was the site of some of the most massive protests worldwide on behalf of the Rosenbergs, it is no surprise that the film was well received, despite its dramatic and factual flaws, when it aired ten years ago as a miniseries on French national television.

It starred well-known French actors Marie-José Nat as Ethel and Gilles Segal as Julius Rosenberg and included archival footage along with its fictional settings and characterizations. Its first U.S. broadcast, on cable televis-

ion in New York several years ago, provoked some particularly harsh red-baiting from Dorothy Rabinowitz in the *Wall Street Journal*.

Filmmaker Stephen Stept has as the protagonist in his 1981 dramatic film, *End of Innocence: June 19, 1953* (Fig. 24), a small Jewish boy. Set in a working-class New York city Jewish neighborhood on the day of the execution, the half-hour film uses the Rosenbergs's execution as a means to examine his family, his neighbors, and the ways of the world.

A discussion of the movie *Daniel*, based on E.L. Doctorow's novel *The Book of Daniel*, occurs on page 124

Fig. 22. The Rosenbergs on their way from jail to court as seen in Alvin H. Goldstein's 1974 documentary *The Unquiet Death of Julius and Ethel Rosenberg*. (Photo courtesy Facets Multimedia.)

Fig. 23. Separated by a glass divider, Julius and Ethel Rosenberg (Gilles Segal and Marie José Nat) speak to each other during prison visiting hours in the 1975 French docudrama *Les Rosenbergs ne doivent pas mourir (The Rosenberas Must Not Die.)* (Photo: SFP/J. Chevry.)

Fig. 24. Concerned and confused about the Rosenberg case, a young Jewish boy stops at a newsstand where the impending executions are the headline story in Stephen Stept's *End of Innocence*, a 1982 American Film Festival finalist.

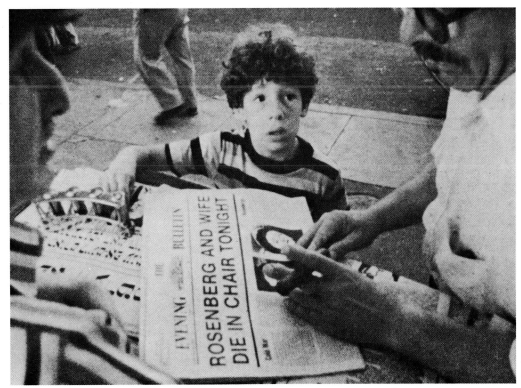

We, The Undersigned Petitioners...

Elizabeth Russell

In the matter of Ethel and Julius Rosenberg
The undersigned petitioners come forward
To confess their guilt.
We hereby affirm
That we too have committed the following crimes, to wit:
Joined unions
Signed petitions
Fought jimcrow
Spoke peace.
(Some of us have typewriters in our homes, and jello boxes,
Yes, even collection cans for child refugees.)
More, we have had access to the secret of our nation's
      strength—
We have passed through our hands the dream of human
      brotherhood
And finding it good have given it freely to our friends...

Fig. 25. Hugo Gellert, *Liberty in Chains*, 1952, charcoal on paper.

At The Last

Anne Lifschutz

"What was the color of the smoke
From Ethel Rosenberg's head?"
A clipped voice asked.

I don't know whether this journalist
Received his answer.
Perhaps he failed
To round out successfully
The story he was paid to write.

Let me tell him now:

It was exactly the same color
As the smoke that rose
Over the crematoria
In Buchenwald, Dachau.

Fig. 26. Michael and Robby after a
Valentine's Day 1953 visit
to their parents at Sing Sing
prison. (UPI/Bettmann
News Photo.)

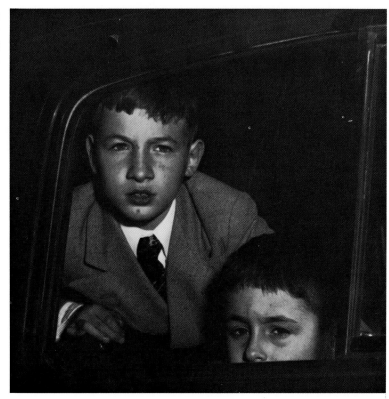

The Children

Three Sonnets by Louis Aragon
Adapted from the French
by Walter Lowenfels

The Question:

And you who plunge your hands into the thunder
The dollar, the Plague, the a-bomb ray gamma
Great masters of fear heroes of Hiroshima
What is it tears your Pentagon asunder?

Italians, Persians, pygmies from down under
Who man your bases France to Panama
What song unites the world's vast panorama
But *Yank Go Home!* Doesn't this make you wonder?

What unknown atom gives you your neurosis?
Or is it Syngman Rhee your faithful double?
Or Chiang Kai-shek who lives by pure osmosis?

Your footsteps tremble. What then is your trouble?
Can two small boys choke your apotheosis
And rip your Pentagonic myths to rubble?

II
The Response:

Yes they're the tar drops in the honey pot
The green leaves that a skyscraper outlaws
America outflanked by two small boys
New York in danger, Cossacks within gun shot.

Such criminals of peace each tiny tot
Their plaintive voices ring out from their toys
But their small quiet stops the world's great noise
Their tears are bombs that make the White House rock

The Pentagon colossus smells a rose
Its thorns he senses pricking his clay feet
He arms himself though why he hardly knows

Cursing us as he stalks his lonesome street
He crushes two small boys with frightened blows
Making us live for them in each heart beat.

III

... And the Moral:

It wasn't enough to put this double love
Of theirs this natural love of sons to death
Even as the whole world sought to their last breath
To keep their own hearts beating. It wasn't enough

To turn the light of Mother Father off
But still these butchers keep on playing deaf
At two small children murmuring in their grief.
What other murders are they dreaming of?

And when their foster parent was found dead
Their lawyer and defender Emanuel Bloch
How could the White House sleep?
                                    Take them from bed
Snuff out their souls and let their pillows rock
Your memories to sleep while in your head
You crush this family with the laws you mock!

Give Us Your Hand
Edith Segal

Tonight
as you quietly draw the curtain
on the day's activity
and reclining
contemplate the fertile promise
of unborn time
imagine
you
are Ethel or Julius Rosenberg
in the Death House at Sing Sing:

The dimness is a fog your eyes defy
Sleep is a luxury long lost…
Time being treasured,
measured by the hurrying steps of death—
even napping is a thief

Suddenly there's light in your cell,
in the prison block,
in the house on Monroe Street
where you lived with your children
in the narrow streets
of New York's lower east side—your city,
light
in every city in the land
in the assembly halls in all the schools,
your school, P.S. 88
where you stood with your hand upon your heart
as you faced the flag and said the words
that were to give your life direction:

With Liberty and Justice for All

Now
you stand at the bars of your cell
with your hands cupped wide at your mouth
and shout to the world at the top of your lungs:

If you sleep while they kill *us*
will they kill *you* while you sleep?

If you ever breathed too deeply
the air of brotherhood,
clasped black and white hands
in your neighborhood

or gave a dime
for democratic Spain

or signed your name
to nominate your choice—
a voice for peace

will they kill *you* while you sleep
if you sleep while they kill *us?*

We yearn to live and see our children grow
but if we burn, part of them
and part of you will turn to dust
and death will haunt our home, our land

Give us your hand!

Let us stand in the sunlight
when the wind is still
and the din of war subsides into the sea

and scales are righted
and our worth declared to be
among the living
to mold the fertile promise
of unborn time

Time!
Tomorrow they die
Unless we make their cry a warning:

Death is in our land!
GIVE US YOUR HAND!

1952

Fig. 27,28.   Morton Sobell holds a rose during a vigil in front of the U.S. Federal District Court in New York to commemorate the sixteenth anniversary of the Rosenberg's June 19, 1953 execution. Five months earlier, Sobell's mother Rose and wife Helen react to news that Sobell is being freed after more than eighteen years in prison, January 14, 1969. (UPI/The Guardian.)(UPI/Bettmann News Photo.)

Free
Helen Sobell

Come, my glorious brother, laugh with me,
Take my hand, my sister, clasp it joyfully—
Children, come, your father stands here free.
It is the birthday of the world.

With work and hope we have hailed your coming,
Gladly bent our backs to bring you here.
We have built for you a place of beauty—
Let us laugh and cry at your rejoicing.

Ours were not the shoulders that were missing,
Ours was not the silent voice unheard.
Together life and we triumphantly
Salute the birthday of the world!

Fig. 29. "Search me!" says Daniel (Ilan M.Mitchell-Smith), when he, his sister Susan (Jena Greca), and lawyer Jacob Ascher (Edward Asner) prepare to visit the children's parents imprisoned on espionage charges in the movie *Daniel*. (Photo courtesy of Paramount Pictures Corporation.)

THE BOOK
—and film—
OF DANIEL

E.L. DOCTOROW

"When I started thinking about the case, the Rosenbergs had been dead for fourteen or fifteen years. I think I was in the army serving in Germany when they were executed, and maybe that's why at the time it was a more remote horror to me than to many others. I was fully sensitive to the McCarthy period generally, but the case didn't propose itself to me as a subject for a novel until we were all going through Vietnam."

E.L. Doctorow's fictional treatments of the Rosenberg years cast a cold-war shadow over the 1970s and early 1980s. His novel *The Book of Daniel,* published in 1971, was critically acclaimed and for many years stood as one of the few important literary works about the McCarthy period. A dozen years later the movie version, *Daniel* (Fig. 29) was released. Although Doctorow wrote the screenplay and Sidney Lumet directed, the film only received mixed reviews and was a bomb at the box office.

The book, though, struck a chord both with Old Leftists who had lived through the McCarthy years and with New Left antiwar activists deep in the midst of a contemporary fight for social justice.

The film had a harder time finding its voice, although it did raise disturbing new questions for a largely uninformed Eighties movie audience. In part because it anticipated the current interest in films with political themes, it attracted considerable media attention. In many cases stories appeared in the news and editorial pages as often as in the entertainment section. A concerned right wing, fearing moviegoers might actually question the media's "happy days" rendering of the period, even trotted out syndicated columnist George Will to trash the film and to execute again the Rosenbergs.

Doctorow emphatically distinguishes between the Rosenberg case and his fiction. "Certainly anyone who knows me knows that if I wanted to write about the Rosenbergs, I'd have called them the Rosenbergs," he says.[2] (In the novel and film the characters are named Paul and Rochelle Isaacson.) "When I wrote *The Book of Daniel* in the late 1960s there were more interesting questions to explore than the aberrant behavior of a pair of old radicals. I was interested in the connection between the New Left and Old Left. What was the role of the radical in America? Was it sacrificial? Why do the left movements always destroy themselves? These questions intrigued me far more than the legal specifics of the Rosenberg case. What I took from the case was the extremity of their legal situation and the use of conspiracy statutes. Those same statutes applied in the 1960s... but failed because the social climate was different."

In the excerpts that follow, Doctorow unerringly portrays the social and political climate of the Fifties.   —R.O.

Notes
1. Interview with Tom LeClair and Larry McCaffery in *Anything Can Happen: Interviews with Contemporary American Novelists,*(Urbana, Ill., University of Illinois Press, 1983).
2. Interview with Arthur Bell, *Village Voice,* September 6, 1983.

Early the next morning, as I was leaving for school, the doorbell rang and I opened the door and two men were standing on the porch. They were dressed neatly, and did not appear to be of the neighborhood. They had thin, neat faces and small noses, and crew-cut hair. They held their hats in their hands and wore nice overcoats. I thought maybe they were from one of those Christian religions that sent people from door to door to sell their religious magazines.

"Sonny," said one, "is your mother or father home?"

"Yes," I said "They're both home."

My mother did not allow me to delay going to school just because the FBI had come to the door. I don't know what happened on that first visit. The men went inside and, going down the splintery front steps, I turned and caught a glimpse of Paul coming out of the kitchen to meet them just as the door closed. My mother was holding the door and my father was coming forward in his ribbed undershirt, looking much skinnier than the two men who rang the bell.

When the FBI knocks on your door and wants only to ask a few questions, you do not have to consent to be asked questions. You are not required to talk to them just because they would like to talk to you. You don't have to go with them to their office. You don't have to do anything if you are not subpoenaed or arrested. But you only learn the law as you go along.

"They don't know what they want," Paul says to Rochelle. "It's routine. If you don't talk to them, they have nothing to pin their lies on. They are clumsy, obvious people."

"I'm frightened," my mother says. "*Polizei* don't have to be smart."

"Don't worry," Paul says. "Mindish won't suffer from anything we said." He is walking back and forth in the kitchen and he is pounding his fist into his palm. "We have done nothing wrong. There is nothing to be afraid of."

It develops that all of Mindish's friends are being questioned. Nobody knows what he is being held for. There has been no announcement on the radio, there has been no story in the newspaper. Sadie Mindish is in a state of hysterical collapse. Her apartment has been searched. Her daughter has stayed home from school. Nobody knows if they even have a lawyer.

The next day the same two FBI men come back again, this time in the early evening. They sit on the stuffed, sprung couch in the living room parlor with their knees together and their hats in their hands. They are very soft-spoken and friendly. Their strange names are Tom Davis and John Bradley. They smile at me while my mother goes to the phone to call my father.

"What grade are you in, young fellow?"

I don't answer. I have never seen a real FBI man this close before. I peer at them looking for super-human powers, but there is no evidence that they have any. They look neither as handsome as in the movies nor as ugly as my parents' revulsion makes them. I search their faces for a clue to their real nature. But their faces do not give clues.

When Paul comes home, he is very nervous.

"My lawyer has advised me that I don't have to talk to you if I don't want to ," my father said. "That particular fact you neglected yesterday to mention."

"Well, yes sir, Mr. Isaacson, but we were hoping you would be cooperative. We're only looking for information. It's nothing mysterious. We thought you were a friend of Doctor Mindish. As his friend, you may be in a position to help him."

"I will be glad to answer any questions in a court of law."

"Do you deny now that you know him?"

"I will answer any questions in a court of law."

The two men leave after a few minutes, and then they sit in their car, double-parked in front of the house, for ten or fifteen minutes more. They appear to be writing on clipboards or on pads, I can't tell exactly. It is dark and they have turned on the interior car light. I am reminded of a patrol man writing a parking ticket. But the sense is of serious and irrevocable paperwork, and I find it frightening. There is some small, grey light in the dark sky over the schoolyard. The wind is making whistling noises at the edges of the window.

"Danny!" Rochelle says sharply. "Get away from there."

My father takes my place at the curtains. "That is outrageous," he says. "Don't you see, it is part of the treatment. They are trying to shake us up. But we're too smart for them. We're onto them. They can sit out there all night for all I care."

The next day is worse. At lunch my father tells my mother he is sure someone has searched the shop. When he unlocked the door this morning, he felt that things were slightly out of place. It wasn't anything he could pinpoint exactly. Maybe the tubes in the trash barrel. Maybe the customer tickets. It was more like a sense of things having been disturbed.

Our lunch is Muenster cheese sandwiches on pumpernickel and canned tomato soup. My father doesn't eat. He sits with his elbow on the table and his hand to his head. He nods, as if he agrees with something he has decided.

"That's it. That's why they came here and asked you to call me home. They could just as easily have come to the store, couldn't they? But they didn't. They wanted to make sure I was home when they wanted to search my store."

My mother discounts this. She says they could have waited until late at night and achieved the same thing. I understand that she is deliberately minimizing the situation. She suggests that perhaps my father is imagining the whole thing about the store being searched. As the pressure increases, she seems to be calming down. Her own hysteria has passed. She is worried about Paul. She is into the mental process which in the next three years will harden into a fortitude many people will find repugnant.

"Did you have your test, Danny?"

"This afternoon."

"Do you know all the words?"

"Yes."

But there are dark circles under her eyes. When I come home from school, the FBI men are sitting outside again in their car. My mother is lying down on the couch with a washcloth across her head. Her left forearm is bandaged. While ironing she gave herself a terrible burn. The edges of our existence seem to be crumbling. The house is cold and Williams has come up from the cellar to say in his deepest voice of menace that the furnace is not working properly and has to be cleaned. He will get to it when he can. I understand this means he will get to it when he does not feel abused by the situation. All my senses are in a state of magnification. I hang around the house feeling the different lights of the day. I drink the air. I taste the food I eat. Every moment of my waking life is intensified and I know exactly what is happening. A giant eye machine, like the mysterious black apparatus at the Hayden Planetarium with the two diving helmet heads and the black rivets and its insect legs, is turning its planetary beam slowing in our direction. And that is what is bringing on the dark skies and the cold weather. And when it reaches us, like the prison searchlight in the Nazi concentration camp, it will stop. And we will be pinned, like the lady jammed through the schoolyard fence with her blood mixed with the milk and broken bottles. And our blood will hurt as if it had glass in it. And it will be hot in that beam and our house will smell and smoke and turn brown at the edges and flare up in a great, sucking floop of flame.

And that is exactly what happens.

If they had something on them before Mindish was arraigned, why didn't they pick them up? If they were suspects before Mindish made his deal, why were they given four weeks to run away, or destroy incriminating evidence, or otherwise damage the case against them? The only answer is FBI stupidity or inefficiency, and that is a reasonable answer but not a good one.

Smoking. In Japan in the 16th century, Christians were winnowed out by having the entire population of a village walk across an image of Christ painted on rice paper and placed on the ground. Those who refused to step on Christ's face were immediately taken out of the procession and hanged upside down over a slow-burning sulpher fire. This is one of the slowest and most painful forms of execution known to civilization: the victim's eyes hemorrhage and his flesh is slowly smoked. His blood boils, and his brain roasts in its own juices. Death may come as late as the second week, without the victim's previous loss of consciousness.

First the strangulation of the phone. There are fewer calls each day. Then a period during which the phone rings once, twice, and is silent. Or I pick up in time, but there is no answer. Finally, the phone stops ringing altogether. It is a dead thing. My father takes to making his outgoing calls in candy stores up and down 174th Street. I enjoy negotiating with him for nickels I happen to have. He needs lots of change, and during the day in school I make a point of trading off quarters for the small stuff. I like to be useful for his evening trips to the phone booth. I make no profit, I merely want to be a help to him. He travels farther and farther from the house, using up phone booths the way he uses up change.

Meanwhile, the newspapers have been reporting a chain action of arrests around the world. An English scientist. An American engineer. A half-dozen immigrants in Canada. Secrets have been stolen. The FBI has been finding these people, and convicting them in the same press release. A chain reaction. My father comes home, not only with the *Daily Worker,* the *Times,* and

Fig. 30. Rochelle and Paul Isaacson (Lindsay Crouse and Mandy Patinkin) share an anxious moment after learning they are under investigation by the FBI. (Photo courtesy Paramount Pictures Corporation.)

the *Post,* but the *Telegram,* the *Tribune,* and even the *News, Mirror* and *Journal-American.* He is reading everything. He speaks of auto-da fé, and I see a Nazi demagogue, Otto Duffy, a sinister European whose Fascist ideas are sweeping over the United States. And it is not just spy arrests, but political trials like Foster and Dennis, and the other Party leaders. It is the defamation of New Dealers like Alger Hiss. It is the Un-American Activities Committee investigations of Hollywood writers. It is the Attorney General's list of subversive organizations. My father paints a picture: our house is completely surrounded by an army of madmen.

One night he reads aloud a *New York Times* story in which it is said that political discussion of any kind has virtually disappeared from college campuses. The *Times* has done a survey. Professors are afraid of being misinterpreted. It is becoming necessary in state universities to sign loyalty oaths.

"You hear, Rochelle? What does it tell you? You know where it ends, Rochelle."

"Shhh, Pauly. You'll wake the children."

I was afraid to go to sleep. I had terrible nightmares which I couldn't remember except in waking from them in terror and suffocation. I was terrified that if I went to sleep, the house would burn down, or that my parents would go away somewhere without telling us. For some reason, the second of these possibilities came to seem more likely. I would lie in the dark and think that I couldn't fall asleep because the minute I did, they would leave me and Susan and go somewhere they had never told me about. A secret place. It's the same thing when you catch them fucking, the same terror of exclusion. Flopping about, completely out of control, these people who control you. Grunting and moaning and gasping, who have told you to tie your shoelaces and drink your

juice. I could feel now in everything since Mindish's arrest, a coming to stay in our lives of the worst possible expectations. The world was arranging itself to suit my mother and father, like some mystical alignment of forces in the air; so that frictionless and in physical harmony, all bodies and objects were secreting the one sentiment that was their Passion, that would take them from me.

Where they might run off to did not occur to me as jail. I thought of it as a harmonic state of being. Gradually, I recognized the location. It was somewhere near Peekskill, when Paul got beaten up. He lay for days on the living room couch-bed with his headaches and puffed mouth, and his broken arm, and Rochelle took care of him. Her ministrations were devoted but practical, like an army nurse in a field hospital. She was as grimly involved as he in what he had done. They didn't seem to notice me. I understood the universe stood in proper relation at last to the family ego.

OH PAULY, OH MY POP, IT'S ALL RIGHT, IT REALLY IS ALL RIGHT. BUT WHY DID YOU HAVE TO GIVE YOUR GLASSES TO MINDISH?

One morning Daniel heard a knock on the door. He recognized the hour. You have to know the house to see what happened. The front door was on the left side of the house as you faced it from the inside. It opened onto a short hall, and on the right-hand side of the hall was the entrance to the living room. Halfway down this short, dark hall was the narrow stairs that went up to the two bedrooms. Under the stairs was the place we kept the carriage and also old newspapers. Just beyond this area was the doorway to the kitchen which was behind the living room in location. I tell you this (who?) so that you may record in clarity one of the Great Moments of the American Left. The American Left is in this great moment artfully reduced to the shabby conspiracies of a couple named Paul and Rochelle Isaacson. They sleep in a foldaway couch-bed in the living room. They bought it from Pauly's older sister, Frieda, my Aunt Frieda, with the mole with one hair coming out of it just above her upper lip, when she moved into a smaller apartment, after her husband died. The front hall is linoleum. A little side table, just out of range of the door when it opens, holds the phone and the Bronx phone book.

When Daniel opened the door, there stood the two FBI agents, Tom Davis and John Bradley. Behind them, across the street, frost in the crotches of the chain link fence of the schoolyard shone in the early morning sun like stars in Daniel's eyes.

"Hi Danny. Is your Dad at home?"

"What is it, Daniel?" his mother called from the living room.

"It's those two men," Daniel replied.

Daniel and the FBI men listened to the sounds of his mother waking up his father. Daniel still held the doorknob. He was ready to close the door the second he was told to.

"What time is it?" said his father in a drugged voice.

"Oh my God, it's six-thirty," his mother said.

She came into the hallway, pulling on her robe. Her long nightgown was thin cotton and Daniel panicked for a second because you could see the tips of her breasts through the material until she wrapped the robe around her and tied the belt. He glanced at the two men in the door to see if they saw, but there was nothing in their faces.

"Morning, Mrs. Isaacson. Can we come in?"

His mother was combing back her thick hair with her fingers. She turned her attention to the two men at the door, who by this time had become acquaintances of a sort. They had cultivated a we're-all-in-this-thing-together kind of approach. The idea in their exaggeratedly wry suffering of my father's verbal abuse and stubbornness was that they preferred having no part of this messy situation, but as long as they were assigned to this job, perhaps some

> "Well now, we don't see things just the way you commies do, Paul."

mutual kindness and even a bit of humor would make it easier for everyone concerned. Once they even alluded to the pressure on them from their "higher-ups."

"Who are these higher-ups?" my father had said.

"Now, Paul, we're supposed to ask you the questions."

"So you're not getting enough out of me," my father said, not without pride.

"You're a tough nut, all right," one of them said. "Next thing we know, you'll be trying to indoctrinate us."

"Well, I'll tell you something. I have answered your questions about me. I have told you my biographical details. I have not answered questions about anyone else."

"You mean like Doctor Mindish?"

"I have said what I mean. But I am curious about you. I am curious that a man of reasonable intelligence like yourself would choose to become a tool of the ruling class. I would like to know what makes you do it? What is your motivation? What are you saying to all the

poor and sick and exploited individuals in this country when you join this Federal Bureau of Inquisition?"

"Well now, we don't see things just the way you commies do, Paul."

Either my mother nodded that they could come in, or they took her silence as permission. I know she would have been anxious to keep the cold out. They walked through the door and immediately there was an electric charge of life just outside, and right behind them came another man, then two more, then a few more, all warmly dressed and well tailored for the harsh autumn morning, a dozen FBI men, all told, bringing into our little splintery house all the chill of the outdoors on their bulky shoulders. They poured through the front door like an avalanche of snow.

"What is it now!" my mother shouted.

"Rochelle!" my father called.

I looked outside. Five or six sedans were double-parked along the street. Another car was pulling up. Two more of the G-men stood on the sidewalk. Another was going down the alley to come in through the basement. In my ears was the crackle of a turned-up police radio.

My father was shown the warrant for his arrest as he sat on his hide-a-bed with his bare feet on the floor. He groped around for his glasses. He told my mother he felt suddenly nauseous, and she had him bend over with his head between his knees till the feeling went away. She was furious.

"What are these men doing here?" she said to Bradley and Davis. "Do you think you've got John Dillinger? What are you doing?" Men were going through the bookshelves, the bedclothes, the mahogany wardrobe closet. Men were marching upstairs.

My mother stood with Susan in her arms and tears coming down her cheeks. Every piece of furniture in the house had been, in some moment of her life, her utmost concern. She had made every curtain, she had scrubbed and polished every inch of floor. This old, leaky, wooden shack we lived in—and what newspaperman who wrote about the trial ever said a thing about the Isaacsons' poverty, the shabbiness of their home with its broken-down Salvation Army furniture and castoffs, and amateur paint jobs, its stained wallpaper where the rain soaked through the front door.

"Murderers!" my mother cried. "Maniacs! Haven't you hounded us enough? Can't you leave us alone?"

She did not appear to realize that my father had been arrested.

I ran upstairs. Two of them were in my room. They examined my dinosaur book, the model airplane I was working on, and the cigar box I used to hold my marbles. They looked under the mattress on my cot, they lifted the linoleum on the floor, they looked in the closet and went through the blankets and sheets my mother kept there, flapping out each one and then throwing it on the floor. They took the crystal radio my father had helped me make, and the table radio, an old metal Edison that I listened to my programs on, pulling out the plug and wrapping the cord around the radio and tucking it under his arm. And in Susan's room one of them opened the belly of her monkey doll with a penknife and stuck his finger in it and pulled out the stuffing. In Susan's room was my grandma's shiny hope chest, and they were going through that, tossing out Grandma's brown picture of her mother and father, and a *siddur*, two down pillows, and some old clothes of hers, and a lace tablecloth with fringe. Mothballs rattled on the floor. Down at the bottom of the chest was a blue, oblong tin with rounded corners. It was my grandma's last tin of asthma grass. One of them picked it up, opened it slowly, sniffed it, replaced the lid, and wrapped the tin in his handkerchief and put it in his pocket.

Daniel ran back to his own room. His own blue tin filled with pennies of peculiar existence had been opened and the pennies scattered on the floor.

Downstairs the place was a shambles. Broken dishes in the kitchen. The newspapers from under the stairs strewn about. One of them was picking out copies of the *Daily Worker*, and issues of other papers with stories about ATOM SPIES arrested in England, Canada and New Jersey. A terrible draft swept through the house now, the front door having been propped open. I looked

outside. Williams stood on the sidewalk. He was wearing his overalls over a grey sweat shirt. He was wearing slippers. He was looking down the alley. And from under my feet came the thunder of garbage cans crashing around the cellar.

I don't know how long this went on. There appeared across the street, along the schoolyard fence, growing numbers of children not interested in going to school. People were hanging out of the windows of the apartment houses on 173rd Street. At each corner of our block a regular police patrol car was parked across the intersection. The FBI radio sputtered like my grandma's asthma grass. Teachers were watching. The FBI men were taking all these valuable things to their cars. I stood at the door and watched, and this is what they took: My crystal radio and my radio for listening. A stack of selected newspapers. My father's International Workers' Order insurance policy for five thousand dollars. A toolbox. A year's issues of *Masses and Mainstream*. And the following books: JEWS WITHOUT MONEY by Mike Gold, THE IRON HEEL by Jack London, STATE AND REVOLUTION by V. Lenin, GENE DEBS, THE STORY OF A FIGHTING AMERICAN by Herbert Marais and William Cahn, THE PRICE OF FREE WORLD VICTORY by Henry A. Wallace, Vice President of the United States, THE GREAT CONSPIRACY by Michael Sayers and Albert E. Kahn, WHO OWNS AMERICA by James S. Allen (the cover shows a fat capitalist with a top hat and a dollar sign inscribed on his belly, sitting in front of a factory on top of a big bag marked *profits*—oh, Red cartoons! Oh, Robert Minor with your sexy goddess of freedom lying raped and bleeding, and your workingmen of the giant arms, and the clasped hands of your black and white brothers, and your ranks of workers advancing toward the cringing capitalist bosses, I salute you! I salute you, Creator of the anti-comic strip! In such bold strokes of the charcoal pencil is my childhood forever rubbed into my subversive brain, oh, Robert Minor, oh, William Gropper, geniuses of the pencil stroke, precision tools of working-class dreams, agitators, symbol-makers, vanguard with your unremitting proprietorship of the public outrage) and THE STORY OF THE FIVE YEAR

PLAN by M. Ilin. This last book is from my room. It is a translation of a primer for Russian children. My father gave it to me and said to keep it in my room until I was old enough to read it. I am old enough, but have not gotten around to reading the first chapter.

On the bank of a large river, great cliffs are being broken into bits. Fierce machines resembling prehistoric monsters clamber clumsily up the steps of a gigantic ladder hewed out of the mountain... A river appears where none existed before, a river one hundred kilometers long... A swamp is suddenly transformed into a broad lake... On the steppe, where formerly only feather grass and redtop grew, thousands of acres of wheat wave in the breeze... Airplanes fly above the Siberian taiga, where in little cabins live people with squinting eyes clad in strange dress made of animal skins... In the Kalmik region, in the middle of the naked steppe, grow buildings of steel and concrete alongside the felt tents of the nomads... Steel masts rise over the whole country: each mast has four legs and many arms, and each arm grasps metal wires... Through these wires runs a current, runs the power and the might of rivers and waterfalls, of peat swamps and coal beds. All this... is called the Five Year Plan.

Daniel stood in the entrance to the living room. He was still in his pajamas. The cold of the morning had driven itself into his chest. It filled his chest and his throat. It pressed at the backs of his eyes. He was frightened of the way he felt. The cold hung like ice from his heart. His little balls were encased in ice. His knees shifted in ice. He shivered and ice fell from his spine. His father was dressed now, standing in his good suit of grey glen plaid with the wide lapels and square shoulders hanging in slopes off his shoulders and the wide green-forest tie and the white shirt already turning up at the collars, buttoning his two-button jacket with one hand, and his face, unshaven, turned in a moment's attitude of trying to remember something, trying to remember as if it was on the floor, this sadness, this awful sadness of trying to remember, so unaccustomedly dressed up in his over-large suit with the pleated trousers and cuffs almost covering his brown wing-tipped shoes, and his other hand rises limply from the wrist, his arm rises, and he doesn't seem to care, attached to a handcuff as the man who holds him captured lifts his hands to light his cigarette, my father's hand going along in tow, the agent cupping his match and lighting his cigarette, and my father's hand dangling, having moved just as far as the other man moved it.

I remember that Susan was crying. "Why they do that to Daddy? Why they do that to Daddy?" over and over, "Why they do that to Daddy?" and that my mother was rocking her, holding her tightly, and swaying with Susan in her arms saying shhhh, shhh... But Susan was hysterical, sobbing with great gasps for air. We have none of us ever had enough to breathe. I kicked the FBI in the shins and I butted them in the groin, and I screamed and raged, and swung my fists at them. I know I hurt a couple of them. But I was shoved aside. And when I came back I was lifted by the hands and feet, and flopping and squirming like a snake, and You leave my pop alone! I'll kill you! I'll kill you! I was dropped behind the stairs in the pile of papers. My father was hustled out the door. I was on my knees, warmed by my own tears, thawed in my rage, and I saw his face as he turned for one brief moment and yelled over his shoulder: "Ascher!"

And then it was terribly quiet. And all the cars were gone, and the gaping people were gone, and the door was closed, and I looked at my weeping mother, and I held her baby daughter for her as she dialed the phone. And I realized my father was really gone.

The Isaacsons are arrested for conspiring to give the secret of television to the Soviet Union...

Elected silence sing to me.

The guard sees him pace his cell. His arm rises, his finger points. Occasionally a sound escapes his pantomime, some release of anguish whose diction is unclear.

He associates with Big Bill Haywood, and with Debs and with Mooney and Billings. All these fighters. The Scottsboro Boys. Their stars illuminate the walls, burn away the humiliation. Debs' cell was enormous, as big as the world. That is what the rulers never learn. The properties of steel and stone are subject to moral law.

Nor is death what it seems to be. When the ruling class inflicts death upon those they fear they discover that death itself can live. It is a paradox. Ma Ludlow is alive. Joe Hill is alive. Crispus Attucks is alive. Even Leo Frank, why do I think of Frank swinging from his tree in Geor-

> I looked at my weeping mother as she dialed the phone. And I realized my father was really gone.

gia, but all right, Frank. The two Italians speak and stir and smile and raise their fists in the mind of history. I am their comrade, they talk to *me*, Sacco makes his statement to *me*.

Socrates was tried. He was found guilty. He was forced to drink hemlock. By this act his persecutors raised to eternal life and consigned themselves to the real death and total obscurity of persecutors everywhere.

Jesus was tried. He was found guilty. He was tortured and executed. If Jesus had not been tried, if he had not been put to death, how would his teachings have endured? The Christians themselves celebrate this fact in their idea of resurrection: He returns and lives with men, in the imaginations of men hundreds of generations later. Of course this doesn't touch the question of how his ideas which were completely Jewish, were perverted by institutions which spoke in his name.

The difference between Socrates and Jesus is that no one has ever been put to death in Socrates' name. And that is because Socrates' ideas were never made law.

Law, in whatever name, protects privilege. I speak of the law of any state that has not achieved socialism. The sole authority of the law is in its capacity to enforce itself. That capacity expresses itself in Trial. There could be no law without trial. Trial is the point of the law. And punishment is the point of the trial—you can't try someone unless you assume the power to punish him. All the corruption and hypocritical self-service of the law is brought to the point of the point in the verdict of the court. It is a sharp point, an unbelievably sharp point. But there is fascination for the race in the agony of the condemned. That is a law, a real law, that rulers can never overcome—it is fixed and immutable as a law of physics.

Therefore the radical wastes his opportunity if he seriously considers the issues of his trial. If he is found guilty it is the ruling power's decision that he cannot be tolerated. If he is found innocent it is the ruling power's decision that he need not be feared. The radical must not argue his innocence, for the trial is not of his making; he must argue his ideas.

His trial is held in a large, shadowed hall. Voices echo. Gestures are solemn, oratorical. In attendance are all the world's history of dead heros of the Left.

But a small elevator brings him up from the basement lockup and with one marshal in front of him and one holding his arm, he steps through the door into the courtroom and the raised judge's bench is off his right eye. He sees a large square room, but a room, not a hall, and the raked jury job has leather chairs of green. The walls are wood-paneled in the same dark wood of the balustrade which separates the trial area from the spectators' pews. The floors are marble. The back doors look padded, and have porthole windows. As he enters no one seems to notice. He sits and he waits. Ascher touches his arm and speaks quietly into his ear. On the other side of Ascher, Rochelle writes on a pad. He is bewildered, his own visions have made him vulnerable. Ordinary people move about the room on obscure business. There are few spectators. He turns in his chair and cannot tell who is press. Everyone looks the same. Everyone is sallow in the light of the courtroom which is a mixture of daylight and the incandescence of weak bulbs. At the same time voices seem metallic, the acoustics of the room are not good. He is reminded of what—a library, a legitimate theater with the fire curtain down, a doctor's office, an indoor swimming pool. He feels slightly ill. He recognizes the feeling, a cavern opening inside him, a cavern of fear, and closing his eyes he sees into its darkness and it has no bottom.

When the Judge comes in from his own door on the other side of the bench and quickly takes his seat, Paul, having been gently suffered to stand on his feet, takes a deep breath. It is to seal the cavern of his nauseating fear. Everyone sits and the Judge, like a businessman starting his day, commences the trial in an efficient, quiet, conversational voice. He does not look down at Paul. He addresses only the lawyers. It is Judge Hirsch. Not having known of his existence even a few short months ago, Paul knows a good deal more about him now, including Hirsch's most intimate professional secret, that he hopes to be appointed to the Supreme Court. All the lawyers in the corridor know this. Hirsch has heard more cases brought by the government in the field of subversive activities than anyone else. He is Jewish. He wears a striped, ivy league tie, the knot of which can be seen under his judicial robe.

Paul realizes that he has to adjust to the reality of the situation. Howard "Red" Feuerman, the Chief U.S. Attorney, is a thin, boyish fellow with freckles, and thin sandy red hair and a tenor voice. He is younger than Paul expected, perhaps his own age, and he too wears a glen plaid suit, of brownish tone, although his fits him better. Feuerman is a war hero. He commanded a destroyer. His career has been meteoric. He is a graduate of St. John's, and is married to an Irish girl and has seven children. Paul runs his hand through his hair. He quickly tightens the knot at his collar. He wishes at this moment, and it is unbelievable to

him, and it shames him but he wishes at this moment he could be back in his cell. On the window ledge, under the bars, he keeps the shoebox with his letters from Rochelle and the children, and his hairbrush, and his toilet articles, and the cigar box with his collection. He has a very good way of folding the extra blanket at the foot of his cot. He might be having a chat now with Doyle, the day guard, a very decent man who has had much sorrow in his life.

But you can see that is part of it too, the enforced isolation, the sapping of confidence so that being with other people in a room without bars is suddenly a terrifying thing. They are counting on just the feelings I am feeling now. I will show them they can count on nothing.

Nevertheless he feels he's lost something even in the few minutes he's been here. A run scored for the other team. Ascher is now up at the bench with Feuerman, and he looks to his left across Ascher's empty chair and catches Rochelle studying him worriedly. Behind them, filing in through the rear doors of the court, are the people from whose numbers a jury will be chosen. Surely it is ridiculous to suppose that even one Communist is among them. He wants to reach out, to touch Rochelle's hand. He puts down the urge. They have agreed to be calm and dignified and under no circumstances make of themselves spectacles for the watching eyes of the press. To show no emotion, to give no satisfaction, to provide no hearts with occasion for scorn or pity. Not pity but justice is what they will have, and not by groveling for it but by demanding it. They have worked it all out—Rochelle has been very emphatic on this point.

He must clear his head and keep cool. What matters is that he maintain his faculties. To analyze the situation and assess it correctly and do what has to be done on the basis of that assessment. He understands that the trial will be held in recognizable New York accents. His adversaries are human beings with jobs to do. They will do their jobs feeling that they honor the standards of

justice. An American flag, a beautiful flag with gold fringe, hangs from a pole which is socketed in a stand behind the judge's bench. I am to be presented as an enemy of this flag. Yet Mrs. Goldstein, my fourth-grade teacher, told me of all the children in my class, I had the finest, straightest salute, and I was commended to the notice of the other children: "The way Paul stands, children, that is the way to stand, nice and tall and with a straight back when you say the pledge of allegiance." The marvelous Mrs. Goldstein. The marvelous smell of the classroom on rainy days, with all the raincoats and rubbers. A schoolroom on a rainy day, steamy with wet raincoats in the closet and wet rubbers. The windows fogged with steam, the rain dripping down the outside of the windows. The hot lunch program. The hot soup. To each other the teachers spoke Yiddish, which was ridiculous because nine tenths of all the children were Jewish and they understood Yiddish from the mothers and fathers, from their grandfathers. The maps that pulled down like shades. The watercolors of Washington and Lincoln and Coolidge framed in glass high on the walls.

All societies indoctrinate their children. The marvelous Mrs. Goldstein in total innocence taught us the glorious history of our brave westward expansion: our taming of the barbaric Indians, our brave stand at the Alamo, the mighty railroads winning the plains. Thus I must understand the nature of the conspiracy against me: it is mounted in full faith and righteousness by the students of Mrs. Goldstein.

He begins to feel better. His stomach is settling. The long drawn out process of picking jurors has begun. He sits with his hands clasped on the edge of the table. He does not stare too intensively at each of these people who may decide his fate. His personal manner will offend no one. His mind is working, and he is no longer stunned. He feels the satisfaction of a soldier having done everything necessary to prepare himself for battle. It is a moment of clarity and exhilaration.

A Time For Remembering
(For Ethel and Julius Rosenberg)
Lewis Allan

We saw you for the first and last time
Lying in your white, silk-lined coffins,
The false mask of peaceful death upon your faces
And the seal of finality stamped upon the moment
In the sobbing hush of sorrow.

This was the end of the end of the end
Of all tomorrows
And the winding commentary of stricken faces
Wrote horror to the act
And the shuffling obituary of the patient feet
Walking, walking, walking
From sidewalk to stairs to chapel
Was a weeping remembrance
More eloquent than monuments.

> *O my Love, my Love,*
> *We meet once more*
> *And so forever part,*
> *O my Love, my Love,*
> *Take this red rose,*
> *This bleeding rose*
> *That is my heart*

Sweet lovers of a cruel age,
All innocence and trust,
Like wide-eyed children
Holding the future by the hand,
Walking in the joy of dear comradeship,
What fearful death,
What dreadful lightning struck you down?

Why did you draw the man-made lightning rage
Of the prison-keepers of Liberty,
Hunted, caged, and tortured
(Oh, so legally tortured)
Before they burnt your bodies
On the altar of their vengeful greed,
Your home destroyed,
Your children orphaned,
And your honest memory
Made prey to all the ravenous vultures
Of these times?

> *O my Love, my Love,*
> *My dearest Love,*
> *We meet once more*
> *And kiss and say goodbye,*
> *Forever and forever lost*
> *Who might have saved our lives*
> *By one small lie.*

On you they vented all their fury
With their carefully calculated,
Stool-pigeoned, informer-framed,
Judas-judged, war-planned murder,
Scrawling a blazing warning across the darkening sky,
Amid the thunderhead of war-clouds
Manufactured here at home,
The smoke of their witches' brew
Mushrooming out of the pentagon pot
And the marble-domed kettle of poisonous intrigue,
Befogging the sharp purpose
Of their hellish plot.

WARNING
VERBOTEN

DO NOT SPEAK OF PEACE
OR YOU WILL DIE
LIKE THESE TWO

DO NOT WORK FOR PEACE
DO NOT THINK OF PEACE
DO NOT SPEAK OF BROTHERHOOD
OR A BETTER WORLD
A WORLD WITHOUT WAR
WITHOUT POVERTY
WITHOUT PROFIT
FOR IF YOU DO
WE WILL BRAND YOU TRAITOR
AND SPY
AND KILL YOU
AS WE KILL THESE TWO
FOR OUR CREED IS WAR
AND CONQUEST
AND PROFIT

WARNING
VERBOTEN

> *O our Loves, our Loves,*
> *Our dearest Loves,*
> *Our Loves, our children,*
> *Our children dear,*
> *Eyes brimming tears,*
> *Hearts full of fear,*
> *Our Loves, our Loves,*
> *Our dearest Loves,*
> *Our longing arms*
> *Are Oh so empty of you here*

Fig. 31. Lisa Kokin, *Remember Ethel and Julius Rosenberg*, 1977, batik, 54 x 40".

Honor
And Truth
And Innocence
Lie dead
And the perjurers
And despoilers
And murderers
In high places
Exchange small conversation
And large stakes

Twenty pieces of silver
In Judas coin
On wide-screen
Cinemascope,
In Red-White-and-Blue
Star-Spangled
Technicolor patriotism,
False as the perjured testimony
And the prosecutor
And the prosecutor judge
And the frightened prosecuting jury.

The switch has been thrown
And the man-made lightning warning
Has flashed across the headlines

BEWARE
OR YOU WILL BE NEXT
IF YOU THINK OF PEACE

It is cocktail time,
It is time for white house parties,
It is time for golf,
It is time for prosecutors-into- judges,
And judges-into-higher- judges,
And atom bomb blast tests
And fall-outs
of radio-active lies ...

Honor
And Truth
And Innocence
Lie dead

Dead and buried deep
Sunk into the secrecy
Of official archives
Carefully stamped
CASE CLOSED

But the case is not closed
And though the dead
Cannot be brought to life,
There will be a strict accounting
In the court of history
And an overturning of decisions
Where headstones on living graves
Will be tumbled,
And prison bars broken
And cell-doors opened
And men and women
Emerge from the living-death
Of unjust sentence
To confront the murderers
And the false accusers
In the great strength
Of their innocence
To right a monstrous wrong
And bring to light
For all to see
Murder most foul.

O my Love, my Love,
My dearest Love,
We meet once more
And kiss and say
  goodbye,
Forever and forever lost
Who might have saved
  our lives
By one small lie

1954

Editor's note: Lyricist Lewis Allan ("Strange Fruit," "The House I Live In"), was the pen name for Abel Meeropol, adoptive father of Robby and Michael Rosenberg.

In That *erev-shabes* Hour

Yuri Suhl

translated from the Yiddish by Irena Klepfisz

Fig. 32. Archie Nahman, *Ethel and Julius Rosenberg*, 1987, stainless steel, brass, on painted plywood, 30 x 17". (Photo:
Steven Borns.)

In that *erev-shabes* hour *
a world stood grief stricken, in tears
while Washington rejoiced over its great victory.
And when *shabes* threatened to disrupt the Sing-Sing celebration
and give the Rosenbergs one more day to live
they eluded *shabes*
and pushed back the clock of the Angel of Death.
Eyeing the Jewish calendar they saw a way
to burn the Rosenbergs
and not desecrate *shabes*.
They'd turn on the current one minute before candle blessing.
Respect for the Jewish God
befits God-fearing people.

In that *erev-shabes* hour
when the June sun was setting a fiery-red
each one was led separately
into the arms of death:

First he
then she—past his empty cell.
But the electric current
which seered their wondrous intellect
illuminated their innocence even more brightly
and lit up millions of minds
with a clear, piercing light.
That moment the world became a mourner
but its sorrow was transformed into rage
and placed the guilty before the world court.

In that *erev-shabes* hour
the judge was stationed at his post
in the judge's chamber on Foley Square
and impatiently paced the floor
unable to stop thinking
of the trial, of the hearing:
Ah, what a distance his sentence had spanned
from the judge's chair
to the electric chair in Sing-Sing.
(Not an easy time, not an easy time.)

Paris, London, Berlin, Rome, the Vatican!
From neighboring Mexico to distant Japan!
From a village in Vietnam
a town in Uruguay
Warsaw and Tel Aviv—
from everywhere came cries of protest.
From everywhere—
mountains of telegrams, mountains of letters.
And the endless ringing of the phone
through the nights of disturbed sleep.
It was a long battle—bitter, hard.
Only, thank God, thank God
it finally ended—
the agony of waiting ended.

At last the radio announced
it was all over—
about ten after eight.
First he… then she…
  He quickly switched off the radio
  grabbed his packed valise
  and ran, ran, ran to the train
  away from the hot stinking city
  to the summer place where his wife and children waited
  Where peace waited for his bruised spirit.

  The train races
  but his thoughts outrace it.
  He sees how his wife sees him in the distance
  and hurries towards him with outstretched arms
  to him, the good husband
  the loyal guardian of his country.
  And he can already hear the children's happy cries
  and now they're all walking together.

  A beautiful night
  God's miracle everywhere
  and what happened at ten after eight
  Is now far away, left far behind.

A beautiful night.
The sky is filled with stars
the high mountains enveloped in velvet silence
and if you listen carefully
you can hear a spring babble
and the snap of the smallest twig.

A beautiful night
a night for deep thoughts and lofty dreams.

On that night
their Michael and Robby became orphans…

On that night
people stood lost in silence
lost in thought
as grief dissolved into rage
and the rage—into clear, piercing light.
On that night
millions of mourners
were transformed into millions of prosecutors
who placed the guilty before the world's court.

*Editor's note: erev shabes means Sabbath eve.

Sunday, June 19, 1955   MORNING FREIHEIT   מאָרגן פֿרײַהײט

אין יענער ערב־שבת'דיגער שעה

(צום צווייטן יאָרטאָג פֿון דער הינריכטונג פֿון
דזשוליוס און עטל ראָזענבערג, דעם 19טן יוני, 1953)

-------------------- פֿון מ. א. סול --------------------

אין יענער ערב־שבת'דיגער שעה,
ווען אַ וועלט איז געשטאַנען אַ פֿאַרקלעמטע אין טרערן,
האָט וואַשינגטאָן געפֿרייט זיך מיט דעם גרויסן זיג . . .
און ווען דער שבת האָט געדראָט די סינג־סינג־שמחה צו פֿאַרשטערן
און שענקען די ראָזענבערגס נאָך אײן מעת־לעת לעבן,
האָט מען זיך מיט דעם שבת אויך אַן עצה אַן געגעבן
און דעם מלאך־המחת־זייגער געטאָן אַ רוק צוריק.
לויט'ן אידישן לוח האָט מען אויסגערעכנט,
אַז אי די ראָזענבערגס וועלן ברענען,
אי מען וועט דעם שבת ניט פֿאַרשוועכן --
מען וועט זיי "גענבן דעם שטראָם" אַ מינוט פֿאַר ליכט־בענטשן.
דעספּעקט פֿאַר'ן אידישן גאָט

Yiddish typography: Joe Kurland

The Rosenberg Cantata
Mike Gold

"The final answer is always with the people."
—Julius Rosenberg

The Beast
I have muddied the People's brain with movies and television
I have deadened their hearts with money and dead art
I have deafened them to the great voices
The People can never hear you
And every bank and steel mill has sworn
That this is the American Century
And the Rosenbergs must die.

All are at the feast of life but you
The auto roads and sunny beaches swarm with happy
          Americans
They rejoice in their autos and frigidaires
And their children play around them in joy
But you have sacrificed your family joy
To your beehive bitter god.

            (*a silence*)
Confess only that you stole the Bomb.
I need your confession
It is a battle won
In the war for the American Century.

            (*a silence*)
Here is the key to your prison
Confess and live.
You can gain the bright crown of success
Confess daily at treason trials and on television
Become famous informers rich and admired like Hollywood
          stars
And your children will have joy.

            (*a silence*)
Be practical, make a deal and live,
Justice and truth are commodities
The world is a jungle,
Its only law victory or death.

Editor's note: This is an excerpt from a
longer poem by Gold

ETHEL

ALICE HAMERS

"My parents were progressive," says playwright Alice Hamers, author of *Ethel*. "That's probably a euphemism for membership in the Communist Party." Jewish, and New York City born and raised, Hamers's family lived in Knickerbocker Village, the same complex as the Rosenbergs. Her mother remembers Ethel wheeling a baby carriage along Cherry Street with other mothers.

Nine years old when the Rosenbergs were killed, Hamers says, "I was devastated by the executions. I took their murders with me to camp that summer.

"Communists and communism never scared me the way it does most U.S. citizens. While there was certainly an unhealthy dogmatism, my experience of communists and communism included a loving family of friends, music, picnics, lots of laughter, many social and political gatherings and activities, and always a profound concern with peace and social justice. I have always wanted more people to have an idea of the Rosenbergs—of communists, progressives—as *I* knew them through my parents and friends, through growing up in the lap of… the [old] left. *Ethel* is a vehicle for that expression."

The play, which has had several staged readings in New York, focuses on the relationship between two women in their sixties, friends of Ethel's from high school. Learning that a writer wishes to question them about Ethel, one eagerly welcomes the chance to talk, the other wishes to leave her painful memories buried. The play also includes flashback scenes like this one of Ethel in her prison cell.

—R.O.

ACT III, Scene 2

September 28, 1952. Early Sunday afternoon. Ethel's cell on death row, women's wing, Sing Sing Prison, Ossining, New York. It is silent except for the occasional callings of gulls and starlings. Once or twice the clanking of a distant steel door is heard.

The cell is small— 6' x 7' with 8' ceiling. In it is a narrow bed, a chair, a small table, a toilet and sink. The nearest window is up and across the corridor from Ethel's cell. There is no light fixture inside this cubicle; rather a bulb is located on the other side of the bars. Ethel has no control over lights on or off.

The scene opens with Ethel alone in her cell, lying on bed, biting nails, setting clippings on corner of the table. A Sunday New York Times *lies spread out over bed. Ethel occasionally turns its pages for distraction. She gets up, paces, sits down on chair in front of table, picks up a pen, writes a few words, sets pen down, up again.*

Enter Matron Bessie Dailey holding a rose in a milk carton hidden behind her back. (Bessie is a composite/fictional character drawn from scant information on Ethel's prison matrons.)
ETHEL: (*Singing loudly, operatically, slightly hysterically*) Happy Birthday to me. Happy Birthday to me. Happy Birthday, dear Condemnednik, Happy Birthday to her… How old am…
BESSIE: (*Presenting rose*) Happy Birthday, dear.
ETHEL: (*Ignoring flower for the moment*) Where have you been?
BESSIE: I was gettin' here. You don't think I'd forget your birthday now, do ya darlin'?
ETHEL: Alas, my dear, how could you? I have reminded you at least a dozen times in the past week… An event is an event around this tomb.

Bessie hands Ethel the rose.

Oh, Bessie…. Ah, this miserable creature has turned thirty-seven years old today… third birthday behind bars… may be my last, eh?
BESSIE: Now you don't want to be talkin' that way… You can have that in your cell; I've okayed it.
ETHEL: A rose in my cell. How generous. I shall take this thorny branch and prick my way out of here. Today's my day, and I have decided I want to go home. Julie comes with me…
BESSIE: I'll pass that message on.
ETHEL: At least the weather shines on me… sort of… and so do you. Thank God you're on today. I couldn't have tolerated anyone else. Not today… not today. What time is it?
BESSIE: About 2:30, sweetheart… What does the paper say?
ETHEL: Oh, what does the paper say… Let's see. (*Holding up paper*)… It says that Julius and Ethel Rosenberg were granted a full pardon by the Supreme Court, which realized the gross miscarriage of justice. It says that they were returned to their rightful place with their wonderful and precious family. It says that the vicious beasts, liars and stool pigeons who put them in the condemned cells have fallen groveling in the dirt, begging forgiveness… including the pathetic little brother (*This is like a knife.*) It says…
BESSIE: You're in spirits today.
ETHEL: Sol was here this week. A visit with my "headshrinker" always helps. No, really, Bessie. People have such funny ideas about psychiatry. I know how you feel, but really he's been…
BESSIE: I didn't say a word now, did I?
ETHEL: And I had a wonderful visit with

Fig. 33. Janet Walerstein Winston, *Ethel's Dream*, 1986, oil, oil pastel on panel, 43 x 45".

Bessie gets up to turn on the radio. Ethel picks up the newspaper and opens randomly to women's pages, looks at fashions. Sound of radio stations switching, finally locating a classical station.

Good, leave that. (*Bessie returns to chair by Ethel's cell*) You know, if you'd let me, I could really dress you up right.
BESSIE: And what is wrong with the way I dress?
ETHEL: Too drab. You need more flash in your wardrobe. More pzazz.
BESSIE: In here?
ETHEL: The more pzazz in here the better. Anyway, you're not in here. You go home after work… Less tailored. You're so attractive; you have such a nice figure; you need clothes that flatter you.
BESSIE: Who do you think I am, Rita Hayworth? I'm…
ETHEL: Look what a nice velveteen choke does for the neck. Look at this dress. This is perfect for you. With my hips it would never work… This dress is more suited to me. Wouldn't it be something to get a dress like this to wear around my cell… Lady Ethel Rosenberg will be giving continual performances at the Grand Sing Sing-on-the-Hudson! How appropriately named. They must have known I was coming… How about this ensemble for my grand finale? Hah!… No, but I'm being serious… I think this is a good style for you; much better than what you're wearing.
BESSIE: I'm comfortable in this…
ETHEL: Comfort? Who thinks about comfort? A little suffering builds character… Believe me… Earrings; you'll need earrings to match… maybe medium-sized button earrings, blue, a dark blue; no, maybe a light blue.
BESSIE: What about shoes?
ETHEL: Of course, the shoes. Open-toed, sling back. Black or blue to coordinate with the earrings. Really, do it.
BESSIE: And to whom, Miss, shall I send this bill?
ETHEL: Send it to J. Edgar Hoover, and sign it sincerely Ethel Rosenberg… It's my birthday, and I can't even see my

the children. You should see my beautiful boys… staying with Julie's mom was too much. As soon as they're more settled in their new surroundings Mike can take piano lessons, and Robby can get into a day school… (*Exploding suddenly*) Who are these snakes that they should pull me from my children… You tell me, Bessie… you tell…
BESSIE: Ethel, honey…
ETHEL: Never mind Ethel honey. What am I supposed to do locked away in this torture chamber? I have a family to raise… You know Robby looks just like me. It's like looking into a miniature mirror. Oh my sweet children, my boys, my boys…
BESSIE: Reach your hand out… (*Bessie takes Ethel's hand. They sit silently for a moment. From outside sounds of gulls can be heard.*)

ETHEL: I don't know how much more of this I can take. I'm exhausted.
BESSIE: You're doin' fine.
ETHEL: I know. Don't say it. Hold on, hang in. What'd you think we're doing? What choice have we got? Who would ever have imagined this!? This is my life!? Why me, God? What did I do to deserve this?
BESSIE: It's not for us to know such things.
ETHEL: I can't understand why I just don't snap. But I don't. I don't. Tomorrow and tomorrow and tomorrow… Oh God, let's get off this. How can you stand me? I sound like a broken record… I can't think for another moment. Turn on the radio.
BESSIE: What do you want, the ball game?
ETHEL: No, music.

husband. What would it hurt? You'd think...

BESSIE: Darlin', don't beat your head against a wall. Where's the use in it?

ETHEL: Where's the use in anything?... But I know there is. I know what Julie and I are doing is what we have to do. I know we're right. I know it... but my babies, Bessie, my babies. Mike understands alot. He had to grow up so fast; but Robby... my poor babies. (*Silence*) We're not getting out of here alive. It's gone too far.

BESSIE: What do you know?

ETHEL: I know. It's right here in the paper. If they can kick Charlie Chaplin out of the country as a suspected Communist, if they can do that to him, what do you think they'll do to the Rosenbergs? Fry 'em. That's what.

BESSIE: Don't you talk like this, you hear me. There are alot of people on your side in this world. Now don't you go and lose your faith. I know it doesn't seem fair, but that's the way life is sometimes. There's no explainin'.

ETHEL: (*Imitating Bessie, but not mocking her*) No, there's no explainin' people who would do such things— burn and torture millions of people. Who are they, Bessie? I sit here day after day and wonder who these people are. What compels them to do this? Who would tear me away from my children like this? I can't...

BESSIE: Forget 'em. Concentrate on the folks who love you. They're the ones'll get you through this life—them and faith. Come on now... Why don't

you keep busy like your husband? Write a letter to him. He gets hurt when he doesn't hear from you. You know how much he loves you. You're a lucky woman; not many women find such a good husband.

ETHEL: I'm so selfish sometimes. But I can't. I'm dying in here. I know, so many thousands of people out there who have taken us in, but it's so hard; it's so hard. You know I got a letter from a Dutch woman who named her baby after Julie and me: "Ethel Julia." Isn't that something? (*Pause*)

BESSIE: That's something, alright!

ETHEL: Do you think I'm terrible? God knows, my mother does. She'd probably pull the switch if she could... my mother and my brother...

BESSIE: You've had no easy time of it Ethel, darlin'. Who knows what gets into folks? (*This situation pains Bessie on behalf of Ethel*)

ETHEL: Waiting to die. I'm sitting here waiting to die, but my life keeps moving on. The kids get older; I get older. Julie... I'm thirty-seven years old—almost forty—a woman. I'm a grown woman. Roll on Columbia... Those miserable, stinking, rotten...

Ethel turns on Bessie.

You think I did something too, don't you?

BESSIE: Ethel!

ETHEL: Oh... forgive me, please, Bessie, forgive me...

BESSIE: (*Moving to leave*) I've got some

things that need takin' care of...

ETHEL: I'm barely human anymore. At least there are Wednesdays... Do you realize that for almost two years I have been allowed to see my husband for one hour a week! And only behind bars! This Wednesday I have a double treat even—my Julie's visit, and then I get to sit alone with the World Series. What more can a gal ask for?

Bessie walks down corridor to exit door.

Come on Dodgers! The champions of the underdog will show those fascist Yankees... You're leaving me.

BESSIE: I'll be back, you know that.

ETHEL: I'll be here. (*Yelling after Bessie*) I'll design more outfits for you... (*To herself*) I need new outfits for myself. Look at these rags. At least some new underwear... (*Again mimicking Bessie's brogue*) O.K. Ethel, darlin', what shall we do with ourself? With this endless time that may end all too quickly.

Ethel alone as at beginning of scene— same kind of search for activity. Tunes into playing radio and sings along with aria which is on. Music fades. Lights dim slowly indicating passing of day. Light outside cell comes on... then lights out... night... sound of rain... Ethel tossing in bed unable to sleep... gets up. Paces. Sings "PEAT BOG SOLDIERS"... Joined by Julius from the distance of the men's wing. Julius's voice fades. Ethel finishes alone. Lights fade.

The Rosenbergs
Ethel and Michael, Robert and Julius
W.E.B. DuBois

*It was the end of a long, dark day; a day of sorrow and suffering. I was
very, very weary. As the night fell and the silence of death rose about me,
I sat down and lay my face in my hands and closed my eyes. I heard my own
voice speaking:*

Crucify us, Vengeance of God
As we crucify two more Jews,
Hammer home the nails, thick through our skulls,
Crush down the thorns,
Rain red the bloody sweat
Thick and heavy, warm and wet.

We are the murderers hurling mud
We the witchhunters, drinking blood
To us shriek five thousand blacks
Lynched without trial
And hundred thousands mobbed
The millions dead in useless war.
But this, this awful deed we do today
This senseless, blasphemy of birth
Fills full the cup!
Hail Hell and glory to Damnation!
O blood-stained nation,
Stretch forth your hand! Grasp it, Judge
Wrap it in your blood-red gown;
And Lawyer in your sheet of shame;
Proud pardoners of petty thieves
Cautious rabbis of just Jehovah,
And silent priests of the piteous Christ;
Crawl wedded liars, hide from sight,
In the dirt of all the night,
And hold high vigil at the dawn!
For yonder, two pale and tight-lipped children
Stagger across the world, bearing their dead
There lifts a light upon the Sea
With grim color, crooked form and broken lines;
With thunderous throb and roll of drums
Alleluia, Amen!

Now out beyond the plain
Streams the thick sunshine, sheet on sheet
Of billowing light!
Above the world loom vast sombre hills
Limned in lurid lightnings;
While from beneath the hideous sickened earth,
The Sea rains up flood on flood to cleanse the heavens.
Twixt Sun and Sea,
Rises the Great Black Throne.
Sternly the pale children march on
Bearing high on their hands, Father and Mother
The drums roll until the Land quivers with pain

And slowly yawns:
The children prone bow down
They bow and kneel and lie;
They lay within the earth's deep breast
The beautiful young mother and her mate,
Straight up from endless depths
Rise then the Bearers of the Pall
Sacco and Vanzetti, old John Brown and Willie McGee.
They raise the crucified aloft.
The purple curtains of Death unwind.
Hell howls, Earth screams and Heaven weeps.

High from above its tears
Drops down a staircase from the Sun
Around it with upstretched hands,
Surge of triumph and dirge of shame,
Gather the mighty Dead:
Buddha, Mahmoud and Isaiah
Jesus, Lincoln and Toussaint
Savonarola and Joan of Arc;
And all the other millions,
In throng on throng unending, weeping, singing,
With music rising heaven-high,
And bugles crying to the sky
With trumpets, harps and dulcimers;
With inward upward swell of utter song.
Then through their ranks, resplendent robes of silken velvet,
Broidered with flame, float down;
About the curling gown
Drop great purple clouds, burgeon and enthral,
Swirl out and grandly close, until alone
Two golden feet appear,
As of a king descending to his throne.
In the great silence and embracing gloom,
We the murderers
Groan and moan:

"Hope of the Hopeless
Hear us pray!
America the Beautiful,
This day! This day!
Who was enthroned in sunlit air?
Who has been crowned on yonder stair?
Red Resurrection,
Or Black Despair?"

Ethel Rosenberg: A Sestina
Enid Dame

The charges against you never did make sense.
Did you steal a bomb or merely type
a letter? At City College, did you sit at the table
and listen to young men argue about revolution?
Did you say to yourself, being a woman,
"Why do they think it will be easy?"

You were a person who quickly learned what wasn't easy.
The world nagged and withdrew. Only your daydreams made sense.
There, you sang opera. Otherwise, you were a woman
who never could please her mother, who learned to type,
who finally married—a personal revolution!—
the man who (they claimed) filmed documents on his secret table.

You insisted it was really an ordinary table.
You'd bought it at Macy's. That was too easy
for jury and judge, whose image of revolution
was violent, apocalyptic, wholly devoid of sense,
removed from a world of children, dirty dishes, typewriters and the unhappiness of men and women.

I picture you in your three-room apartment, a woman
singing snatches of arias to yourself as you set the table,
loving and hating the house. I know the type.
Scraping and rearranging; refusing to take things easy.
Foreboding washes over you, an extra sense.
Mopping the floor, you dream of revolution.

In those days, there was only one revolution
going, and though it viewed people as workers, not men and women,
you signed its petitions, sens-
ing that freedom begets more freedom. Let's table
the next, obvious discussion: how few things are easy,
how people usually react according to type.

You hardly appeared at your trial, in spite of the type-
face in the headlines distorting your revolution,
mistranslating you. On the other hand, you weren't easy
to understand, or even to kill. A stubborn woman,
you made them do it twice. And somewhere else, at our table,
we—who believed in last minute miracles—sat quietly, emptied
  of sense.

You've been dead most of my life. I'm the type of woman
who questions what's easy. At night with crystal and table,
I beg ghosts out of dead revolutions to come to me, to talk sense.

Fig. 34. Georges Salendre, *The Rosenbergs*, 1953, stone.

Fig. 35. Gene Epstein Richmond, *The Family*, 1978, oil pastel, collage.

DANNY BOY
Edna Toney

Although Edna Toney came of age in the Thirties and Alice Hamers in the Sixties, both have written plays that bring into focus the human dimension of the Rosenberg case and the toll the McCarthy years took on so many.

Toney's play *Danny Boy*, written in the mid-Seventies, emphasizes the betrayal of "Eve Rothman" (Ethel Rosenberg) by her brother "Danny Goldman" (David Greenglass). Toney's is a simple evocation of the struggle to maintain dignity which Eve and her husband Jesse (Julius) exercised. The play was produced at the Mid-Hudson Arts and Science Center in Poughkeepsie, New York.

"In 1950," Toney recalls, "I was a playwriting student at Columbia University. I was also a political dissident, married and had two small children. The more the media featured weird accusations against the Rosenbergs, the more I felt that in this mad McCarthyite atmosphere it could easily have been Edna and Anthony* instead of Ethel and Julius."

After the Supreme Court decided not to review the Rosenberg case and the couple was executed, Toney says she "purchased a copy of the trial records and read them all the way through." She decided then and there to write a play about the case, a scene from which is excerpted below.

—R.O.

Scene III

It is a week later, close to noon. Jesse, in a neat business suit, sits at the kitchen table with a cup of coffee and a newspaper. He is scanning a page, occasionally picking up a pencil and circling a small area. After a few moments the front door is heard opening and closing. Eve enters wearing a street dress, a hat and carrying a handbag.

EVE (*dazed*): Home already? My goodness, I didn't realize it was nearly suppertime. (*She takes off hat, puts*

*Editor's note: Anthony Toney is one of the artists in the exhibition.

down handbag.) What shall I cook? I haven't even thought about it? (*She leafs through the mail.*) I went straight to the hospital from taking Susie to nursery school… Still nothing from Marie… I can't get over it… (*Takes a letter from envelope.*) Your thirteenth college reunion. Are you going?

JESSE: I'll wait for the twenty-fifth so we can all compare potbellies.

EVE: It's not till October. You might change your mind.

JESSE: I might.

EVE (*picking up another envelope*): Parents' Night for Second Graders, June 23. 8 P.M. That's next Tuesday? Who'll go?

JESSE: You go.

EVE: I'm in such a terrible state from all this terrible business…

JESSE: Exactly why you *should* go. It'll make a nice change.

EVE: I wouldn't be able to concentrate…

JESSE: There's nothing much to concentrate *on*. As I recall the one I attended last year at P.S. 11, first they tell you individually how brilliant your child is and then everybody gets coffee and cake.

EVE: I'll decide later. (*Picks up another envelope*). What's this? I don't see a signature or a name. Where's the envelope?

JESSE: It didn't come in one.

EVE: So how then?

JESSE: Slipped under the door.

EVE: And no name… (*reads aloud*) "Why don't you move out? We'd like to keep this a nice building minus the stigma—of notoriety." (*Flings the letter down*). What kind of talk is that? We didn't do anything? All right, my brother is accused of something and his name is in the papers. Right away that means he's guilty and we're guilty by association… These people… these anonymous people should be ashamed of themselves, whoever they are… (*Picks the letter up again and examines it closely*). Whoever *she* is, probably. It's kind of a ladylike handwriting, thin, curly letters and a very good quality paper, the kind we can't afford. Mrs. 6B, she could afford it. Or Mrs. Langdon. Or that snooty Mrs. Hoyt.

JESSE: Or none of the above. Calm yourself, Eve. This is something we have to bear for awhile, along with the occasional nut phone call.

EVE: Was there? Did anybody…? While I was gone?

JESSE: Yeah. One. (*She groans.*) Try to think of them as pathetic, powerless people hoping to give themselves a sense of power.

EVE: I can't. I just want to punch them in the nose.

JESSE: But it's not possible to do that, is it? So you have to put them out of your mind and go about your affairs. (*He comes out of the kitchen, puts an arm around her, guides her to an armchair where she sits down.*) It can't last forever. (*He goes back to the kitchen and newspaper. Eve changes from shoes to house slippers. There is silence for a moment.*)

EVE: What an awful person that Rachel is. Who could possibly live a decent life under her influence? Imagine I come to the hospital bringing a little cheer-up gift in all good will—which she never acknowledges. Just looks at me with eyes of stone. She didn't say it straight out but in a dozen different ways she hints that *I* am really to blame for her accident. Over and over again she stresses one point: Last Wednesday, when Danny was arrested, if she hadn't been left all by herself, if *I* had come over when she telephoned, she wouldn't have been wandering around in the dark—in her own living room you hear—and tripped over the rug and broken her leg. *Me*, she was suddenly so anxious to talk to. *Me*, who she never once telephoned before, couldn't wait to hang up on, never invited over… Believe me, Danny must have plenty to put up with. Did you ever hear of such a thing? (*Jesse shrugs his shoulders*). Such behavior is not significant?

JESSE: Not the way you think.

EVE: What way then, may I ask?

JESSE: You're both blaming each other so you won't have to blame the real culprit.

EVE: Such an expression. "The real culprit." Maybe you think he *is actually* an atomic spy.

JESSE: No, no, I don't. (*Upset, he drops what he is doing, comes into the living room.*) But he must have done *something*, Evie. You simply won't get that through your head. The FBI doesn't move in with a charge like that and make a big, dramatic arrest unless they have something on him.

EVE: What? Some little thing that when it's all past and done with, they could still hold it over his head?

JESSE: What does that mean? (*Eve is silent, flustered*). Are you finally admitting he did something in the army? (*She is suffering, but still silent.*) Don't you think *they* have all the facts? Am I the last one to be told? Damn it, what was it? (*He keeps staring at her. Then something dawns on him.*) Wait a minute, wait a minute. That time in '46 you said he phoned you from New Mexico that he was transferred from the Los Alamos plant to somewhere in Colorado, somewhere very unspecific, somewhere very indifinite. For about six months—he was in the stockade, wasn't he? (*Reluctantly, she nods*). For what?

EVE: Walking out with a part.

JESSE: Oh my God. It's even worse than I thought.

EVE: But he just took it to get a few dollars. He wanted to buy himself…

JESSE: The reasons don't matter.

EVE: But the dealer who bought the part was from around the area. Right in the same town. He could be brought here by Danny's lawyer. He could reveal the truth.

JESSE: He'll reveal what he's told to reveal. If they're going to rig the important part of the case, they won't hesitate to rig the rest.

EVE: But why must they rig anything? Why must they do this to poor Danny?

JESSE: In theory you know the answer very well. We discussed such matters often enough. But when it deals with Danny you just won't face the fact. And the fact is that he happens to fit in to the scheme of things. There's a brand new war to plug. It'll need plenty of plugging, too. Americans aren't very enthusiastic about defending Korea, thousands of miles away, from the Chinese Communist menace. So they're going to bring in an *American* Communist menace, start the flag-waving and the draft registration.

(*Sighing.*) I wouldn't want to predict the outcome of this case.

EVE: What could they do to him?

JESSE: That depends on how much hysteria they manage to whip up. It doesn't have to make sense. Just one big lie repeated over and over can do it. The newspapers and radio will go along as they've done with the red-hunting circus in Congress.

EVE: We must get him a better lawyer.

JESSE: Better lawyers cost better money. We don't have it.

EVE: Rachel said the $1000 downpayment for the partnership went fast. First they were hoping to leave the country with it after their neighbor mentioned getting a visit from the FBI. And then… and then it happened and now it's all gone for the lawyer's retainer fee. To be fair, Jesse, in that agreement you made with him, he still has another $2500 coming.

JESSE: *Also, to be fair*, business is just about at a standstill, thanks to Danny Goldman. (*She looks bewildered.*) You know, Evie, I've mentioned this several times since the damned arrest but it never seems to register. There are no new orders. There are many cancellations of recent ones. We—I— am controversial. Controversial. The dirty word in business. (*Laughs grimly.*) Well, at least I'm related to a Somebody now, whether he deserves the title or not. But the fact remains that those in the business are avoiding me since the news is out that my former— and very recent—partner is a suspected atomic spy. The last two days I had nothing to do in the shop. Sent the workers home. Why do you suppose *I'm* home at this hour?

EVE: At this hour? What time is it? (*Looks at her watch.*) Oh. Jesse, I've been so stupid. I didn't realize. My mind has been so preoccupied. And the worst part is it's all so terribly unfair to you. I bothered you and pestered you and pushed you to take the boy in and now you're bearing the brunt.

JESSE: Don't torment yourself with these thoughts, Evie. A lot that comes about is due to sheer chance. In this case it happens to be *your* brother. It could

just as easily have been my brother, Harry, for instance. He's hinted more than once that his dress house and all the rest of them on Seventh Avenue for that matter are mixed up in organized crime. So he's been lucky. And Moe down on Wall Street. If the Securities and Exchange Commission ever looked into some of these deals he's bragged about privately. Well, he's been lucky, too, so far. Anyway, the moral of the story is, why not look at the bright side? Why not be glad Goldman and Rothman weren't *actually* partners when the arrest was made? Why not be glad we didn't agree to his panicky request for getting him a loan? (*Eve cannot repress a groan.*) Eve, you didn't.

EVE: No. (*He sighs with relief.*) But I tried. Only banks don't lend to women.

JESSE: Well, I never thought the day would come I'd be happy about a reactionary policy but this is definitely the day. (*He picks up newspaper and pencil.*)

EVE: What are you doing?

JESSE: Tell you later. It's almost time to pick up Susie, isn't it?

EVE: Yes, yes… (*She starts changing back into shoes.*)

JESSE: Mom called.

EVE:.What did she say?

JESSE: Oh, one thing and another. Mainly she was concerned at finding the breadwinner home so early in the day. When I explained my predicament—not all of it, just the least scary aspects—temporary financial embarassment and like that—she offered, listen to this, Evie, she offered me $200 secretly saved up from all her sons' regular weekly donations. I had to refuse, considering that *one* of her sons is not going to be making that regular weekly donation for a while.

EVE: You mother is a good woman.

JESSE: Yeah. Rosie Rothman is O.K.

EVE: (*Looks at her watch.*) Five to twelve. I'll run the two blocks. Susie gets anxious if I'm late.

JESSE: And remember, hold the fort. All will be well. (*They embrace. Eve runs out.*) See you soon. (*He goes to*

the phone with paper, dials a number.) Hello?… I'm calling in reference to the ad you ran in this morning's *Herald-Tribune*. Has that job been filled yet?… Oh good. Yes, I would be very interested… Yes, I have quite a bit of experience. Five years besides three in the Army Signal Corps. There I was chief inspector on transmitters… Oh sure, I've got all the certificates and documents necessary… Well, I haven't been working for anybody else. I had my own shop… Well, there was an illness in the family and I couldn't give it my full attention and so the accounts dropped off. You know how it is with a small shop… The name? Liberty Radio Parts… Mine? Jesse Rothman… You know me? I don't ever recall… Oh, I see… Yeah, I understand… Sure, sure, business is business… Yes, indeed, we all have our families to care for… Thanks for your good wishes. Goodbye. (*He hangs up, turns a page in the newspaper, another marked area, dials a number.*) Hello… I'm calling in reference to your ad in this morning's *Herald-Tribune*. Thank you… Yes, I'd like to ask a few questions. First of all, how long is the training period?… I see… And what's the salary during this time … That's not very much, is it?… No, I never sold insurance before… Well, I'm sure you're right. I'm sure there is a large, waiting market out there… Well, I might try it. Would that be the address that's in the ad? (*Doorbell rings. He calls to offstage.*) Just a minute. (*Then back to the phone*). Third floor, Suite Two. (*He writes it down hurriedly.*) Yes, I got it… My name? How come you want my name?… Oh, that's nice. Everybody likes to be welcomed… It's Rothman. R-O-T-H-M-A-N. Correct… First name?… um… Joseph… And thank you. Goodbye. (*He hangs up, throws down pencil and newspaper, then walks offstage to open front door. A moment of silence. Then Jesse slowly backs into living room, hands up, horror written all over his face.*) Who are you? What do you want?

THE PUBLIC BURNING

ROBERT COOVER

Fig. 36. Janet Wallerstein Winston, *Execution I*, 1986, acrylic and pencil, 19 x 19".

Robert Coover's novel *The Public Burning* is a savage political fantasia. It attempts to re-create the political maelstrom swirling around America during the McCarthy era. It is a highly controversial book, with a crazily plausible Richard Nixon as narrator, and the Rosenbergs's execution set as a Times Square spectacle directed by Cecil B. De-Mille.

It took more than two years and three publishers before *The Public Burning* (originally titled *The Public Burning of Julius and Ethel Rosenberg—An Historical Romance*) was finally published by Viking Press in 1977, but even then things didn't go smoothly.

Although he was familiar with the Rosenberg case, it was only while teaching at Bard College in 1966 that Coover was struck with the idea of writing about it. By accident, Coover came across John Wexley's 1955 account, *The Judgment of Julius and Ethel Rosenberg*, and was surprised that his colleagues and students had no memories of the case despite it then being only 13 years old. Except for those who worked to save the Rosenbergs, at the time Coover believed the case was an "absolutely forgotten moment, erased from the tribal memory."

Initially, he conceived of the story as theatre—re-creating a public burning in Times Square with Uncle Sam as master of ceremonies. "The piece was a sort of a Happening, very much influenced by the street theatre of the times . . . a whole circus event originally, with high wire acts," Coover remembered. By 1969, though, after three years of research, the story evolved into a novel.

In looking for a narrator, Coover sought a character close to, but not a central player in, the Rosenberg drama, and considered both the warden and the executioner at Sing Sing. But after Richard Nixon was elected president in 1968, Coover knew the zealous Fifties Commie-hunter and Eisenhower vice president would be perfect for the job.

The book passed from Dutton to Knopf, before Viking finally published it. Knopf monkeyed around with it the longest, hiring an army of lawyers to read the manuscript and fearing a lawsuit from former President Nixon, among others. (They even went so far as to convene a panel of outside lawyers, including the dean of the Columbia Law School.)

Once Viking agreed to publish it, Coover's troubles were still not over. The publisher's lawyer wanted major changes in the manuscript, including removing all living characters, a change Coover refused to make. Eventually, he had to hire his own lawyer. "I didn't make any money on the book," Coover says. "I spent it all on legal fees, just getting it into print."

Remarkably, 70,000 copies *were* printed, a large run for the highly respected but not widely read author. Viking, recognizing the possibility that a relative or an actual living character in the book might seek an injunction to halt its release, wisely sent out bookstore copies a month before the scheduled publication date.

Once the book hit the stores, reaction was immediate and intense. Although it was well received in many quarters, reviewers on the right slammed it hard, more for its politics than for its literary merit. Syndicated columnist George Will played book critic with a vicious attack, describing the novel as "a violation of the ethics of literature," a comment which darkly hints at censorship. (A few years later, Will would try his hand at film criticism, using his column to lambaste the movie version of E. L. Doctorow's *The Book of Daniel*).

Despite, or perhaps because of the furor, the book made it onto the *New York Times* best-sellers list for a week before Viking unceremoniously pulled all the publicity. It was an act of self-censorship that still rankles, Coover recalled. The Bantam paperback edition had a short shelf life, too, and was shredded after two months.

Nevertheless, the book was particularly well received overseas. In Britain, Penguin published a successful edition, which, like the American edition, is out of print. As of today, *The Public Burning* is available only in French and German.

However, English-language readers may again have an opportunity to read the novel—without having to go to the library or used bookstore—since Coover says he is considering a revised version, a little faster-paced and a little shorter. In the meantime, here are excerpts from the original edition.

—R.O.

Groun'-Hog Hunt

On June 24,1950, less than five years after the end of World War II, the Korean War begins, American boys are again sent off in uniforms to die for Liberty, and a few weeks later, two New York City Jews, Julius and Ethel Rosenberg, are arrested by the FBI and charged with having conspired to steal atomic secrets and pass them to the Russians. They are tried, found guilty, and on April 5, 1951, sentenced by the judge to die— thieves of light to be burned by light—in the electric chair, for it is written that "any man who is dominated by demonic spirits to the extent that he gives voice to apostasy is to be subject to the judgment upon sorcerers and wizards." Then, after the usual series of permissible sophistries, the various delaying moves and light-restoring countermoves, their fate—as the U.S. Supreme Court refuses for the sixth and last time to hear the case, locks its doors, and goes off on holiday—is at last sealed, and it is determined to burn them in New York City's Times Square on the night of their fourteenth wedding anniversary, Thursday, June 18, 1953.

There are reasons for this: theatrical, political, whimsical. It is thought that such an event might provoke open confessions: the Rosenbergs, until now tight-lipped and unrepentant, might at last, once on stage and the lights up, perceive their national role and fulfill it, freeing themselves before their deaths from the Phantom's dark mysterious power, unburdening themselves for the people, and might thereby bring others as well—to the altar, as it were—to cleanse their souls of the Phantom's taint. Many believe, moreover, that such a communal pageant is just what the troubled nation needs right now to renew its sinking spirit. Something archetypal, tragic, exemplary. Things have not been so good since the new war began—especially since the Chinese Reds came swarming across the Yalu and put our boys to rout— there's a need for distractions, and who knows? done right, it could bring a new excitement into the world, lift hearts, get things moving again, maybe even bring victory to the Free Peoples of Asia, courage to the rioting workers in enslaved Eastern Europe, fertility and tax reductions to the nation, all this is possible. And though the delays in the courts have at times perhaps been worrying, it is all coming together now in this time and place like magic. Fourteen, after all, symbolized fusion and organization, justice and temperament; the City is this year celebrating the tercentenary of its own founding as New Amsterdam, its axis the Times Tower is in its Silver Anniversary year, and the Statue of Liberty—Our Lady of the Harbor, Refuge of the Destitute, Ark of the Covenant, Regina Coeli, Mother Full of Goodness, Star of the Sea and Gem of the Ocean—is sixty-nine; Times Square itself is an American holy place long associated with festivals of rebirth; and spring is still in the air. It is even hoped that a fierce public exorcism right now might flush the Phantom from his underground cells, force him to materialize, show himself plainly in the honest electrical glow of an all-American night-on-the-town, give Uncle Sam something to swing at besides a lot of remote gooks.

Weeks before, the designated area is cordoned off with police barricades and a stage is erected at the intersection of Broadway and Seventh Avenue on top of the information kiosk. This stage is built to simulate the Death House at Sing Sing, its walls whitewashed and glaringly lit, furnished simply with the old oaken electric chair, cables and heating pipes, a fire extinguisher, a mop and bucket for cleaning up the involuntary evacuations of the victims, and a trolley for carting the corpses off. The switch is visible through an open door, stage right, illuminated by a hanging spot. Other elegantly paneled doors, right, exit off to press and autopsy rooms, and upstage left another door leads in from the "Last Mile," or "Dance Hall." Over this entry, which the Rosenbergs will use, a sign is tacked up that reads: SILENCE. Details from the set of the Warden's Office in *The Valiant,* a one-act melodrama by Holworthy Hall (*pseud.*) and Robert Middlemass about a condemned man wrongly accused, produced in the early thirties by the Clark House Players on the Lower East Side and featuring starry-eyed sixteen-year old Ethel Greenglass, are incorporated (a telephone instrument, a row of electric bell buttons, a bundle of forty or fifty letters, etc.), partly to make Ethel feel more at home, partly to impress upon her the ironies of her situation, partly just to surprise her with a little jolt of déjà vu.

Special seating sections are set up out front, camera platforms are built, backstage VIP passageways, wedding altars, sideshows, special light and sound systems. The streets funneling into Times Square are hung with bunting (the Square is not a square at all, of course, and from above the decorated area looks a little like a red-white-and-blue Star of David); traffic is rerouted so as to cause maximum congestion and rage; a solid belt of fury at the periphery being an essential liturgical complement to the melting calm at the center; and billboards and theater marquees, the principal topographical feature of the district, are consecrated to the display of homespun American wisdom:

EVERY MAN MUST CARRY HIS OWN HIDE TO THE TANNER

OUR LIVES ARE MERELY STRANGE DARK INTERLUDES IN THE ELECTRICAL DISPLAY OF GOD THE FATHER!

AMERICA THE HOPE OF THE WORLD

NICE GUYS FINISH LAST

THREE MAY KEEP A SECRET IF TWO OF THEM ARE DEAD

An Entertainment Committee is appointed, chairmanned by Cecil B. De Mille, whose latest success was last year's Oscar-winning *Greatest Show on Earth,* with assistance from Sol Hurok, Dan Topping, Bernard Baruch, the AEC and Betty Crocker, Conrad Hilton, whose Albuquerque hotel figured prominently in the persecution's case against the Rosenbergs, Sam Goldwyn and Walt Disney, Ed Sullivan, the director of the Mormon Tabernacle Choir, the various chiefs of staff, Sing Sing Warden Wilfred Denno, the Holy Six, and many more. They audition vocalists, disk jockeys, preachers, and stand-up comics, view rushes of Uncle Sam's new documentary on the two little Rosenberg boys intended as a back projection for the burnings, commission Oliver Allstorm and His Pentagon Patriots to compose a special pageant theme song, assign a task force of experienced sachems to work up a few spontaneous demonstrations, and hire a Texas high-school marching band to play "One Fine Day" from *Madame Butterfly,* "The Anniversary Waltz," and the theme from *High Noon,* said to be a particular favorite these days of President Eisenhower. The President, just back from a week of moralizing and whoopee in the Badlands and Oyster Bay, has been visited at the White House this week by the Singing Cowboy Gene Autry, and Gene has been invited to render "When It's Twilight on the Trail" and "Back in the Saddle Again" at the electrocutions. TIME , the National Poet Laureate, celebrating this spring his own thirtieth birthday, is asked by the Committee to read a commemorative poem, an American middleweight championship bout between Bobo Olson and Paddy Young is appended to the program, and someone hires Harry James and His Orchestra to play overhead on the Astor Roof. Efforts are made to rush through a new ordinance allowing the sale of liquor in city theatres, and thus by extension in Times Square on Thursday night. The weather has turned hot, and in such a pack-up it will help if there's something with which to wet the whistle. As the day draws near, a massive contingent of New York State Troopers is dispatched to Ossining to relieve the 290 overworked prison police now guarding the Rosenbergs and to escort the atom spies to the city—and all of the other principals in the case are to be brought here as well: the Judge and jury, prosecution team and witnesses, including Ethel Rosenberg's kid brother David Greenglass, the Los Alamos soldier whose self-incriminating evidence almost single-handedly brought about the convictions of Ethel and her husband and got them condemned to the electric chair. This chair, now looming stark and fearful on the Times Square stage, is the singular responsibility of State Executioner Joseph P. Francel, World War I veteran and Cairo, New York electrician. Francel, who was badly gassed in the war, is a professional who has hastened hundreds of malefactors to their deaths—in fact, he is celebrating his own fourteenth anniversary this year as Sing Sing Executioner, having first been appointed on Columbus Day, 1939, and will receive a bonus $300 for this double bill. All of this is taken as a good omen.

Deep in the inner sanctum of the Federal Bureau of Investigation, high up on the fifth floor, J. Edgar Hoover, the world's most famous policeman, lost for a moment in reverie and congratulatory telegrams (he is this year celebrating his Silver Anniversary as America's Top Cop, his career being contemporaneous with that of Mickey Mouse), jumps clean out of his chair. What? What! He stumbles about confusedly, scattering dossiers, old $2 betting stubs, and comic books depicting his own life saga every which way. Holy Moley! This is terrible! His heart is palpitating, his florid face is splotchy, his trigger finger has gone cold and limp as a wet noodle. It's times like these when John Edgar Hoover of the FBI wishes his mother were still alive. Of course it's a spy ring, has to be, it always is. I *mean*, there's only one secret, isn't there? We had it, now they've got it, it's that simple. He's been warning them this would happen since 1937. The enemy within. Now, just look! Jumping Jehosaphat! And if they could penetrate Los Alamos, they could penetrate Congress or the White House, or even—he pushes the thought out of his mind and, glancing edgily over his shoulder, scrambles frantically for the intercom buttons. Goodness! he's all thumbs! This is worse than the day he tried to put the cuffs on Old Creepy Karpis! He whacks the intercom with his thick fists and cries: "The secret of the atom bomb has been stolen! Mobilize every resource! Find the thieves!"

With Uncle Sam at Burning Tree

I was sitting on the floor of my inner office, surrounded by every scrap of information I could find on the Rosenberg case, feeling scruffy and tired, dejected, lost in a surfeit of detail and further from a final position on the issue than ever, when the bell on my clock rang twice for a quorum call. it was late, goddam late, I thought Lyndon Johnson had long since given up. I desperately wanted to get rid of this atom-spy affair and go home—if I left the damned thing now, I'd just have to come back, and then where would it end? Why the devil had Uncle Sam got me into this?

Fig. 37. Mark Yankus, *Untitled*, 1984, photo collage, 8 x 8".

Just to convince me of the enormity of their crime? But I was already convinced. How many Americans had died and would die because of what they had done? Would the Reds have dared invade South Korea, rape Czechoslovakia, support the Vietminh and Malayan guerrillas, suppress the freedom-hungry East German workers, if the Rosenbergs had not given them the Bomb? We were headed, truly into a new Era of Peace after World War II, our possession of the ultimate weapon and our traditional American gift for self-sacrifice would have ensured that—and we might even have helped our friend Chiang return to the Chinese mainland where he belonged, loosened things up a little inside Russia to boot—but the Rosenbergs upset all that. When the Russians tested their first A-bomb in 1949, I was one of the first to hit at Truman's

failure to act against Red spies in the United States. And then when they got Fuchs in England in 1950, I called for a full congressional investigation of atomic espionage to find out who may have worked with Fuchs in this country—I moved quickly, caught most Congressmen napping, got most of the headlines. And deserved them. No, Dick Nixon knew what was going on all right, and was quick to say so, that's how I beat that fancypants movie star for Senator that year, and even though finally I didn't have all that much to do with the Rosenberg case itself, I always felt that—indirectly anyway—it was my baby.

All the more so when you considered that it was my successful pursuit of Alger Hiss which had given courage and incentive to the entire nation, made Communism a real issue, restored the dignity and prestige of HUAC, changed the very course of America and the Free World, and ultimately had made these electrocutions possible. In Whittaker Chambers's new best-seller *Witness*, he wrote: "On a scale personal enough to be felt by all, but big enough to be symbolic, the two irreconcilable faiths of our time—Communism and Freedom—came to grips in the persons of two conscious and resolute men . . . Both knew, almost from the beginning, that the Great Case could end only in the destruction of one or both of the contending figures, just as the history of our times . . . can end only in the destruction of one or both of the contending forces!" And hadn't I been the catalyst that gave Whittaker and the Free World victory? To hell with your goddamned "McCarthy Era"! *I'm* the one!

President Eisenhower, of course, has long insisted that "the church, with its testimony of the existence of an Almighty God is the last thing that it seems to me, would be preaching, teaching, or tolerating Communism," but even the President is said to be taking a hard second look this morning. For a starter, the Chief has turned over to Edgar Hoover's G-men the names of 2300 clergymen who signed a "special plea for clemency for the Rosenbergs," as well as the list of 104 signatories to a follow-up letter, taken to be the hard-core Comsymp preachers. "The Rosenberg campaign," warns Harold Velde's Early Warning Sentinels, has "afforded the Communist conspiracy a momentous opportunity to remount a long-planned invasion of the churches of America!" FBI undercover mystery man Herbert Philbrick thinks many of the 2300 are dupes, "unsuspecting victims" sucked in by the wily Angels of Darkness at the center, but turncoat Joe Zack Kornfeder, former bigwig in the American Communist Politburo, disagrees:

REP. GORDON SCHERER, OHIO: Among those two thousand ministers were, however, some just idealists and pacifists, were there not?

JOE ZACK KORNFEDER: I do not think so. I think that those two thousand were pretty close to the machine.

Demonstrators, moving past the White House this morning toward the Supreme Court, are actually carrying blow-up posters of the Son of God Himself, with the text:

REWARD

—For information leading to the apprehension of Jesus Christ . . .
Wanted—for Sedition, Criminal Anarchy, Vagrancy, and Conspiracy to overthrow the established Government . . .
Dresses poorly . . . has visionary ideas, associates with common working people, the unemployed and bums . . . Alien—believed to be a Jew . . . Red Beard, marks on hands and feet, the

> To hell with your goddamned "McCarthy Era"! *I'm* the one!

result of injuries inflicted by an angry mob led by respectable citizens and legal authorities.

I had always had this instinct, I always knew who had it, whether at school, in downtown Whittier, or in Washington. I learned right away to talk things over with Dr. Dexter, president of the college, and Dean Horack at Duke, with Herman Perry, manager of the Bank of America in Whittier, with Herbert Hoover and Murray Chotiner, Karl Mundt and Christian Herter, Tom Dewey, Foster Dulles and his brother—there was a certain vibration they had, and I always felt it. And who was Julie Rosenberg hanging out with? Losers like Morton Sobell and Max Elitcher and William Perl and Joel Barr. Collecting money for the Reds in the Spanish Civil War and signatures for the Scottsboro boys. Organizing the Stu-

dents' Strike for Peace. Instead of telling his deans and teachers how much he admired them, he insulted them. A great deal of time during the trial two years ago had been spent on describing the Rosenbergs' adolescent activities, what was termed their "premature anti-fascism." The defense objected, but this was demonstrably relevant, not to show "motivation," as Judge Kaufman allowed, but to reveal the hidden patterns of developing heresy.

The first thing I did when I went to Whittier College was help found a new fraternity, the Orthogonians (actually, we called ourselves the "Square Shooters"), which was a kind of bridge between the old-line Franklins with their fancy-dress rules and right-wing pride, and the more open but disorganized and apathetic independent students. Athletes mostly, Chief Newman's boys, but we ran the politics and social scene as well. We met once a month down at Sanders' cafe for our traditional symbolic meal, or sometimes I took the whole fraternity to Grandma's house, and she and Mom fixed the beans and spaghetti. I was always generous like this. The Square Shooters was a real fraternity, all right, with all the usual, hoopla, horseplay—I'll never forget our christening ceremonies at a Wednesday-morning chapel service when Sheik Homan tried to break a bottle of Old Taylor over my head!—and campus politicking, but we were also innovators. True, we had "secret" symbols—a boar's head and a square with "Beans, Brawn, Brains, and Bowels" as the four corners—and mottoes and special handshakes and I even composed a chapter song: "All hail the mighty boar, Our patron beast is he!" But at the same time, we got rid of the evening dress, fought against exclusivity, even initiated a Negro football star, shocked the whole campus with our risqué vaudeville skits and plays, most of which I wrote, and made a virtue of being a good guy instead of a rich guy. I've been making bridges like that between tradition and innovation ever since. In a very real sense, Julius Rosenberg was going to the electric chair because he went to City College of New

York and joined the American Students Union when he was sixteen. If he'd come to Whittier instead and joined my Square Shooters, worn slouch sweaters and open collars with the rest of us, it wouldn't be happening. Simple as that.

Tricia and Julie were running up and down the stairs screaming, and I could hear Pat calling them down to the table. Breakfast was cooking. I had expected an upset stomach this morning, but instead I was simply hungry. I hoped that Pat grasped the fact that I was in a major crisis and was fixing corned beef hash for me with an egg on it. That I hadn't come to bed all night, that I'd slept with my clothes on the living-room sofa, should be enough of a clue. Probably not, though. She could be pretty insensitive.

I discovered, inspecting my face closely, that I'd somehow missed a patch of beard under my chin. Still not as alert as I ought to be. Hard to focus. I hadn't completely shaken off all that happened last night. I had awakened with an erection, for example—luckily, Pat had come down to call me before the girls had seen it—and it still hadn't gone away. I plugged in the razor again, grimacing at my face. Well, TIME's right, I admitted, lifting my "fat cheeks" and staring down past my "duck-bill nose," it's true, I'm no goddamn Millard Fillmore. But then, what the hell, neither was Abe Lincoln. Once, a little girl came up to me with a newsmagazine photograph to sign. After I'd autographed it, she thanked me and said: "It's an awfully good picture. It doesn't look like you at all." I wondered afterwards if someone had put her up to it. But people have often registered an odd kind of surprise on first meeting me face-to-face. They tend to stare at my nose as though measuring its breadth, lost there and unable to find my eyes again. So, all right, I've often said that there wasn't much that could be done with my face. In that regard I'm my own severest critic: it isn't perfect; it's never going to be.

Cartoonists had had a heyday with it. Not even Julie Rosenberg, who had a genuinely sinister mug, right down to the weak chin, pointed nose, and pen-

cil-line moustache, had had to take the kind of punishment I'd received every week from Herblock and the others. Picasso had actually made the sonuvabitch look handsome, very Anglo-Saxon, where Herblock always showed me as a jowly, wavy-haired, narrow-eyed tough, linked usually with McCarthy and Jenner, and with suggestions of some bad odor about me, like a little boy who'd just filled his pants or something. He hadn't given any of us a day's rest since we came into office back in January, you'd think we were invading Mongol hordes or something, instead of fellow Americans. His cartoon Ike looked a lot like Jiggs from "Bringing Up Father," only daffier, he drew Herb Brownell like a kind of Dracula, and Joe McCarthy was shown as a sweaty, hairy, cleaver-wielding tramp. I don't know about these other guys, but cartoonists

> Picasso had actually made the sonuvabitch look handsome, very Anglo-Saxon.

had alays had fun with my face. Already back at Whittier College, they were happily nailing me with a few harsh lines: a solid black bar for eyebrows (no eyes), a stretched ski-slope S for a nose, a small sour turndown comma for a mouth encompassed by curly black hair cut square, little parenthetical ears, meat-platter cheeks, and a stiff neck—just three mean marks and a dark frame. I didn't mind. It was one of the consequences of power. If not a condition: maybe politicians needed faces like that to become recognizable. Something to set you apart: people respected the almost magical force emanating from archetypes, no matter what sort, or who put them there. Or maybe the caricature came first and the face followed.

"What's that, John?" I asked.
"I said, there's supposed to be twelve

thousand of them here today, Mr. Nixon," my chauffeur said.

I realized we'd been slowed to a crawl, and there was a terrific traffic jam up ahead of us around Dupont Circle. I clutched my newspaper. "Twelve thousand what?"

"Demonstrators. You know, the atom spies . . . "

I saw them now, moving down Connecticut toward the White House. "Can't we—can't we do something—?"

"I can try to cut north up toward Howard University, then down Capitol . . . "

Howard was a Negro university and there were a lot of those people in the pro-Rosenberg movement. I felt a sudden twinge of distrust: was John leading me into a trap? "We don't have time to go to the office now," I snapped. "We'd better get straight to the White House!"

"Yessir. I'll try to cut down to the Mall."

But at Washington Circle on Pennsylvania, seven blocks from the White House, there was no movement at all: a solid mass of traffic, people, placards, and photographers. John swerved left, and left again, but all the cars were bumper to bumper, and people were running back and forth in the streets. I was nervous, so I decided to distract myself by working the Times crossword puzzle. I found it on a back page, nested among book ads. My eye fell on the first clue, 1 Across: That's easy, I thought with a shudder: GOOF. I suddenly saw the puzzle as a kind of matrix, a field of play which mirrored the structure of the newspaper and thus history itself, the paradigmatic range of "news" and possibility, crossed with real "time-arrow chain-of-events," I felt like Alice lost on her chessboard. I read the clues: why all this business about plays, food, cartoonists, rats, God, women, and cosmetics, I wondered? AHAB was there, SAN ANTONIO, NEGRO, and ROAMERS. 23 Down: HEAT. I dragged my eyes away from the crossword puzzle to the book review: it was about an "atomic thriller," Atom at Spithead. Even before I saw it, I knew it would be something like this. Adlai Stevenson's Campaign Speeches were being advertised, and a novel called The Singer Not the Song: "He could not resist using the girl as one last diabolic weapon..." From all over the page, words jumped out at me: S O C I A L I S M ... B U C H E N W A L D ... EISENHOWER ... FRANKENSTEIN ... BLOOD ... TENEMENT ... REVOLUTION ... CHECKMATE— we were stopped dead. "I'll walk, John! I cried. I ripped the crossword puzzle out and stuffed it in my pocket, jumped out of the limosine.

Once on foot, I found it much easier to keep moving. Not so many people as it had seemed inside the car. Just enough, together with the sightseers, to bottle up traffic at the intersections and make it seem worse than it was. It also helped that they were mostly moving in the same direction. At first, I supposed they were headed for the White House, and I decided to circle around behind them, past the Treasury and in by the East Wing, but once I reached the back of Lafayette Square, I could see they were all moving on east. It took me a panicky moment to realize that their objective was not my Senate Office Building, but only the Supreme Court. But though I felt relieved by that, I had to recognize that the worst, nevertheless, was still before me: crossing the park and Pennsylvania Avenue through all this lawless rabble to the White House gates. I began to regret leaping out of the car so impulsively like that.

A mob, you see, does not act intelligently. Those who make up a mob do not think independently. They do not think rationally. They are likely to do irrational things, including even turning on their leaders. Individually, people in a mob are cowardly; only collectively, goaded on by a leader, will a mob appear to act courageously. A mob is bloodthirsty. A taste of blood will whet its appetite for more violence and for more blood. Nothing must be done which will tend to accentuate these characteristics. A mob has lost its temper collectively. An individual dealing with a mob must never lose his or he will be reduced to its level, and become easy prey for it. He must be as cold in his emotions as a mob is hot, as controlled as the mob is uncontrolled, concentrating entirely on the problem which faces him and forgetting about himself, keyed up for battle but not jit-

tery. Since those who make up a mob are basically cowards, one must never show fear in the face of a mob, blocking out any thought of it by a conscious act of will. Since a mob is stupid, it's important to confront it with unexpected maneuvers: take the offensive, don't panic, do the unexpected, but do nothing rash. I knew all this. Nevertheless, I was scared shitless and could hardly think.

Intuitively, I just kept moving. I put the U.S. Chamber of Commerce at my back like a big brother and plunged straight ahead into the park and toward the White House. I saw it, I knew it immediately: this crowd is all unfriendly— the Phantom has touched them, I thought, he's invaded them, they're all contaminated, we will have to liberate them all, as we've done with the Rosenbergs. I kept my head ducked and bulled hopefully ahead—so far they hadn't noticed me. Just a block, that damned square, but it seemed endless—I felt like I was crossing all of Gettysburg. I prayed to God to get me through safely. I prayed to Uncle Sam, I prayed to Pat. "In the name of Jesus Christ!" I whistled softly between my clenched teeth. What troubled me most was the complete unreasoning hate in their faces: this mob, I recognized, is a killer mob! I suspected some of them were even doped up, and I feared that, if they saw who I was, they'd get out of hand. They carried placards, shouted, and seemed to be picking up things they might throw. It made me almost physically ill to see the fanatical frenzy in the eyes of those teenagers; anyway, something was making me quite ill. I felt absolute hatred for the tough Communist agitators who were driving children to this irrational state, and I wanted to shout at them, or scream, or bite them or something, but somehow I kept a grip on myself, knowing that above all I had to control my emotions and think calmly. The test of leadership is whether one has the ability, as Kipling said, to keep his head while others are losing theirs. By this time, I was virtually running, shoulders hunched like a fullback, snorting desperately.

I slowed. I noticed I was drawing a lot of attention. I worried I might have a

heart attack. Or some other kind of seizure, I could hardly breathe. The mob turned toward me and started to close in. It was essential, I knew, that I bust right through: if I turned back now, it would not be simply a case of their bluffing out Richard Nixon, but of the United States itself putting its tail between its legs and running away from a gang of Communist thugs. For an instant, the realization passed through my mind: *I might be killed!*— and then it was gone, mind and all. They were nearly on me. I stopped abruptly. Then I lurched forward. Everybody must have been surprised: as I plunged on, straight at them amazed at my own impetus, the mob stumbled backwards. In a larger sense, I recognized, this was another round in a contest which has been waged from the beginning of time between those who believe in the right of free expression and those who advocate and practice mob rule to deny that right. I might have calmed myself with such a thought, but there was no time—one of the ringleaders, a typical case-hardened Communist operative, stepped into my path, blocking me off, a look of cold hatred in his eyes. And I realized then, as this was going on, that right here was the ruthlessness and the determination, the fanaticism of the enemy we faced! That was what I saw in his face. This was Communism as it really is. He opened his mouth—I felt like I was back in the lion's cage with Sheba. *Oh my God—!*

"Excuse me, Mr. Nixon," he said, the rest closing up behind, forcing me to pull up short. "Could I have your autograph?"

"What?" I shouted. This startled them and they fell back a step. I noticed for the first time that the placards they were carrying read DEATH TO THE JEWISH TRAITORS! and THE HOT SEAT FOR THE ROSENBERGS—SIZZLE 'EM! It came to me then that this was my own constituency. The range and scope of this crisis began to fall into a pattern. *"Can you have my autograph?"* I yelped, repeating his question to give myself time to think, and also, hopefully, to stop my hands from shaking. I groped for words, for a phrase, something tough and pun-

gent I could exit on. I wanted to do more than simply mouth prepared platitudes, but my mind was completely locked up, like the traffic around Washington Circle. All I could think of was: everyone in politics knows a Vice President cannot chart his own course, it's not my fault! They stared at me, somewhat amazed. A young college boy with a friendly smile was carrying a big picture of the electric chair with the legend HOME COOKING, KOSHER STYLE!, and I saw a priest with a sign that read THE ROSENBERGS ARE MORTAL ENEMIES OF THE ENTIRE HUMAN RACE! I realized it was going to be another hot day. I was sweating like a stoat. "The issue is not whether or not I can give you my autograph," I said at last, leaning toward them as a coach would lean toward his players in a huddle, *"but rather the survival of the nation itself!"* I gazed at them with a very heavy look, and the few who were still smiling went blank, their jaws dropping. For a fraction of a second there, I gave them all a sense of what it felt like to be at the center of things, drew them all into the High Councils of Power, showed them a glimpse of the brink and its peril. Then I smiled, nodded, clapped a shoulder, waved to someone at the back as though recognizing him, and lunged on through. They parted in astonishment. This has been very successful, I thought.

Except for the mounted U.S. Park Police, some parked buses, and a couple of lonely Red Top cabs that had managed somehow to get through the traffic jam further up the street, Pennsylvania was empty as I crossed it. A long way across, and I felt very self-conscious. Then, off to my right I saw them: the real demonstrators, marching toward me, seven abreast, down Pennsylvania, headed toward the Supreme Court. What now? I wondered, freezing in my tracks: should I stop and confront them?—and nearly got run down by a trolley car whistling up from behind. Jesus, I thought, picking myself up and scrambling on across the goddamn street, this is going to be one helluva day. At the White House gates, still hurrying forward, I looked back over my shoulder at the crowd in Lafayette

Square thinking: you've got to be careful in a situation like that, you have to think all those things through—and plowed into a child standing there on the sidewalk. I glanced around. Luckily, no photographers had seen this. I set the boy back on his feet, brushed him off, skinny little kid, about the age of my daughters, with big dark eyes and baggy pants. Like the waifs out of those Horatio Alger novels. Very intense and even, somehow, mysterious. I'd given him a thumping whack and he wasn't even crying. He looked up at me as though he were lost, as though looking for a friend or a father, and I thought: he's beautiful, this child! He reminded me of all those March of Dimes posters. I wanted to hug him to my breast, to protect him from all this, to kiss him, I wanted to reach into my pocket and give him something. "Don't be afraid, son," I whispered. His nose was running. I wiped it with my own handkerchief. "It's all right." He gazed up at me with those soulful eyes, parting his small lips—I *know* this child, I thought. As though from a dream, a beautiful dream. I seemed to recall green hills, a rippling brook, a rustic cabin, and inside—and then I realized who it was he looked like. I pushed him away in alarm, wiped my hands nervously on my pants, and, shuddering, hurried on through the White House gates. That haunting face: it belonged to Ethel Rosenberg.

At home meanwhile, the President's Cabinet has been called into morning session, the Sing Sing prison officials and Times Square program committees have been put on alert, the Nine Old Men have arrived at the Supreme Court. The Senate, not to miss any of the action, is in recess today, but the House of Representatives is heavily engaged upon major legislation, and the situation there is reported to be "one of anxiety and suspense." Between votes, Congressmen spend a lot of time at their phones. At the White House, queues of visitors are already forming up, waiting for the doors to open, and the guards are jittery: almost ten thousand tourists out here this morning, what if just one of them—? "Simple duty hath no place for

the twitters!" Uncle Sam admonishes them in firm Quaker cadences, watching the Vice President squirt across Pennsylvania Avenue from Lafayette Square out of the corner of his eye. "Chins out, chests up, lads, discipline is the soul of an army, and if any strange fruit attempts to haul down the American flag, shoot him on the spot!" He grins thoughtfully to himself as the Veep bowls over a little kid; then he ducks into the White House through a back entrance, meditating on Moe the necktie-peddler's observation in *Pickup on South Street:* "He's as shifty as smoke, but I still love him."

At the Supreme Court, Chief Justice Fred Vinson takes his seat under the clock in front of the tall Grecian columns and red plush curtains, hastens perfunctorily through the opening rituals, and announces abruptly: "We think the question is not substantial. We think further proceedings to litigate it are unwarranted. Accordingly, we vacate the stay entered by Mr. Justice Douglas on June 17, 1953!"

There's a moment of shocked silence in the packed courtroom—it's come so fast it's caught everyone by surprise, some still haven't taken their seats—then a burst of cheers and boos. The defense attorneys, dark with anger, leap from their chairs, tipping them over, scramble toward the bench—but Justice Robert Jackson objects to the "irregular manner" in which the new lawyers have entered the case, and they are ordered to carry on their unpleasantries elsewhere. Justice Tom Clark notes that the Court has now considered this case seven times, and a moment of awe grips the courtroom— *the seventh occasion!*

But Justice Hugo Black, dissenting from the 6-to-2 majority opinion and doubting the Court even had the right to vacate the stay of a fellow Justice in the first place (". . . so far as I can tell, the Court's action here is unprecedented . . ."), argues crabbily that "it is not amiss to point out that this Court has never affirmed the fairness of the trial!" There he goes again. "What," the people mutter, "is Black and white and Red all over?"

Justice William Douglas, facing possible impeachment, insists bluntly that "the cold truth is that the death sentence may not be imposed for what the Rosenbergs did unless the jury so recommends," but before he's even had a chance to get it all out, Manny Bloch is on his feet, asking for more time to rewrite the clemency appeal, arguing that the doubts of three Justices (Frankfurter has snuck out unnoticed for the time being) is "a matter which is appropriate for consideration on a petition of mercy." He's wearing a brand-new suit, having dumped coffee on his old one this morning: no peace, saith the Lord, unto the wicked.

U.S. Acting Solicitor General Bob Stern snorts at this argument, but Justice Black, cantankerous as ever, points out that clemency from the President is all but pleaded for in the majority opinion itself, which says plainly: "Vacating this stay is not to be construed as endorsing the wisdom or appropriateness to this case of a death sentence." Stern, who is as aware as Black is that this is a mere protective maneuver by the Court to avoid any hint or complaint of error, says flatly that no more time is needed, and the Court, thinking about this for a full fifteen minutes (the stage is built, after all, and this show is ready to go on), agrees. No more delays. Even Douglas caves in now and votes with the majority, leaving Black alone in his bilious dissent.

The spectators, reporters, court buffs rush from the courtroom, spreading the word to the thousands left outside, all of whom now grab up their children and cameras and race to the White House: *It is nearing High Noon, and now President Dwight D. Eisenhower alone stands between the atom spies and death.*

The Cabinet Meeting

Our laughter was interrupted by a messenger from the Supreme Court: all nine Justices had arrived and the Court was sitting. The Attorney General glanced cooly at his watch, then said: "In just a few moments, Chief Justice Vinson is expected to announce that the Supreme Court is vacating Douglas's stay. As soon as possible after that, the President must issue a final denial of clemency, which we've already drafted, and then the Justice Department will follow with its announcement that the Rosenbergs will be executed tomorrow night at the latest."

Someone pointed out that that was the Sabbath.

"We're not going to burn them on Sunday!" the President shouted, rearing up from his doodle, his blue eyes flashing.

"No General, the *Jewish* Sabbath," Herb explained. "These people are Jews."

"Oh, all right, then," said the President.

All of this was just a joke, everybody was just trying to calm down.

The Attorney General pondered the

> "We're not going to burn them on Sunday!" the President shouted. "No General, the *Jewish* Sabbath.... these people are Jews."

problem a moment, then said, "Well, in that case, we'll finish it tonight. We'll set up as soon as the Court stops sitting."

"Before sundown," someone said. "It starts at sundown, their Sabbath."

"Right, sundown. Thanks."

Friday. Sunset. The two thieves. Jews condemned by Jews. Some patterns had been dissolved by the overnight delay, it was true, but others were taking shape. Uncle Sam could not be entirely displeased, I thought. But the President only belched grumpily and shifted in his seat. He said he still didn't understand what the issue in the Supreme Court today was, still didn't see why there had been this delay. If they were guilty, they ought to be punished; if not, let them go. The speech-writer Emmett Hughes, once part of the retinue surrounding the National Poet Laureate, scribbled away, his dark brows bobbing, taking notes on all this for posterity—not what he was being paid to do, but you could spot these parasites a mile away. I supposed, no matter how tight a ship you ran, there'd always be one of these guys slipping in. "I must say, I'm impressed by all the honest doubt about this expressed in the letters I've been seeing," the President said. Was this true, was he really unable to understand so simple a point of law, or was this too part of his disguise? The good soldier, forthright and true, the man of arms too honest to grasp the devious men of letters? Sometimes simple people are more mysterious than those of us who are more complex.

Herb explained once more about the 1917 Espionage Act and the 1946 Atomic Energy Act. As soon as he said that the issue was purely technical, I thought: he's just given it all away, he's just told them Douglas was right. Just as, in a purely technical sense, Don Wheeler was also right in calling for Douglas's impeachment. But I also knew Eisenhower would not realize this, or would not seem to. Was he testing us, I wondered? I recalled his offer—his challenge, rather—to reopen this case at any time before the executions if any one of us believed that to do so would serve the best interests of the United States. Thus, each of us was on the spot....

"Well, the proof of admission there's no frame-up," I said, "is the complete silence of the Phantom-controlled press in the Soviet Union and elsewhere. It's obvious they're expecting the Rosenbergs to confess and they don't want to look like a bunch of clowns. And I'll tell you something else. Morton Sobell's wife said something very recently out in Far Rockaway. She said: "Julius and Ethel could save their own skins by talking, but Julius and Ethel will never betray their friends!" I mean, it's obvious, isn't it?" Of course, I'd got this from a guy who'd got roughed up at that meeting and so was pretty biased, and a right-wing Jew at that, nervous about the anti-Semitism the Rosenbergs could arouse, but that hardly mattered, I understood the essential truth of it and so did everybody else around the table.

Except perhaps the President. He scowled and unwrapped a cigar. "Well, now," he said, "if the Supreme Court decides by, say, five to four or even six to three, as far as the average man's concerned, there *will* be doubt—not just a legal point in his mind." He was himself that average man he was talking about, of course. This was the secret of his success. He really was average, a cheerful unimaginative boy from Abilene, and yet he was also the man who won World War II, so that just showed what an average man could do. So long as he was an American. Uncle Sam always chose his disguises to fit the times.

"Well, who's going to decide these points," Brownell argued, "pressure groups or the Supreme Court? Surely, our first concern is the strength of our courts. And in terms of national security, the Communists are just out to prove they can bring enough pressure, one way or another, to enable people to get away with espionage. I've always wanted you to look at evidence that wasn't usable in court showing the Rosenbergs were the head and center of an espionage ring here in *direct* contact with the Russians—the *prime* espionage ring in the country!"

The President stared blankly at Brownell, then lit his cigar. "My only concern is in the area of statecraft," he said. "The *effect* of the action." He understood: it was as though he hadn't even heard Brownell's offer to look at the secret evidence. If there was any. It was strange that no one questioned Brownell on this, even though nobody had ever seen this material, Eisenhower especially.

In Memoriam: Ethel Rosenberg
For Miriam
Louise Bernikow

After the years wiping china clean
Pouring coffee from your breasts in a flowered dress,
Typing at night—his letters—
Incantation at the typewriter:
Let me be—let me speak—let me be.

After the years of believing more than they
Typing a world no one would read but yourself,
Knowing the melody, singing your way
Through orchards of diapers,
After all that, naturally
He went first
And you heard the current coming
Like the sound of typewriter keys
Like rain
You sang
Incantation in the electric chair
And burned
Like Joan
Slowly,
With your feet on the ground.

Fig. 38. Robert and Michael Meeropol. (Photo: Lionel J-M Delevingne.)

If We Die
Ethel Rosenberg

You shall know, my sons, shall know
why we leave the song unsung,
the book unread, the work undone
to rest beneath the sod.

Mourn no more, my sons, no more
why the lies and smears were framed,
the tears we shed, the hurt we bore
to all shall be proclaimed.

Earth shall smile, my sons, shall smile
and green above our resting place,
the killing end, the world rejoice
in brotherhood and peace.

Work and build, my sons, and build
a monument to love and joy,
to human worth, to faith we kept
for you, my sons, for you.*

Ossining, N.Y., Jan. 24, 1953

*later changed to "for our sons and yours."

CHECKLIST
UNKNOWN SECRETS:
ART AND THE ROSENBERG ERA

Dimensions are given in inches; height precedes width precedes depth.

Kim Abeles
Other (In Memory of Ethel and Julius Rosenberg), 1987
Altered chair, copper, foil, wire, photographs and typewriter
36½ x 25 x 19
Lent by the artist, courtesy Karl Bornstein Gallery, Santa Monica
Plate 35

Dennis Adams
Bus Shelter I, 1983
Photograph
30 x 40
Courtesy Nature Morte Gallery, New York
Plate 50

Dennis Adams
Bus Shelter II, 1986
Photograph
30 x 40
Courtesy Nature Morte Gallery, New York
Plate 51

Victor Arnautoff
In Memoriam, 1953
Oil on canvas
12 x 24
Collection Robert Meeropol
Plate 53

Robert Arneson
2 Fried Commie Jew Spies, 1987
Bronze
11 x 30 x 19
Courtesy Allan Frumkin Gallery, New York
Plate 32

Doug Ashford
April 6, 1951. Room 110, The Federal Court, N.Y., N.Y. and Nine of the Jurors, 1987
Acrylic on ten photographs
Nine parts: 5 x 7; one part: 11 x 14
Overall dimensions variable
Lent by the artist
Plate 25

Karen Atkinson
Era After Era, 1987
Photographs, wood, paint, and transparencies
120 x 108 x 12
Lent by the artist
Plate 29

Gary Bachman
The Eye Never Sees What Flies Into It, 1984
Formica, wood, clock and graphite on paper
Two panels: 24 x 24 x 9 each
Overall: 24 x 54 x 9
Lent by the artist
Plate 17

Rudolf Baranik
Banners, 1953
Oil on canvas
52 x 37
Lent by the artist
Plate 14

Rudolf Baranik
Dictionary of the 24th Century (excerpt), 1987
Photostat
52 x 37
Lent by the artist
Plate 15

Terry Berkowitz
The Children's Hour, 1987
Mixed media with sound
24 x 72 x 24
Lent by the artist
Plate 26

Angel Bracho and Celia Calderon
We Have Not Forgotten the Rosenbergs, 1954
Woodcut
36 x 26
Collection Rob Okun and Deborah Kruger
Plate 6

Chris Bratton
Quiz Show, 1988
Television, videotape, stainless steel, and motor
78 x 24 x 20
Lent by the artist
Plate 57

Luis Camnitzer
The Rosenberg Project, 1986
Mixed media
73 x 34½ x 32
Lent by the artist
Plate 34

Sue Coe
Needs of the State, 1987
Mixed media on paper
91 x 60
Courtesy Sally Baker, New York
Plate 21

Adelyne Cross-Eriksson
American Justice (Save the Rosenberg Couple), 1953
Wood cut
7½ x 5
Collection Rob Okun and Deborah Kruger
Plate 54

Mort Dimondstein
Priming the Witness, 1955
Oil on masonite
18 x 36
Lent by the artist
Plate 5

Fred Ellis
Cold War Warrior, 1952
Pencil on paper
14½ x 11
Collection Ben and Beatrice Goldstein
Plate 8

Ralph Fasanella
McCarthy Era-Gray Day, 1963
Oil on canvas
40 x 70
Lent by the artist
Plate 56

Ralph Fasanella
McCarthy Press, 1963
Oil on canvas
40 x 70
Lent by the artist
Plate 39

Rupert Garcia
Ethel Rosenberg, 1980
Pastel on paper
40 x 30
Lent by the artist, courtesy Iannetti-Lanzone Gallery,
San Francisco
Plate 42

Rupert Garcia
Julius Rosenberg, 1980
Pastel on paper
40 x 30
Lent by the artist, courtesy Iannetti-Lanzone Gallery, San Francisco
Plate 41

Hugo Gellert
Morton Sobell, 1954
Charcoal on paper
8 x 10
Collection Dr. Helen L. Sobell
Plate 11

Hugo Gellert
Embraced by Posterity, 1953
Pencil on paper
22 x 30
Collection Rob Okun and Deborah Kruger
Plate 10

Cook Glassgold
Ethel and Julius Rosenberg: The Atom Spy Hoax, 1979
Acrylic on canvas
36 x 30
Collection Unity Center, New York
Plate 55

Alex Grey
In Memory of Julius and Ethel Rosenberg, 1987
Oil on wood and goat skulls
30 x 26 x 7
Lent by the artist, courtesy Stux Gallery, New York
Plate 27

Marina Gutierrez
Remembering the Rosenbergs, 1987
Acrylic on aluminum with mixed media
50 x 44
Lent by the artist
Plate 22

Jerry Kearns
Capitol Punishment, 1987
Acrylic on canvas
50 x 120
Courtesy Kent Fine Art, New York
Plate 19

Rockwell Kent
Book Burners, 1951
Lithograph
13¾ x 9⅝
Collection Ben and Beatrice Goldstein
Plate 12

Rockwell Kent
The Judgment of Julius and Ethel Rosenbeg, 1955
Woodcut
12 x 16
Collection Dr. Helen L. Sobell
Plate 13

Margia Kramer
Covert Operations, 1987–88
Phototext panels on wood screen with videotape and pamphlet
Overall: 78 x 66 x 66
Lent by the artist. Special thanks to Walter and Miriam Schneir and Marshall Perlin for their help in locating documents; to the MacDowell Colony and Yaddo for their support.
Plate 40

Fernand Léger
Liberty, Peace, Solidarity, 1952
Silkscreen
32 x 30
Collection Robert Meeropol
Plate 33

Leon Marcus
Roy Judas Cohn (Blessed be Thy Holy Name), 1986
Pencil, oil and ink on paper and oak display cabinet
22¾ x 13
Lent by the artist
Plate 30

Leon Marcus
Through the Keyhole, 1954
Oil and crayon on canvas
48 x 36
Collection Ruth and Bert Lessuck
Plate 44

Paul Marcus
The Greatest Show on Earth, 1987
Woodcut
78 x 112
Lent by the artist
Plate 9

Arnold Mesches
The Kiss, 1954
Casein on paper
10 x 3
Lent by the artist, courtesy Jack Shainman Gallery, New York
Plate 16

Arnold Mesches
The Funeral #2, 1955
Oil on Canvas
36 x 24
Collection August and Rena Maymudes
Plate 4

Arnold Mesches
The Judge, 1956
Oil on masonite
24 x 30
Lent by the artist, courtesy Jack Shainman Gallery, New York
Plate 3

Louis Monza
The Couple that Paid, 1953
Oil on canvas
20 x 16
Collection Randall Morris and Shari Cavin Morris
Plate 43

Francisco Mora
Help Stop This Crime, 1952
Woodcut
23½ x 15¾
Collection Rob Okun and Deborah Kruger
Plate 7

Antonio Muntadas
6/19/53, 1987–88
Mixed media
Dimensions variable
Plate 49

Alice Neel
Eisenhower, McCarthy and Dulles, 1953
Oil on canvas
30¼ x 22
Courtesy Robert Miller Gallery, New York
Plate 20

Lorie Novak
Past Lives, 1987
Color photograph
36 x 29
Lent by the artist
Plate 31

Lorie Novak
Untitled, 1987
Color photograph
36 x 29
Lent by the artist
Detail on cover

Saul Ostrow
Balancing Justice (Idealism and the Media Will Make you Blind),1987
Wood, plexiglass, gold leaf, and transister radio
Overall: 78 x 48 x 9
Lent by the artist
Plate 46

Pablo Picasso
Untitled, 1952
Lithograph
14 x 20
Collection Michael and Robert Meeropol
Plate 1

Adrian Piper
Xenophobia I: Anti-Semitism, 1987
Wood, masonite, cracked glass, and photographs
36 x 24
Lent by the artist
Plate 48

Archie Rand
Pendulum, 1987
Acrylic on canvas
42 x 60
Courtesy Phyllis Kind Gallery, New York and Chicago
Plate 38

Martha Rosler
Unknown Secrets, 1988
Two parts: silkscreen and photograph on paper,
90¾ x 54½; cloth and wood assemblage,
28 x 18
Overall: 90¾ x 85; and text handout
Lent by the artist
Plate 45

Juan Sanchez
The Rosenbergs: Framed Conspiracy, 1987
Oil and mixed media on canvas
46 x 68
Courtesy Guariquen, Inc., Bayamon, Puerto Rico
Plate 36

Peter Saul
Ethel Rosenberg in Electric Chair, 1987
Acrylic and oil on paper
60 x 40
Courtesy Allan Frumkin Gallery, New York
Plate 24

Greg Sholette
Men: Making History, Making Art: 1954, 1987
Left panel text: U.S.-CIA backed coup topples Guatemala's President Arbenz–1954–U.P.I.
Right panel text: American artist Jackson Pollock weaves an image of chaos with paint
Cibachrome, "photo-diorama" and polyester resin bas reliefs
20 x 72 x 3
Lent by the artist
Plate 18

Kenneth Shorr
Commemorative Governmental Portraits, 1987
Photographs, steel, plexiglass, oil paint, and canvas
Four panels: 50 x 60 each
Plaque: 8 x 10
Overall dimensions variable
Lent by the artist
Plate 47

Deborah Small
Witch Hunt, 1987
Acrylic on wood
96 x 120 x 12
Lent by the artist
Plate 28

Anthony Toney
Procession, 1954
Oil on canvas
72 x 48
Collection Whitney Museum of American Art, New York
Plate 52

Patty Wallace
Spy vs. Spy/Tic Tac Toe, 1986
Nine Ektachrome photographs and black tape
Each: 11 X 14
Overall: 42 x 51
Lent by the artist
Plate 37

David Wojnarowicz
The Anatomy and Architecture of June 19, 1953 (for the Rosenbergs), 1987
Acrylic and collage on masonite
36 x 36
Courtesy Gracie Mansion Gallery, New York
Plate 23

Wordsworth
Untitled: Homage to Ethel, Julius and Morton, 1987
Cloth and grommets
48 x 72
Lent by the artists
Plate 2

*Not illustrated:
Dennis Adams
Maquette for Bus Shelter II,
1984
Aluminum, plexiglass, fluorescent light and Duratrans on wood base
15¾ x 23½ x 17½
Courtesy Nature Morte Gallery, New York

LENDERS TO THE EXHIBITION

Kim Abeles
Doug Ashford
Karen Atkinson
Gary Bachman
Sally Baker
Rudolf Baranik
Terry Berkowitz
Karl Bornstein Gallery, Santa Monica
Chris Bratton
Luis Camnitzer
Mort Dimondstein
Ralph Fasanella
Allan Frumkin Gallery, New York
Rupert Garcia
Ben and Beatrice Goldstein
Guariquen, Inc., Bayamon, Puerto Rico
Marina Gutierrez
Iannetti-Lanzone Gallery, San Francisco
Kent Fine Art, New York
Phyllis Kind Gallery, New York and Chicago
Margia Kramer
Ruth and Bert Lessuck
Gracie Mansion Gallery, New York
Leon Marcus

Paul Marcus
August and Rena Maymudes
Michael and Ann Meeropol
Robert and Ellen Meeropol
Arnold Mesches
Robert Miller Gallery, New York
Randall Morris and Shari Cavin Morris
Antonio Muntadas
Nature Morte Gallery, New York
Lorie Novak
Rob Okun and Deborah Kruger
Saul Ostrow
Adrian Piper
Martha Rosler
Jack Shainman Gallery, New York
Greg Sholette
Kenneth Shorr
Deborah Small
Dr. Helen L. Sobell
Stux Gallery, New York
Unity Center, New York
Patty Wallace
Whitney Museum of American Art, New York
Wordsworth

ROSENBERG CASE BIBLIOGRAPHY

Coover, Robert. *The Public Burning.* New York: Viking Press, 1976.

Doctorow, E.L. *The Book of Daniel.* New York: Random House, 1971.

Fineberg, Solomon Andhil. *The Rosenberg Case: Fact and Fiction.* New York: Oceana Publications, 1953.

Freed, Donald. *Inquest.* New York: Hill and Wang, 1970.

Gardner, Virginia. *The Rosenberg Story.* New York: Masses and Mainstream, 1954.

Goldstein, Alvin H. *The Unquiet Death of Julius and Ethel Rosenberg.* New York and Westport Conn.: Lawrence Hill, 1975.

Meeropol, Robert and Michael. *We Are Your Sons: The Legacy of Julius and Ethel Rosenberg.* Boston: Houghton Mifflin, 1975; University of Illinois Press, 1987.

Millet, Martha. *The Rosenbergs: Poems of the United States.* New York: Sierra Press, 1957.

Nizer, Louis. *The Implosion Conspiracy.* Garden City, N.Y.: Doubleday, 1973.

Philipson, Ilene. *Ethel Rosenberg: Beyond the Myths.* New York: Franklin Watts, Inc., 1988.

Radosh, Ronald and Milton, Joyce. *The Rosenberg File: A Search for the Truth.* New York: Holt, Rinehart and Winston, 1983.

Root, Jonathan. *The Betrayers.* New York: Coward-McCann, 1963; London: Martin Secker and Warburg, 1964.

Reuben, William A. *The Atom Spy Hoax.* New York: Action Books, 1954.

Schneir, Walter and Miriam. *Invitation to an Inquest.* New York: Doubleday, 1965; New York: Pantheon, 1983.

Segal, Edith. *Poems and Songs for Ethel and Julius Rosenberg.* New York: National Committee to Reopen the Rosenberg Case, 1983.

Sharp, Malcolm Pitman. *Was Justice Done? The Rosenberg-Sobell Case.* New York: Monthly Review Press, 1956.

Sobell, Morton. *On Doing Time.* New York: Scribner, 1974.

Rosenberg, Ethel and Julius. *Death House Letters.* New York: Jero, 1953.

Rosenberg, Ethel and Julius. *The Testament of Ethel and Julius Rosenberg.* New York: Cameron and Kahn, 1954.

U.S. vs. Rosenbergs, Sobell, Yakovlev, and David Greenglass. Transcript of Trial. New York: Committee to Secure Justice for Morton Sobell.

Wexley, John. *The Judgment of Julius and Ethel Rosenberg.* New York: Cameron and Kahn, 1955.